25

THEY CALLED IREDELL COUNTY HOME

INTERESTING PEOPLE WHO WERE BORN OR LIVED IN IREDELL COUNTY, N.C.

BY

O. C. STONESTREET

O. C. Stonestreet

From the Same Author:

A Brief History of Cool Spring School (1998)
Tales of Old Iredell County (2012)*

Soon to Come:

Military Intelligence Beats None at All
Vacationing on the Islets of Langerhans
Paranoia for Fun and Profit

* PUBLISHED THROUGH CREATESPACE.COMV

Copyright © 2013 O. C. Stonestreet

All rights reserved.

ISBN: 1492330477

ISBN 13: 9781492330479

Library of Congress Control Number: 2013917204
CreateSpace Independent Publishing Platform
North Charleston, South Carolina

DEDICATION

With much love, I dedicate this book to my two grandsons, Blake Alexander Stonestreet and Ryan Mason Stonestreet.

BACK IN IREDELL

by Mrs. Sallie Floyd Watson

That you, Jim? So glad to see you.
Been a-lyin' here alone;
Waited till you'd get the message,
(You don't mind me if I groan).

Stopped to look around a little?
Biggest crop you ever see,
Finest farm in all the county.
Jest wish you was fixed like me?

That's all so, I know it, Jimmy,
Yes, I'm rich, but oh, I'd be
Jest as poor as in the 'Sixties
If 'twould bring my wish to me.

Jest to be a boy in Iredell,
Jest to hear the mocker's tune,
Catch a fish in Davis' mill pond
Some good cloudy day in June.

'Member how we chased them squirrels
In old Colonel's bottom land?
And rabbits when the snow came early,
Thick as jiggers in the sand?

Then, when we was gettin' older
Come the days of 'Sixty-one.
'Course we 'listed, mind it, Jimmy?
Why, a fight them days was fun.

An' the Blues went off so gayly!
Marched and fought and starved and bled;
Oh, the broken hearts in Iredell
When we counted up our dead!

Wounded, ragged, starvin', heart-broke;
I came home in 'Sixty-five
Saw old Iredell and my Hannah,
Thanked God then I was alive.

Seemed I couldn't make a livin'.
Everybody said, "Go West!"
Knew my Hannah'd go where I went,
Thought I wouldn't mind the rest.

Well, we moved West in a schooner,
Hadn't much to take along.
Tented 'til we built a dug-out;
Bought this land for just a song.

Worked from one week's end to 'tother,
Little richer every year.
Hannah said I'd die a rich man;
She did her part—never fear.

But, you see, we lost our Robbie—
Went so sudden just from play
And poor Hannah never questioned,
Jest got weaker every day.

Guess she broke her heart for Iredell—
Women never like the West—
Said folks hadn't time to neighbor,
Said they hadn't time to rest.

Said, the night when she was dyin',
"Oh, the clay out here ain't red!
Make my grave in Fourth Creek churchyard,
Let me rest when I am dead."

Doctor said 'twas all the fever
But it hurt me even then.
Now I know how she was feelin',
Oh, for Iredell once again!

"Do you want to see a preacher?"
Can you call me William Wood
Back across the shinin' river
From the presence of our God?

Why, he's comin' now to meet me!
Who's that standin' on his right?
Hannah, Robbie, Back to Iredell!
Jim, I'm goin' home tonight!

—*Statesville Daily, July 21, 1930*

INTRODUCTION

An interesting assortment of people have called Iredell County, North Carolina, home, both before and since it was established as a county in 1788. Some of these folks were born here and have become relatively well-known close to home, while others moved away and rose to prominence and are better-known elsewhere. A few of the people in this book were not born in Iredell County, but became citizens of the county, and subsequently rose to prominence here. I consider them all to be "Iredellians" and feel they deserve a place in this book.

I have arranged my subjects in alphabetical order, generally going by the name they were called, but not always including titles such as "Professor," "Doctor," "Reverend" and such.

There are some interesting Iredellians about whom I have already written in my 2012 book, *Tales from Old Iredell County*, and I refer you to that book for their stories. Among them are: Selma Hortense Burke, artist, humanitarian and educator; Dr. James W. Davis, surgeon; centenarians Matthew Gibbs and Patrick Gracy; "Little Joe" Gilland, of Barium Springs; Helen Celeste Henkel, Iredell school superintendent; George Lee Moose, Iredell's caveman; Hugh Lawson White, Whig presidential candidate; and others.

Among the ranks of the 70-some people included in this volume are seven educators, six soldiers, five public servants, four aviators, four poets, four medical people, three athletes, three ministers, three entertainers, two writers, two sailors, two scientists, two newspaper editors, a merchant, a farmer, a pioneer, a judge, a salesman and a partridge in a pear tree.

There are also a handful of people who might be classified as "historian," although none of them wrote professionally. Without them, we likely would not have known about some of the others.

In addition, we have a number of people in this volume who cannot be satisfactorily put into just one box. For instance, we have the Rev. Dr. Elijah F. Rockwell, who although not a county native, may be considered Iredell County's first historian. Rev. Dr. Rockwell also was a minister and a teacher. The Rev. Dr. Alexander Means was probably the closest Iredell has come to producing a true Renaissance Man; he was a teacher, a scientist, a physician and a minister. The Honorable Augustus Leazar was a teacher, a newspaper editor and publisher, a state legislator and an administrator of the state prison system. Mary Martin Sloop was a physician, a writer, a teacher and social worker.

Then there was "Professor" James Walker Sr., who was a poet and a teacher. And where do we put Shelley Frontis? He was a poet and a mayor of Mooresville, but also was the town's first trained dentist. And so it goes.

There are as many, if not more, Iredellians who deserve to be in a book such as this, and perhaps there will be enough interest to support a "*They Called Iredell County Home, Volume II*" in the future.

I have taken the liberty of tweaking the original articles which appeared in area newspapers. In some cases I made grammatical and spelling corrections, in other cases I moved sentences and paragraphs around, and in several instances I have added more (or corrected) information on a subject.

As before, I have included a bibliography for those who want to know where I got my information and to encourage readers to do further research on their own.

I don't know anything about Mrs. Sallie Floyd Watson except that her poem appeared in a 1930 issue of The Statesville Daily and I thought it deserved a wide audience and so used it as a sort of poetical introduction. Perhaps someone knows more about Mrs. Watson and will contact me. Also, I was unable to locate a photograph of Ralph Sloan. Perhaps someone has a photo of Ralph Sloan they would share with me.

Remember the first word we learned in the old Dick and Jane primary readers? You don't? Well, it was "Look!" You never know what you may find. I hope you may come across an old friend or two as you read this book or that you may meet an interesting person for the first time. They, as we, called Iredell County "home."

—O. C. Stonestreet

Bradford's Crossroads

Iredell County, N.C.

ACKNOWLEDGMENTS

Once again I must thank my wife Judy for her help and forbearance, my son Chris for his (unacknowledged) co-authorship of the article about Homer Meyers Jr., and to the editors and publishers of my original articles.

Much gratitude goes to those who work in the Mooresville Public Library and the Iredell County Public Library in Statesville, particularly to Mr. Joel Reece of the James Iredell Room.

Also, thanks go to Mr. Ken Harris Jr. for the photo of his father, the Hon. Ken Harris; to Dr. Steve Hill for photos of Mac Gray and Quincy Sharpe Mills. Rev. Homer Keever's daughter, Mrs. Nancy Keever Andersen, supplied me with a photo of her father. My appreciation goes to Dr. Felton Thomas for the photo of his brother, Lt. David Thomas, USAF; to Mrs. Martha Dobson for her photo; to Mr. Jimmie Allie for the photo of Mary C. Holliday; to the Summers family for their photo of Yeoman 3rd Class Richard N. Summers, USN; to Lorri Hafer for the photo of her mother, Mary Mayo; and to Mr. Chris Holliday for the photo of Norman "Butch" Small.

Wendy Carroll graciously allowed me to use the photo of her father, author Ted Taylor, with his canine friends.

Thanks also go to the Crossnore School for the photo of Drs. Eustace and Mary Sloop; to Principal James Coleman of the Antioch Christian Academy in Lumberton for the photo of Judge Harris' headstone; to the Williams family for the photos of Mr. and Mrs. S. Clay Williams; to the Brantley family for the photo of David Henry Brantley; and to the Frontis family for the photo of Stephen Frontis Jr.

Jan Blodgett of Davidson College Archives supplied me with the photograph of the Rev. Dr. E. F. Rockwell.

Mr. Gary Leveille, of Great Barrington, Mass., helped me with a photo and research on Thomas Jefferson McKinley.

Mr. David L. Morrill, of Sylacauga, Alabama, supplied helpful information on Mooresville motorcyclist Gray Sloop.

The Office of the Mayor of Charlotte, N.C., allowed me to use their photographs of the Hon. Ben Douglas and the Hon. Stan Brookshire.

Finally, I would be remiss if I failed to acknowledge the invaluable assistance of my two four-legged Scottie research assistants, Misses Molly Carol and Nessie Grace, without whom this book would have been possible, but not as much fun.

THEY CALLED IREDELL COUNTY HOME

George Amox

I had seen George Amox standing there on his corner mornings as I drove into work at the R&L and had stopped and had spoken with him a little. On July 3, 2006, I invited him to join me at the office and have a cup of coffee and talk with me. The following was printed on the front page of the R&L the next day.

* * *

On almost every workday morning for more than two years, George Amox has been standing on the corner of Statesville's Front and Center streets by the Civic Center, holding a large American flag. He attracts the attention of the drivers and passengers of the vehicles going by.

Amox was born in Savannah and raised in east Texas and in Flat Rock, N.C. He enlisted in the Army in 1960, ending his military service as a staff sergeant in the 82nd ("All-American") Airborne Division. He served in the States, Germany, Korea and Vietnam. He moved to Statesville when he got out of the service in 1973.

Amox is on total disability and has diabetes and melanomas and other health problems. He will likely loose his right eye. The doctors at the VA hospital in Salisbury say this is due to his exposure to Agent Orange, a sprayed chemical defoliant used by the U.S. military in Vietnam.

Amox has a wife,Peggy, two daughters and a son and three granddaughters and is expecting another grandchild in September (of 2006).

On Independence Day and every day, Amox, who will be 65 next week, has a lot to say about freedom, the flag, the military and veterans.

* * *

R&L: Why are you standing out there, at Front and Center, in almost any kind of weather?

GA: I'm out there to honor the men and women who have died for this country in our military. Did you know that some 38 servicewomen have died in Iraq or Afghanistan?

I originally was going to do this for only two weeks. I started doing this at Radio Road where it crosses over I-40, but the Highway Patrol said I couldn't stay there. People thought I was trying to commit suicide or something, so the Highway Patrol told me I had to move.

R&L: Why aren't you there every day?

GA: Sometimes I'm going to the VA hospital in Salisbury, and sometimes I stay home because my wife, Peggy, is in poor health, and she's my first priority. Thank God for that VA Hospital. They've been very good to me.

R&L: What do you think the flag stands for?

GA: The flag stands for the freedom we have and for those who gave their lives for that flag. And it stands for all of us.

R&L: What kind of responses do you get?

GA: I have a lot of people salute—not me but the flag. A lot of people wave, honk their car horns. I salute firemen, policemen and EMTs. They're going in harm's way, too.

R&L: You get some bad responses too, don't you?

GA: Yeah, a lot give me the finger. I used to keep count on how many gave me the "bird," but my wife said to quit counting; they're not worth counting. One guy throws rocks at me. He's hit me in the chest and has hit my truck a couple of times.

R&L: Why do you think they act this way toward you?

GA: I guess they don't realize why I'm out here. Maybe they're mad at the president, mad about the war, so they take it out on me.

I like President Bush, but I don't agree with everything he's done. I didn't like Bill Clinton, but I supported him because he was the commander-in-chief.

Some people have tried to give me money, but I won't take it. One fellow wadded up $25 and threw it to me; another fellow stuffed a $10 bill in my pocket and ran away, but I'm not trying to raise money, and I'm not begging. I gave the money to some veterans I know who really needed it.

I tell people that if they want to give money to veterans, go see the Marine Corps League down in Troutman.

It sounds strange, but I don't want people to see me. I want them to see that flag; it's all about our country, not me. One guy asked me if I was selling flags. I said, "Yeah," and he asked, "How much?"

I told him, "About $10 million each."

He said, "No, seriously." I told him I was serious and I asked him how much freedom was worth.

R&L: Don't you get a little lonely standing out there in the rain some of these mornings?

GA: Well, sometimes one of my granddaughters will stand with me. But I'm not lonely. I'll tell you the truth—I'm not by myself. There's some 58,000 who died in Vietnam who are standing right there with me, plus those of our troops who've died in the Middle East.

Standing there with the flag has done me more good than anything else I could have done. It's therapy; I can talk about Vietnam now. On my truck a bumper sticker says, "Support Our Troops." What more can I say?

"Gerri" Benfield

Her boss told her she'd never make it, but she proved him wrong.

Geraldine "Gerri" Benfield is a retired paramedic, the first female hired by the Iredell County Emergency Medical Service, which was established in 1975.

Gerri was a role model and a pioneer, but she didn't think about that at the time. She got her start when Linda Fleming, the wife of Iredell EMS Director John Fleming, urged her to apply for a job. This was in November of 1978.

"She [Linda] called me and told me they wanted a female in the county EMS. She called me two or three times and told me to get my resume in, to go see John and talk to him," Benfield recalled.

Benfield already had two and a half years of nursing education and had worked at Davis and Iredell Memorial hospitals almost continually for 22 years. And she was certified as an Emergency Medical Technician (EMT). "I got bored at the job I was doing in manufacturing," she said. "I had worked in the emergency room but hadn't been in an ambulance that much. I knew I wanted to get back in the medical profession. That was my life."

But she suspected that working in a moving ambulance might be something of a challenge. "I thought it couldn't be much different from working in a hospital, but there were a lot of differences," she said. "For one thing, trying to treat someone in the back of a moving ambulance, and going to the scene of a wreck and picking up injured people—I had never seen or done anything like that before."

She also thought she might have trouble picking up a very heavy stretcher.

She was tested early.

One day after John hired me, they got a call and he said to me, "Come on. Let's see if you really want to do this."

"It was a car wreck or something and he asked me when we got through and were back in the truck, "Do you think you can do this?" And I said, "Yes, it doesn't look that hard to me."

Gerri would spend more than 18 years on the job before retiring in April of 1994.

THE EARLY YEARS

Benfield spent the first five years working on the convalescent unit, "picking up patients from hospitals and taking them home, or the other way around, or from a rest home to the hospital when it wasn't an emergency situation."

That kept her and a man, Howard Doyle, working on the 8 a.m. to 5 p.m. shift. The regular EMTs were working 24 hours on, then 48 hours off.

"Some of the men thought that it was not the woman's place to be on a truck out in the middle of the night, picking up people," she said.

Part of that attitude may have been because the EMS base—little more than a trailer—had limited sleeping quarters and crews working emergency response worked 24-hour shifts.

"When the base was moved to the Water Street location, I had my own bathroom and bedroom, and it wasn't long after that until John Fleming called me into his office and asked me if I wanted to try working a 24-hour shift. But he made the request with a prediction. He looked at me and said, 'I don't think you're going to make it,'" she recalled.

"He didn't know how stubborn I was. I would have made it or else," she said.

That first week of emergency calls was rough.

"Just the fact that you were there on call for 24 hours in Statesville, and that base got more calls than anywhere else in Iredell County made it hard," she recalled. But once that week was over, she had been accepted by some.

Having a good partner helped, she said. "Paul Campbell was my partner. He more or less broke me in to the job. He was a good, easygoing type of person. I looked on him like he was my older brother."

But that didn't mean that the other men didn't test her with pranks and off-color jokes. In fact, they tested her for a year to see if she could handle it.

"I was kind of uptight when I started. They tried to get me out in the first year, but that was because they'd never had a female in there, and I think if they had a female in there that was not as stubborn as I was, she'd have never made it," Benfield stated.

"They'd tell jokes that weren't—shall we say, politically correct?—just to see what I'd do. They'd look at me to see what my reaction was. I soon learned not to react at all, like I never heard them."

Her attitude was to stick with it.

"I thought, 'You can do whatever you want to me...I don't care...I'll find a way to get even and most of the time I did, even if it wasn't anything but knocking the hound out of them on the shoulder. I'd walk up and punch them with everything I had...it was my way of dealing with a bad situation. But then if my partner wanted to hit me back on the shoulder, he'd hit me a couple of times, I'd say, 'Not too hard, please.'"

Eventually she was accepted and seen as just one of the guys.

"I guess they were waiting to see if I was going to make it or if I was going to flunk out," Benfield said.

"But apparently they didn't have that many women apply when there were openings. The next female after me was Pat Painter, and then Ann Lunsford moved down from the communications department."

SUPPORT AT HOME

Through it all her husband watched her back.

"People would say to him, 'Why is your wife working for the EMS?'" Benfield said. "And I said to let me handle it. I can handle any problem that they throw at me, and I think I did pretty well."

As the job changed over the years, so did Gerri Benfield.

"Paramedics could do a lot more things by the time I retired. They started IVs, administered drugs and were even intubating patients. Once you got to the intermediate level, you were taught how to begin to read an EKG [heart monitor] strip, plus you had to do all the bookwork, going through all these classes—and you had to be re-certified every two years," she said

But at the time, she never saw herself as a pioneer. "It was more just something I wanted to do."

Though she's been retired for some time now, she says she still misses the job. "I miss the companionship more that I do the work. I enjoyed the work; I liked my patients, and it hurt me when we'd bring one in to the hospital a last time...But mostly, I think I miss being able to go into the base and chat with the crews on duty...It was like a small family."

J. D. Beshears

I met with Mr. Beshears, 90, on Thursday, October 15, 2009, at the small museum on the campus of Barium Springs. He drove over alone from Clemmons in his Buick. It was cool and rainy that day and we both wore baseball hats and wind breakers. We shook hands and then walked around the museum together, looking at the hundreds of photos and other memorabilia on display there before we sat down for the interview. He and his two brothers were in several of the photos.

Despite the grimness of some of his experiences, Beshears smiled and laughed frequently as he told his story.

More than 200 of Barium's young men and women served their country in World War II; 15 are known to have died in service, including Ben Morrow, mentioned below, who survived the Death March but died in May of 1942 of dysentery.

* * *

James Dixon Beshears, born in 1919 in the Hanes community near Winston-Salem, says he traveled half-way across the world just to get back to where he started. He now lives in his home beside his only son, Jim, in Clemmons. He is one of a rapidly diminishing group of American veterans of World War II once known as "The Battling Bastards of Bataan."

"J.D.," as he is called, came to live at Barium Springs Home for Children in 1929 after his parents died. His father passed away when he was 9 years old and then five months later his mother died while giving birth to her 10th child. J. D. and Howard and Lacy, the three youngest boys, came to Barium. He graduated from Barium's McNair High School in 1939.

He regularly attends the annual reunions held in August at the Home and attended the one just past. "Barium's changed since I grew up here, but it's still home," he said.

HOME AT THE HOME

At Barium he milked cows, fired the boiler that produced steam to cook with and worked on the Home's truck farm, planting beans and corn and watermelons.

"We grew all the vegetables that we ate at the Home. I remember we had a little celery patch down near the creek that we worked by hand as you couldn't get a tractor in there."

It wasn't all work, however. He was on the school's football and wrestling teams for four years. The Barium Tornadoes were the state champions in wrestling several years while Beshears was on the team.

After graduation his first job was in a cotton mill in Virginia, then he worked as a plumber's helper in Statesville and then had a job with Gilbert Engineering out of Greensboro, doing surveying for home sites in Virginia.

OFF TO WAR

"Me and Ben Morrow joined the U.S. Army Air Corps in May of 1941. They were drafting boys at that time and I didn't want to end up in the infantry."

He trained at Savannah Air Base, Ga., and after training traveled by train across the country to San Francisco, Calif., arriving there on November 1, 1941. From there he went by a ship, the SS *President Coolidge*, to Manila, the Philippines, arriving there on November 20th. He was a buck private, a one-striper, on the bottom rung the military rank ladder.

His Air Corps job was in ordnance- he was part of a crew that would load bombs into a small truck and take them out to bombers. They also would put the fuses in the bombs.

"Where we lived we called it 'Tent City,' as there was no permanent barracks," he recalled. "We delivered the bombs to Clark Field. There was a lot of chaos at that time after we learned that the Japanese bombed Pearl Harbor. The next day our boys, that is, the pilots, wanted to bomb the Japanese on Formosa, but the U.S. hadn't declared war yet. Our planes took off before dawn and flew around and then landed to be refueled at lunch time. That's when the Japanese planes came in.

Our guys were expecting a big flight of planes from San Francisco and people were out near the runway waving and all and that's when the Japanese started dropping their bombs on our planes. That night we went to pick up some bombs at the air base and took the bombs up to a landing strip in the mountains. Two B-17s came in the next day, December 10th. We loaded them with the bombs we had brought up. Captain Colin Kelly was one of the pilots and they took off to bomb the Japanese troop ships in the harbor. That's when Capt. Kelly got killed."

Capt. Colin Kelly was successful in bombing a Japanese cruiser with his plane, although his B-17 was strafed by a Zero and disabled. Kelly stayed with the crippled, burning aircraft until the other members of his crew had bailed out. He was posthumously awarded the Distinguished Service Cross and was regarded at the time as America's first hero of World War II.

Loading those bombs that night was the only time Beshears got to do his official job, the job he had been trained to do, in the Army Air Corps.

THE SURRENDER

Now and then Beshears thinks about the surrender of Bataan, the largest surrender of an American army in history. Of the 75,000 surrendered there were about 12,000 Americans, the rest Filipinos and Chinese Filipinos. Some of those who surrendered were able to escape and fought on as guerrillas in the mountains.

The number who died on the forced march to Camp O'Donnell is impossible to calculate accurately, but estimates are that 5,000 to 10,000 Filipinos perished along with 600 to 650 American servicemen.

"General [Edward P.] King did the right thing, I believe," said Beshears. We fought for four months. President Roosevelt and them in Washington said not to surrender, but those back in the States didn't know the situation. Gen. King knew what the actual situation was."

THE BATAAN DEATH MARCH

"We were marched to San Fernando, then we were stuffed into boxcars. We were packed so tight that the dead didn't have room to fall down. No water, no food and God it was hot. When we marched we weren't allowed to get out of ranks. I was weak; I'd had malaria. I was tired, had been about ready to quit, but

I would never have surrendered on my own. We had only got about a third of a ration before we surrendered. The bombs and artillery pounded us all the time.

"My job had been to bring ammunition up to the front lines in the jungle. When we left we were supposed to set the ammo dump off, but if we had, then the infantry would be trapped, so we didn't blow it.

"I'd say I walked about 65 miles, from San Fernando to Camp O'Donnell, a prison camp. I saw them [the Japanese] hit the Filipinos who came out to the roads and tried to give us something to eat, maybe a little ball of sugar or rice, while on the march. The Japanese would beat or kill them, hit them with bamboo sticks in the back or on the top of the head. I, personally, didn't see them kill American prisoners, but we had no water, no food, except once I was issued a ball of rice; it was about the size of a softball. We stayed at one place, just an open field for three days, no tents, cover, food, anything. I guess they were waiting for more guards to join them.

"On the march if you didn't move quickly enough they'd hit you with bamboo sticks. Once we got to Camp O'Donnell they died like flies, the Americans and the Filipinos.

"I remember a Japanese general spoke to us soon after we arrived. I remember he said, 'We are enemies and will always be enemies.' I think that was General [Masaharu] Homma. After the war they hung him."

From O'Donnell they went to Cabanatuan Province. "The Japs made us into what we called 'Blood Brothers.' That meant that if you escaped or tried to escape, they'd kill the other nine men. We went together even when we had to go relieve ourselves at night.

"At Cabanatuan they put us on a Japanese ship, 2,000 of us in two holds. Guys were sick, there were no facilities, many had diarrhea, and they took us to Seoul, Korea, then to Mukden, Manchuria, on a train. At Muken they put me to work in a textile factory. I ran a loom making canvas. I also got to work on a farm detail—we 'plowed with a shovel.' There I was half way around the globe working on a truck garden like back at Barium Springs and then in a textile mill like I had worked in back in Virginia!

END OF THE WAR

"We saw American planes fly over from time to time. This was in July and August, 1945. We didn't know the A-Bomb[s] had been dropped. A plane flew over one day and dropped three bombs. There was a Japanese aircraft factory nearby it was trying to hit. One bomb blew a hole in the ten-foot wall. Another bomb exploded inside the camp and killed 19 of our guys. The third bomb hit the camp latrine, but thank God, it was a dud.

"Later an American plane flew over and five people bailed out over the camp with some radio gear. They were a Japanese interpreter, a Chinese interpreter and three stateside Yanks. The Japanese held them for about an hour, then they were allowed to set up the radio gear. On the radio the Japanese at the camp learned that the war was over and that they had surrendered. They had to keep the guards separate from us for their safety, 'cause there were a lot of grudges. They had to stack their rifles like we had had to do back at Bataan.

"When I had stacked my rifle, I had thrown away the bolt so it couldn't be used. The next day they started dropping food to us by parachute.

GETTING HOME THE HARD WAY

"I got on a train in Mukden and from there went down to Korea, and got on an American ship, I forget the name, and went to Okinawa. Well, the ship was hit by a typhoon and then hit a Japanese mine. It didn't sink her, but she did take on a lot of water before they got the compartments sealed off. Another ship gave us a line and helped tow us into Okinawa. That mine killed eight sailors in the engine room and two men like me who had been POWs.

"At Okinawa I got on a plane and got to Manila. The tire on the plane blew out as the aircraft landed. The pilot just barely got it stopped before it went off the runway. There was a Displaced Persons Center in Manila. I got on a ship to go to the U.S. On the way out of the harbor our ship hit a sunken ship and we were delayed for another three days or so making sure our ship was still seaworthy.

"We were supposed to come into the U.S. at San Francisco and my brother, Howard, planned to meet me there. He was still in the Navy. "Well, they rerouted us to Seattle, Wash. I remember seeing the harbor and the lights at night and it was so beautiful to finally be back home. They kept me in a hospital there in Fort Lewis, Washington, for a while and my brother Howard found me. Next they put me on a hospital train that took me to Asheville, North Carolina, to Moore General Hospital where I stayed for a while. My other brother, Lacy, who had been in the Navy but was now discharged, met me there. I finally got back to home about Thanksgiving. The war had ended in August and I was still a buck private."

In 1947 Beshears married Maxine, a Forsyth County girl and the couple had a son whom J. D. lives beside today. Beshears found employment with the Western Electric Company in Winston-Salem, from which he retired in 1982.

After Maxine died of cancer, he remarried, this time to a former Barium Springs girl named Evelyn, but that marriage ended in divorce. He plays a lot of golf these days, usually five times a week. He is a member of the American Ex-Prisoners of War organization.

Beshears credits his general good health and well-being to a higher authority. "I've got a good co-pilot," he says with a chuckle. "You know, the Big Guy upstairs. I prayed a lot during the war, still do, and it helps."

Beshears was among the 73 surviving veterans at the Bataan Death March Survivors Reunion that was held in San Antonio, Texas, this past May [2009]. At that reunion the Japanese ambassador to the United States, Ichiro Fujisaki, formally apologized to the survivors on behalf of the Japanese government.

"There were about 500 people at the banquet that was held that Saturday night. I listened to him," said Beshears, "but I never did hear him say that his government was sorry for the way they treated us POWs or for Pearl Harbor or for anything else."

FORGIVE AND FORGET?

"I've heard preachers say to forgive and forget, but you can't forget. I don't believe that. You have flashbacks. I would accept a Japanese family as neighbors if they moved in beside me, and if you bought a Japanese car, then that's your business. But I ain't going to buy one and I don't eat sushi. I can't see myself going into a Japanese restaurant."

We shook hands again as J.D. Beshears put on his ball cap. The cap had an embroidered American flag and eagle and the words: "These colors don't run."

DORIS WAUGH BETTS

The April 24, 2012, edition of the *Record & Landmark* carried the obituary of North Carolina writer and Statesville native Doris Waugh Betts, 79. I did not personally know Doris Betts, but I knew who she was. I had a file on her, hoping someday to do an interview, and I have one of Mrs. Betts' books in my library, *The Astronomer and Other Stories.* One of the eight stories in the collection is "Spies in the Herb House," which is set in 1940s Statesville and centers on the old Wallace Brothers Herbarium that stood about where the Plaza Apartments Building now stands.

The story's first paragraph reads as follows: "To be a child in the tall house where I grew up in Statesville, North Carolina, was to live marooned on an island. Along the front limit of the large yard ran a busy highway which—for several centuries—I could not grow old enough to cross. In back, the lot became a garden and fruit orchard before it stopped at the edge of the railroad tracks where I was not allowed to play. Twice a day the last surviving steam engine in that part of the state puffed slowly by towards Taylorsville, and twice a day I stood in the limits of a honeysuckle bank to wave to the engineer. Sometimes he put out a hand the size of my head, and waggled the fingers inside his striped denim glove."

I did some research on the late Mrs. Betts. When she was a little girl she lived at 819 West Front Street. She learned to read when she was four and composed poems in her head. Her mother wrote the poems down and saved them for her daughter. She attended Mulberry Street School. Both of her parents worked in a cotton mill; her father, William, was a weaver. She graduated from Statesville High in the Class of 1950 where she was voted "Most Talented" by her peers her senior year. At that time she lived at 233 Kelly Street; she used to sing, played the piano and was in several plays at Statesville High where she was regularly listed on the honor roll.

It was while she was at Statesville High that she began to write. The editor of the old *Statesville Daily Record* began carrying a high school column by her in 1949. He referred to her as "Doris 'I wanna be a journalist' Waugh. Some people just know what they want to do sooner than others.

Her first solo journalistic effort appeared in the October 22, 1949, *Statesville Daily Record*, her column called "Hitting the High Spots." She began what became a career captivated by words with the following paragraph:

"Up to this time, I had visualized a columnist as a miraculously resourceful person, bursting with original ideas, and dashing off his material nonchalantly in about 15 minutes. After a nerve-wracking hour of pacing the floor, tearing out hair by the handful, and pounding on a poor defenseless little table, my opinion has undergone a few major alterations. At any rate, this is the first of a series of columns on life at Statesville High School...."

The next week, Oct. 29th, she had another column ready, which began, "With six headaches, three packs of typing paper, and one column to my credit, it has occurred to me that there must be an easier way to make a living. I am considering basket-weaving as a profession."

Basket-weaving's loss is our gain; she continued to write for the *Daily Record* through 1949 and 1950, then it was off to Women's College in Greensboro to be a journalist, but became an English major, rather than a Journalism major. She was the first member of her family to go to college. Her first work of fiction was a short story published in *Mademoiselle* magazine when she was 21.

She worked a variety of jobs. Her first job was playing piano at Bunch's Music Store in Statesville. Later, as a student at Greensboro and as the wife of a law student, she worked in a jewelry store, and then she worked as an office manager of an advertising firm and held a full-time job at the *Sanford Daily Herald* for two years.

Even though she had not completed her bachelor's degree requirements at WC (now UNC Greensboro), she was hired as a fill-in to teach freshman writing at Chapel Hill for one semester in 1966. And teach she did for the next 30-some years, retiring in 2001. She was very popular with her students.

She also racked up a ton of awards and recognitions. She published her first novel at age 22. Six of her first seven books won awards. Mrs. Betts became alumni distinguished professor of English. She authored six novels and three short story collections. She was awarded six honorary degrees, and was a Guggenheim Fellow. One of her novels was a Book-of-the-Month Club selection, while another was a National Book Award finalist. In 1982 she was the first woman and probably the first teacher without a degree to be elected chair of the Chapel Hill faculty. Her 1956 novel, *Tall Houses in Winter*, was set in her hometown and is said to have set Statesville on its ear.

Her short story, "The Ugliest Pilgrim," in her collection, *Beasts of the Southern Wild and Other Stories*, and said by some to be the most widely printed of her stories, became an Academy Award winner as a short film titled *Violet*, and in 1998 was the basis of an off-Broadway musical that won the New York Drama Critics Circle Award.

She liked to write about the common people "muddling through life" the best they knew how, and was proud of her origins: common people, who were "not very well off and hard working." She once described herself as a "recovering Calvinist" and there is much of a religious nature in her work, but it is a questioning type of faith that she seemed to like to explore in her characters. Her people have difficulty with fitting a vision of a benevolent God into what happens in real life.

In a 1990 talk given to the First ARP Church in Statesville, she observed that "...the purpose of religion is not to get us into Heaven, but to get Heaven into us." She was an elder in her church and had taught Sunday school. In a 1995 interview she said that her characters "are puzzled by the mystery of human life, and I work to alert their eye to the possibility that God is alive and well."

Betts' own life reflected this inner struggle as she had to deal with the death of her husband, Lowry M. Betts, who was a judge, in 2007, and the death of a daughter, LewEllen, in 2011. A son and a daughter survived her.

In 1995 Mrs. Betts replied to a letter sent to her by Pam Reich's second-graders at Statesville's Northview Elementary School. Her reply, which was published in the *Record & Landmark*, told of her love of books and reading.

"Many years have passed since I was in the second grade at Mulberry Street School," she wrote, "but I still remember that when we came back from lunch in the cafeteria, (Mrs. Leinster) would read to us out loud.... I think now that the important thing was to hear stories of all kinds, and that I was learning new words and ideas from every page. I hope all of you are learning to love words and stories, too."

Doris June Waugh Betts helped all of us to learn to love words and stories.

REVEREND AND MRS. A. S. BILLINGSLEY

Following the Civil War there were two classes of Northern people who came to the South. The first were those who sought to enrich themselves at the expense of the Southern people. It was said that these low class persons carried all their belongings in a cheap suitcase of the day made of a carpet-like material and so were called "carpetbaggers." To have been called a carpetbagger in the South in those days was about the vilest thing that a person could be called.

The second group to come South were those who sincerely had the best interests of the Southern people in mind, both whites and the former slaves, now called "Freedmen." However, these people who had the best of intentions were sometimes suspected of being members of the first group, and their efforts were not fully appreciated and socially they were often shunned by fellow whites.

Reverend Amos Billingsley and his wife were members of this second group. The couple led interesting lives and deserve to be better known in Iredell County for the work they did. In the Reverend's obituary printed in *The Landmark*, it was noted that "his early work in this section was anything but pleasant...and in his work among the colored people he received no countenance from his white neighbors and practically no recognition, social or otherwise."

Amos Stevens Billingsley was born in 1818, near East Palestine, Ohio, the son of Robert and Jemima Austin Billingsley. He was a graduate of Jefferson College in Pennsylvania (B.A., 1847) and Western Theological Seminary, in Allegheny, Pennsylvania, in 1850. Licensed by New Lisbon Presbytery, United Presbyterian Church in the USA (1851), he was ordained by Lisbon Presbytery on January 10, 1854. He was a pastor to the Slippery Rock Presbyterian Church in Lawrence County, Ohio, until 1857, when he went to the West as a Presbyterian missionary.

He served as a minister in the then-Territory of Nebraska around Brownsville, Nemaha County, from July 22, 1857, to April of 1861. The Presbyterian Church in Brownsville, Kansas, was organized October 31, 1858, by Rev. Billingsley, who was its first pastor.

At the time Fort Sumter was fired upon—April 12, 1861—Rev. Billingsley had just left the Nebraska Territory for the Colorado gold fields. A diary that he kept recording births, deaths, marriages, etc., has been preserved on microfilm by the Nebraska State Historical Society:

"I preach'd last sab[bath] in the a.m. in a log house in Leavenworth Gulch to a very good cong [gregation] comparatively—nearly everybody turned out—Day—wet, cool. Preach'd with my overcoat on. In the P.M. at 5, I preached in a new building near the Express office, which was open at both ends, and 8 or 10 hands [workers] busily at work right close by joining the same building who made such a noise erecting a theatre that it was very difficult to speak or hear. Yet we had a good attentive cong [gregation] . . . . It is a very good field for Christian effort. Harvest great—laborers few." Source: *Diary of Amos S. Billingsley,* July 2, 1861.

He was elected chaplain of the Colorado House of Representatives in 1861 and in December of that same year he organized the First Presbyterian Church of Denver. The church had 18 members, of whom 11 were women. Rev. Billingsley remained with the church for only four months. He was still in Denver when the Emancipation Proclamation was issued by President Lincoln on January 1, 1863.

This event may have been the catalyst that caused Rev. Billingsley to return to the East. He went to Washington, D. C., and at some time was officially made a chaplain of the Union Army, one of 2,398 men of the cloth who were commissioned by the Federal military. Military chaplains, both Federal and Confederate, performed a variety of tasks. Working in prisons, hospitals and camps and near the battlefield, they delivered sermons, visited patients, wrote letters for injured men, and helped, spiritually as well as physically, with burials.

While in the District of Columbia he visited the Douglas Hospital, in his words, "preaching to the sick and wounded soldiers lying upon their narrow couches." He later visited Chesapeake Hospital where he preached to sick and wounded members of a black regiment.

Next, he went by ship to Beaufort, North Carolina, then in Union hands. By the time he arrived, Billingsley was so seasick he could hardly walk. Recovering, he visited soldiers' camps, chaplains' quarters, hospitals and met with delegates of the Christian Commission. From Beaufort he went to Plymouth, N.C., arriving there on December 19, 1863, and began his work among the 2,000 garrisoned troops which he described as "almost entirely destitute of preaching." On January 9, 1864, he was mustered in as Chaplain of the 101st Regiment, Pennsylvania Volunteers. His work there continued until April 17, 1864, when Plymouth was attacked by Confederate forces under Gen. Robert Hoke, "which resulted in our capture after a hot siege of three days."

Rev. Billingsley and other members of the 101st Pennsylvania were sent to Libby Prison in Richmond, Va. After a short stay there he was exchanged and went to the U.S. General Hospital at Annapolis, Md. From there he went to the federal hospital at Fortress Monroe, Va., one of the largest military hospitals of the war. After three months there, he went to the U.S. General Hospital at Hampton, Va., where he remained until several months after the war ended in April, 1865.

The Reverend collected the testimonies of ill and dying soldiers and these, along with his descriptions of his captivity at Libby Prison and his work in the Union hospitals, formed the basis of his first book, *From the Flag to the Cross; or, Scenes and Incidents of Christianity in the War.* (Philadelphia: New World Publishing Company, 1872). The book's subtitle is: "The conversions, prayers, dying requests, last words, sufferings and deaths of our soldiers, on the battlefield, in hospital, camp and prison and a description of distinguished Christian men and their labors."

In his preface he states the book's purpose, "...there seems to be a demand for another [book dealing with the Civil War], giving a more detailed account of the sufferings, piety, and heroism of the private soldier and patient in the hospital. Thus far there seems to be a tendency in the historian to ascribe too much honor and glory to the officer, and too little to the private soldier."

The wounded men the chaplains saw were, of course, both Union and Confederate. Here Rev. Billingsley describes visiting the wounded in a makeshift hospital following the capture of Plymouth, N.C., by the Confederates: "Several of our wounded were put in the same hospital with theirs. On one occasion I went in to see three of our men lying crowded in a room with theirs, and while conversing with and pointing them to Christ, a small, wounded North Carolina boy, who seemed to be in deep anguish, beckoned me to come to him; and as I approached him, he put out his feeble hand, grasped mine, and earnestly said, 'Will you please pray for me?' I knelt by his side, asked God to lead him to repentance, forgive his sins, and save his soul. He thanked me most heartily. The approach of death seemed to knock the spirit of rebellion out of him. He seemed very tender, penitent, and anxious to be saved. The scene was solemn and impressive. Bidding him farewell, I said to him, 'Trust in the Lord, and prepare to meet thy God.' He died soon after."

Six years after the end of the Civil War, in March of 1871, Billingsley and his wife, the former Emily Hamilton (1825-1908), left their Ohio home and settled in Statesville. Why they decided to come to Iredell County and why at that particular time remain mysteries. They both were soon teaching in the new freedmen's schools in the county. The fact that they were Northerners and that they worked with the freedmen (former slaves) and the freedmen's children aroused suspicions in the white community, which generally shunned them.

The duo also started churches for blacks in the area including the Second Presbyterian Church of Statesville (in 1896) on East Front Street, the present location of the *Record & Landmark's* office. The church was renamed "Broad Street Presbyterian Church" in 1918 after it moved to 214 E. Broad Street, and today the "descendant" of the church the Billingsleys started is known as Calvary United Presbyterian Church, located at 500 South Green Street.

It must have been painful for Rev. Billingsley when in 1884 the congregation of Second Presbyterian Church, which he had organized, insisted that they wanted a minister of their own race to lead them. The May 16, 1884, *Landmark* reported: "For a good while past a part of the colored Presbyterian congregation of this place has been dissatisfied with the pastor, Rev. A. S. Billingsley, so much so that one-half the congregation has not gone to church within the past two years except on communion and funeral occasion." The specific reasons for this "dissatisfaction" are not known, but clearly the presiding elders and a good part of the congregation felt the need to be independent of Rev. Billingsley.

When Rev. Billingsley refused to step down from the pulpit, certain members of his congregation actually locked him out of the sanctuary. He broke the lock and went in and preached anyway to four or five congregants.

Following this incident he relinquished his ministry at Second Presbyterian, but continued to preach in the county churches: Logan Presbyterian Church, Cameron Presbyterian Church and New Center Presbyterian Church until a year or two before his death. He also preached at Freedom Presbyterian Church. New Center Church, which was located just west of town near today's Statesville Regional Airport, eventually merged with today's Logan Presbyterian Church in the Scotts community.

A well-educated and well-to-do man, Rev. Billingsley was the author of several books. Two were published during his lifetime. The first was the before-mentioned *From the Flag to the Cross....* He also wrote *The Life of the Great Preacher Reverend George Whitfield, Prince of Pulpit Orators, with The Secret of His Success, and Specimens of His Sermons* (Philadelphia: W. Ziegler & Co., 1878). Another of his books was *The Life of St. Paul,* which was not published during his lifetime.

Posthumously, his writings about the West were published by the Colorado State Historical Society in 1963 as *The Journal of Amos S. Billingsley: A Missionary in the Colorado Gold Fields, 1861-1862, and Chaplain of the House of Representatives.*

Besides his work here in Iredell County, Rev. Billingsley was also on the Board of Trustees and was later President of the Board of Trustees of Biddle University (now Johnson C. Smith University) in Charlotte. This institution of higher learning, which was and still is affiliated with the Presbyterian Church, was begun in 1867 as Biddle Memorial Institute. Its name was changed to Biddle University in 1876, and then changed to its present name in 1923. Rev. Billingsley was awarded a Doctor of Divinity degree by Biddle University. In his will Rev. Billingsley left funds for scholarships for Biddle students who sought to become ministers and also in his will he left the University his vast personal library.

Rev. Dr. Billingsley died on October 12, 1897, in Statesville. He was almost 80 years old at the time of his passing. Following her husband's death, Mrs. Billingsley took her husband's body to Ohio for burial, then she returned to live in Statesville. When her health began failing, she moved back to Ohio in June of 1900 after a total residence here of almost 30 years. She survived a stroke in 1904 and passed away in Ohio in 1908.

It took many years and difficult labors, but eventually the duo's works were recognized and appreciated by the black and white citizens of the town. As one writer expressed it, "When Amos Billingsley came in March of 1871...he came to a land of foes; he met cold words and unfriendly glances on every hand. When he went to his reward his senseless clay was followed to the car which bore him to his final resting place by a crowd of sorrowing hearts."

Rev. and Mrs. Billingsley are buried in the Glenview Cemetery, East Palestine, Columbiana County, Ohio. The couple had no children.

Besides the couple's religious work, there were two other major ways in which they impacted the life of the black citizens of Statesville and, to a lesser degree, the lives of the white citizens and that is the Billingsley Hospital and the Billingsley Memorial Academy.

THE BILLINGSLEY HOSPITAL

This is the story of Statesville's first hospital. It may also have been the first municipal hospital in the state. One of the provisions of Rev. A. S. Billingsley's will was that funds—in the amount of $5,000—were provided for the erection of a charity hospital in Statesville and when it was completed that it be turned over to the town. The hospital was to be for both races, but with separate rooms. There was a proviso in the will that the property would be used only for hospital purposes and if it were abandoned as a hospital, the property would revert to the Billingsley estate.

However, there was no provision in the town's charter for the operation of a municipal hospital or the means to run it, and the aldermen believed that the hospital, even though it would do much good, would be another weight on the already-burdened tax payers' shoulders. As *The Landmark* stated, the aldermen "were perplexed."

An arrangement was worked out and accepted by which Drs. Henry F. Long and W. Junius Hill would take charge of the hospital, equip and run it, "bearing all expenses themselves," and they would have whatever proceeds derived from paying patients. They also agreed to receive and treat all charity patients within the town's borders, with the town paying for the cost of board for the patients. Other town doctors in the community could send patients there and also treat them there.

The cornerstone for Statesville's first hospital was laid on September 7, 1899, and was inscribed, "The A. S. Billingsley Hospital, 1899." Under the stone was a sort of time capsule containing a Bible, Rev. Billingsley's book, *The Life of George Whitfield*; a town directory, documents pertaining to the hospital, a list of all of Statesville's doctors and some other items.

The Billingsley Hospital, located off Park Street at what is now Park Terrace, was completed and admitting patients by early September of 1900 with five patients admitted by the first week of the month. Although not completely finished, *The Landmark* proclaimed the new two-story building as one of the best, if not the best, of its kind in the state.

At that time a north wing was used for female patients and a south wing was for male patients. There was an operating room in the center of the facility lighted by a skylight. There were also four general wards and 12 private rooms. Two dining rooms, a cooking room and storage spaces were housed in the basement. When finished, the hospital was expected to be able to accommodate 40 patients.

Later the "colored" patients would find themselves roomed in the basement, a modification that Rev. and Mrs. Billingsley never intended. The January 19, 1904, *Landmark* reported, "The mayor and hospital committee, who were authorized by the board of aldermen to make arrangements at Billingsley hospital for colored patients, have decided to dig out the basement of the hospital and arrange two suitable rooms for that purpose. The expense of the addition for the accommodation for the colored patients will be met with about $100 raised by the Alpha Book Club and donated for that cause."

Associated with Drs. Long and Hill were Drs. Thomas E. Anderson and M. R. Adams. These four men, along with Rev. W. R. McLelland, a Presbyterian minister, made up the Board of Regents of the Billingsley Hospital Company. Dr. Adams was the company's first president. Miss Mollie Walker, an experienced nurse, was in charge of day to day operations.

A kind of progress report of the hospital was printed in 1902, covering improvements made over the previous 12 months. At that time Drs. Long and Hill were the managers, and both were surgeons. Other staff members included an anesthetist, Dr. R. A. Campbell; superintendent of nurses Miss Anne Ferguson, and nurses Misses Kate Karcher, Lucy Davidson, Maggie Moose, Laura Mae Pitts and Lois Boyd.

As part of its charter, Billingsley Hospital operated a school of nursing beginning in 1901. In 1903 the graduates were the above-mentioned Misses Kate Karcher, Maggie Moose and Lucy Davidson.

In 1901 the hospital performed 74 operations, and had treated 55 female patients and 19 male patients. There had been but three deaths—all of them followed operations for appendicitis.

In 1903 Drs. Long and Hill handed over management of the hospital to Nurses Miss Anne Ferguson and Miss Lucy Davidson. The school continued to operate its school for nurses.

In mid-1904 the hospital reported that within the preceding forty days eleven cases of appendicitis had been reported and ten of the cases resulted in successful surgeries at the hospital. This was, by far, the most common operation performed at the facility.

In spite of successes, there were frequent appeals for financial support for the hospital. A street fair was organized in April, 1904, and contributions were solicited almost from the start. Several letters of praise appeared in the newspaper. One from a Mr. Flake T. Burke appeared in 1902 following his successful appendectomy. Mr. Burke first praised the "kind and attentive nurses" and continued, "I would like to say a word in honor of the Billingsley hospital. It is a good place for the sick. It has two of the best doctors in town at its head, and six as nice young women as can be found anywhere for nurses....God bless the hospital work!"

Similar sentiments were expressed by a lady signing herself as "S.F." in July of 1904, concluding with the sentiment, "The writer endeavors, Mr. Editor, thus to express somewhat of the gratitude and affection due for recent treatment from the dear ladies now in charge of the institution founded by the man to whom Statesville owes so much."

In spite of this, the hospital was often closed and then re-opened. In November of 1905 the town's aldermen were discussing closing it. In 1907 it was re-opened. A concert was held for the benefit of the hospital in 1908.

Dr. Long left Billingsley Hospital in 1905 when he opened his own private hospital on North Center Street.

By 1914 the building was idle again and the Iredell County Civic League—"that body of public spirited women of the county"—proposed running it. It had been under a Dr. Yount, who gave it up the previous December to devote his efforts to his own private practice.

According to the late Homer Keever, the Billingsley Hospital managed to run sporadically until 1920, when the facility housed patients during the flu epidemic of that year. It was in 1920 that the Carpenter-Davis Hospital opened in Statesville, which further drew away patients. After the flu crisis was over, the Billingsley Hospital building was never again used as a hospital. The structure was sold by the city in 1926 and recycled as an apartment house until 1946, when it was torn down by the Barnes Company.

Even before the demolition of the building there was a movement among the town's black citizens to erect what was to be called the "Billingsley Memorial Hospital," solely for blacks. This began in December of 1943, during World War II.

There are numerous references to fund-raising efforts for the Negro hospital in the old *Landmark* and *Statesville Daily Record* newspapers of the late 1940s through the early 1950s. Some headlines give an indication of what was happening: "Colored People Want New Hospital" (1943); "$4,268.43 Raised for New Hospital" (1944); "Mrs. J. F. Cannon Gives $1,000 for Negro Hospital (1945); "The Billingsley Hospital Here Is Given Approval" (1950); "Negroes Need $22,000 More to Build

Hospital" (1951); "Negro Hospital Jeopardized by Mounting Costs" (1951).

Thousands of dollars were raised towards a hospital for the blacks of Statesville and the county, but the project eventually failed as the Civil Rights Movement began and black citizens began to insist on patient equality in the existing hospitals of the county.

As Iredell historian Homer Keever stated it, "The Billingsley Hospital was a reality; Billingsley Memorial was just a dream."

THE BILLINGSLEY MEMORIAL ACADEMY

In 1901 Mrs. Emily Hamilton Billingsley, the widow of Rev. Billingsley, as a continuation of her and her late husband's missionary and social work in Iredell County, donated $1,100 for the establishment of an academy and industrial school for black children in Statesville. By August of 1901 six acres of land on South Green Street "near the colored graded school" had been purchased. Additional funds for the school came from the Women's Fund of the Freedmen's Bureau and $450 from what was then referred to as the "Northern" Presbyterian Church. Another $250 was pledged for the school by local individuals.

In the academy's charter it was specified that the academy was to be connected with the church led by Rev. S. F. Wentz, who had already started a school in the basement of his church.

A brief article in a June, 1903, *Landmark* reported what had been accomplished so far: "H. A. Hunt of Charlotte has drawn plans for Billingsley Memorial Academy which Rev. Samuel Former Wentz, colored, proposes to build in Statesville...It is to be of brick, 43 x 92 feet, three stories and a basement. It will be located in southeast Statesville. The first floor will contain a chapel, recitation and sewing rooms and office. The second and third floors will be used for dormitories, bathrooms and closets. The building will probably cost between $6,000 and $8,000."

Ground was broken during a rally held on August 9, 1905, at the site near "the colored graded school" on South Green Street. According to Statesville resident Mrs. Louise Moten, the Billingsley Academy stood between the side of Calvary Presbyterian Church and Dockery Street, facing South Green Street.

The Landmark described the Academy as being a pet project of Rev. Wentz, who had been raising funds for the building for several years. By the time of the ground-breaking he was reported to have raised $3,150, of which $550 went for the land. Some $600 was said to have been pledged by "colored" citizens and it was thought the project would require about $500 more, this in addition to the $1,100 donated by Mrs. Billingsley. Later reports were that $125 was raised during the ground-breaking rally.

Early in 1906 construction was underway, with Mr. D. A. Morrison as the contractor. The dimensions of the building were now reported to be 50 by 57 feet and three stories high, the first story to be of brick and the other two stories to be of wood.

The cornerstone was laid September 6, 1906, as part of a rally and farmers' conference, and an "entertainment" was also held in the basement of the building. Large crowds were reported to have attended, the stated purpose being to raise monies for the academy and "to stir up the colored people of the community on education." The president of Biddle University in Charlotte was one of the speakers and the Rev. Wentz spoke out against strong drink and vagrancy and the lewd women and low class people he said who hanged around the depot. Another $60 to $80 was raised for the school.

Rev. Wentz ran the academy that year with the help of two other teachers and they taught 95 pupils. In 1909 Rev. Wentz was still principal teacher and had three assistant teachers serving around 125 students. In 1911 the faculty consisted of one male and three female teachers, with 85 to 110 students. In 1913 there were still four instructors dealing with 109 students.

Besides contributing to the education of the community, the academy was often a center of other social activities. A barbecue was held at Billingsley Academy as part of the Fourth of July celebration in 1908. The academy's auditorium was used as a sanctuary while the "colored" Baptist Church on Green Street was being enlarged in 1915. In 1918 Miss Mary Charlton announced that the upcoming black teachers' examinations would be held at Billingsley. What *The Landmark* described as a "Colored Baby Contest" was held in October of 1922, the competition being open to "the best all-around baby from 5 to 12 months old."

In June of 1923 Prince Madarikan Deniyi, said to be a noted lecturer and journalist from Nigeria and a member of the Yoruba tribe spoke at Billingsley on "The Bright Side of Africa. Prince Deniyi spoke in costume, and both white and black people were invited to hear him.

Rev. Wentz ran the school and his church until 1914, when he took a position at Grace Presbyterian Church in Winston-Salem. He was replaced in both positions by the Reverend Zander Adam Dockery. The Reverend's wife, Anna Tamer Dockery, also taught at Billingsley.

A 1928 item in *The Landmark* told of a planned dormitory to be erected on the southern side of the Academy by the Home Missions board of the Presbyterian Church (U.S.A.), which was to house about 100 students.

Among the few brief items about the school in the local newspapers was one from 1931 reporting that the Billingsley students had held an athletic contest with students of Morningside High School. There were three events mentioned: a mile relay race, a pole vault and a three-mile run. Billingsley was reported to have beaten the team from Morningside in all three contests. Dr. M. H. Horrington, a sponsor, said that the he hoped the contest would become an annual event, but this writer has found no further references to this.

The Billingsley Memorial Academy is said to have closed during the Great Depression. It was in operation from about 1906 to sometime in the 1930s, about a quarter of a century. The Billingsley Hospital was in operation for about 20 years. The contributions of Rev. and Mrs. Billingsley should not be forgotten. In particular, the Billingsley Academy should be remembered; perhaps an elementary school in Statesville could carry on the name and heritage.

"Billingsley Elementary School" has a nice ring to it, doesn't it?

DAVID H. BRANTLEY

Here's a story of a local veteran who had much to be thankful for: surviving the most terrible war in our nation's history and arriving home safe and sound. And we should be thankful that this story was preserved for us to read. The reason for that is from 1904 through 1917, the good ladies of the local unit of the United Daughters of the Confederacy, the Battle of Bentonville Chapter, made an effort to collect accounts of the Civil War from local surviving veterans. Someone evidently had observed that the Thin Gray Line was becoming noticeably thinner and grayer with each year's passing.

The ladies were successful in their endeavor, collecting twenty-two such accounts: reminiscences of soldiers, letters sent home, descriptions of life at the home front, and a portion of a diary. One of the accounts preserved was penned by David Henry Brantley, a respected citizen of southern Iredell County.

Mr. Brantley, although he served only for about a year, dictated a very clear and colorful account of some of his adventures in the War of Northern Aggression to his daughter Etta (Mrs. Chal. E. Cornelius) on April 25, 1913, twelve years before his death.

The following document is Mr. Brantley's account, and it appears in print with the kind permission of the Battle of Bentonville Chapter of the United Daughters of the Confederacy. A few minor changes have been made in the interest of readability, but the words are Mr. Brantley's, dictated from memory of events which had occurred about fifty years before. Creswell Springs, incidentally, was a spa and rest resort south of Mooresville across the railroad tracks from the Fleetwood Mobile Homes plant.

Private Brantley was a member of Co. "G," 38th Regiment North Carolina Troops, known as "The Rocky Face Rangers," which was made up mostly of Alexander County men, but also had a fair number of Iredell men in its membership.

Private Brantley surrendered with Lee's Army of Northern Virginia at Appomattox Court House, Virginia, on April 9, 1865, and within a day or two began the long walk home to Iredell County. He was accompanied on his trek by Private George Lee Kistler of Mount Mourne, who had just been paroled from Company "I" of the 7th North Carolina.

* * *

I will give a short sketch of what I saw and experienced in the Sixties.

When I was about 15 years of age, I heard the First Secession Speech by R. I. McDowell at Creswell Spring. He said the Yankees would not fight, we could whip them with Barlow knives and corn stalks. The blood lost would not stain his white pocket handkerchief, but it was not that way.

I saw the first company organize in south Iredell, Company "I" of the 7th Regiment. I felt like volunteer[ing] but was too young. Well, in 1864 [came the] call for 18 [year old] boys, that was my age. I went to Camp Vance near Morganton, drilled and guarded deserters. I made several trips to Raleigh, after a few months was sent to Richmond, Va., from there to Petersburg, Va., in the ditches on the Weldon Railroad. [I was] Assigned to Company G, 38th N.C. Troops, Scale's Brigade, A. P. Hill's Corps, Wilcox's Division, Lee's Army.

The camp was made up from Iredell and Alexander County. After a few days we were ordered to Chapin's Farm below Drewry's Bluff north of James River where the negro fight was. The Yankees had re-cruited their ranks with negroes, was a great number slaughtered, no quarter was shown. The battle began in the evening. We lay on our arms until midnight, were ordered to our left to build breastworks, no tools save Bayonets to gouge dirt with—our hands to shovel— by day we had the dirt bountiful to cover our heads. Was heavy sharp-shooting up to noon, then the Yankees withdrew. We were ordered back to the ditch from where we started.

After a few days went to Bellville, next ordered back to Malvin [Malvern] Hill in the ditches, next ordered to Virgin Mills. We formed a line of battle, lay on our arms until late evening, ordered to relieve Heth's Division. As we went in, the wounded were lying on each side, shot every shape that could be thought of. Some were praying, singing, hollering, swearing- it made us feel pretty bad. At night the battle stopped to bury dead and care for the wounded.

We were ordered to our left in ditches with orders not to raise our head above breastworks—very heavy shooting in front. West Matheson from near Statesville, Iredell Co., our Ensign, was killed near me. He would stand up, took my gun and said he was going to shoot a Yankee in his head to save his overcoat. While up, a ball hit him in the back of head & came out in front—he died in one hour.

The Yankees ceased firing about noon and withdrew. We were ordered back to the ditches from whence we came. Picket duty near the enemy.

I saw nine deserters shot at stakes Jan. 1865. I was detailed assign to Engineer Corps & sent to Sutherland Station, 11 miles from Petersburg on the Southside Railroad to construct abatises for the Breastworks. There were men from all Southern states. We had a fine time—so much to do each day. We could do our task in two hours, then were at liberty to visit around in country foraging.

The people were very nice to us & gave us something to eat. Ash cake was a great dish in Virginia & was with me. Last of March our play-house was broken up. Captain McGinnis and I went down to Petersburg on Saturday for rations. I stayed over night—went to the concert—it was over about 10 o'clock. I came out on the street, the earth

48

was in a quiver, cannons were roaring five miles around. Mortar shells were like throwing balls over the house, was a pretty sight to stand off & view at night.

It was getting late. I went to Garret Hotel and registered, gave ten dollars & went to bed. The inmates were very excited. I slept fine until the porter came & woke me up about day. He said the Yankees had broken the lines & I had better move, which I did.

Shells were falling in the streets, rolling. I dashed across to the Southside Depot. Shells were falling all about. The train started, we went a few miles and Sheridan's cavalry dashed in tearing up the track while the train was stopped. We took the spyglass and saw the movement of the army at a distance. Railroad track was repaired, we went to Southerland Station Farm.

Our men made breastworks out of fence rails & had a battle. I stood and saw it. When the balls came falling around, I moved to other quarters. At 1 o'clock a courier came & ordered us to go to Appomattox River. In our route the road was full of people who had been to church. Scared almost to death when they saw us, not knowing the Yankees were so near. We arrived at the river but could not cross, saw Wilcox's courier drowned.

We went up the south bank in a zigzag move, more fast than slow. About dusk we crossed a stream on a raft of rails, which was very dangerous. When we had gotten up a hill (I do not know where) we lay down to rest. Before day we had to move. Some time that day we came to Deep Creek. McGowan's Brigade was trying to make a floating bridge with rails & gun slings. Had stacked their arms, the water was very deep, would swim a horse.

In a few minutes the cavalry commenced fighting down the creek. Our cavalry came dashing back, some of the horses fell down. The riders never waited for them to get up, but ran on. McGowan's men left their guns and we all ran up the creek a half mile, some one had cut a big pine across. So many of us were on at a time the log would sink 8 or 10 inches. If we had not been scared, we could not have crossed. After we were over & went on a few miles we came to more water. There was a pontoon bridge across & here we rested. The next place of importance was Burkesville Junction, where was a battle.

The next place was Farmville. Train was standing full of ladies & gents scared no use talking. Shells were falling fast, no time for us to stop. We made another move. Sheridan's cavalry dashed in and set our wagon train on fire. Our men run them back, they would run in every day. We did not have many guns. We had to change our course very often. How the time passed, I did not know how. I knew when the 8th of April was. I was detailed to help drive some cattle back 5 miles after night to Pickett's Division. When we had gotten there had to bring them back.

Twelve o'clock night we lay down and had gotten to sleep, ordered up & move on. About daylight we came to a halt near Clover Hill Court House, Appomattox County. Gen. Lee was battling in front, the first part of the day news came that General Lee had surrendered which made us feel—I don't know how to express it—It was not long before Generals Lee & Gordon came.

General Lee made a short address, said, "I have done the best I could—the war is over—you will be paroled & go to your homes & there remain undisturbed."

He seemed very much affected that day.

I visited the field hospital, saw a great number of wounded. Saw Dr. Surgell cutting off legs & arms. I think I saw a big wagon load lying in the farm's yard. I felt very sorry for them on the close of the war.

Our bill of fare was parched corn, Sunday, April 9, 1865. Monday 10th Yankees gave us rations. They commingled with us very fondly—they were glad the war was over—they were surprised to know that Lee had such a small army, they said they felt as if they had not done any thing. They did not fire any salutes.

I saw Grant's army form what they called a hollow square & General Lee's army marched between & stacked arms. He had 10,000 stands. The cannon were packed in the field near us—we that had no guns didn't go after that was through. Generals Grant, Sheridan, Thomas—in our camp on the 11th Wednesday afternoon, we were paroled.

We did not know what to do, no conveyance, a long way to walk. Well, Mr. Lee Kistler & I started home together—we had nothing to eat—had to beg, that fell on me, by time we got home I was an expert beggar.

We came near Lynchburg, crossed Campbell County. I started each day afternoon for supper, then early in morning for breakfast. I always got a piece of bread. When we passed the before mentioned county, next Bedford, then Pittsylvania, then Henry & came to North Carolina at Leaksville.

"We came to Stanton River, no way to cross. We went up the river, we came to a canoe landing. Sambo came over with his hog trough. Lee in one end, I in the other, Sambo in the middle. River high water level with top floating down below landing.

We landed alright, I gave tin cup, Lee a pair of hose—no breakfast—was a wealthy family on the hill, named Jones. I called on the good lady for bread—she invited me to the table. I called Lee. She set water, towel & soap. We took a bath & went to the table with three pretty red-headed girls to wait on the table. Bread, bacon, coffee, pickles—the way we eat was a sin. When we were full I asked bill, nothing, she looked above for her pay. I thanked her and departed. We remember her ever since.

We wag on until we strike Leaksville, N.C. A good man invited us to breakfast, he gave us water, soap, and set down one more square meal.

Next place was Madison, Rockingham Co., & took dinner. That was up in the evening. We crossed Dan River, came in the direction of Kernersville. We never saw a railroad after we left Appomattox, Va., until we came to the railroad bridge beyond Salisbury. We left Lexington to our left. It seems we missed all towns, we came to Yadkin crossed on railroad bridge from there to Salisbury. [Union Gen. George] Stoneman had been there a few days before, the depot was still on fire. We rested a few minutes, then came out 6 miles and got some bread to eat & went out to woods for bed.

The next morning we struck the Sechler Springs Road. I called at house for bread, black girl came out, said Boss was at prayer, he got through and came out. I asked for bread, he said he did not have one bit in the world. I told him I would pay for it if he would take my money. He went & brought me some bread. I gave him 5 dollars in Confederate money. The last debt I ever paid with that money. I thought his religion was like the money—not worth much. We arrived home in the afternoon, change clothes & eat a square meal.

The end.

* * *

Mr. Brantley died on October 3, 1925, and is buried in the graveyard of Centre Presbyterian Church in Mount Mourne. By the way, this story ends on a rather happy note: Mr. Brantley's grandson, Fred Gray Brantley, married Mr. Kistler's granddaughter, Willie Kistler. Both families reckon that their connection can be traced back to their grandfathers' long walk home together from the War.

PAUL BRENDLE

"People ask me what I do in winter when there's no baseball. I'll tell you what I do. I stare out the window and wait for spring."
-Rogers Hornsby

With the approach of opening day of Major League Baseball, the Hot Stove League, that mythical winter fellowship of die-hard diamond prognosticators, disbands until next the fall. For one Iredell County resident in particular, the coming of baseball season is like the return of an old friend.

One-time pro baseball player and actor Bob Uecker may have been called "Mr. Baseball" by TV's Johnny Carson, but around the Cool Springs community when someone says, "Mr. Baseball," they're probably referring to "Coach" Paul Brendle.

Paul Richard Brendle, born in Forsyth County in 1926, came to Iredell when his father, mother, sister and two brothers moved here when he was three and a half years old. His father, Thad Brendle, who was in the furniture business here, played some semi-pro baseball for a Winston-Salem team as a young man.

"That's the true harbinger of spring, not crocuses or swallows returning to Capistrano, but the sound of a bat on a ball."
-Bill Veeck

Paul Brendle began an association with our national game while he was a student. "Baseball started for me on the playground at Wayside Elementary School. Then in the 7th or 8th grade, our principal, Mr. J. T. White, organized a school team and we really played baseball at other schools. We traveled in a car pulling a trailer, with six or seven little boys in each," he said.

His preparation for what would eventually become his career continued at Cool Spring High School. There for three years he played first base and some basketball under principal and coach Mr. Royd Blaine Madison. A popular student, Brendle was president of the senior class the year he graduated, 1944.

"You gotta be a man to play baseball for a living, but you gotta have a lot of little boy in you, too."

-Roy Campanella

From Cool Spring High he went into the Navy on July 6, 1944, at the age of 17. Brendle served on an LST (Landing Ship, Tanks) as an ablebodied seaman supporting the invasion of Iwo Jima and then the invasion of Okinawa. Besides being a deckhand, he also manned a 20 mm antiaircraft gun in the ship's bow. At one period during the heaviest of the fighting, Brendle and his shipmates manned their battle stations for 32 hours straight. The ship's cooks brought them sandwiches and strong Navy coffee to keep them awake.

"If you had to go to the head (Navyese for 'bathroom')," he recalled, "you had to get someone to take your place until you got back."

His ship, LST-823, was credited with shooting down one Japanese kamikaze plane. The enemy aircraft crashed into the sea close enough that Brendle was able to see the pilot's face. After Japan's surrender, Seaman Brendle was attached to an Air/Sea rescue unit. He was dischagred from the Navy on July 4, 1946, two days shy of two years of active duty.

"A good friend of mine used to say, 'This is a very simple game. You throw the ball, you catch the ball, you hit the ball. Sometimes you win, sometimes you lose, sometimes it rains.' Think about that for a while." -from the 1988 movie,
"Bull Durham"

Following military service he went back to school on the G. I. Bill, to Mitchell Junior College in 1946 for two years where he played basketball and baseball. At the same time he was playing first base for Diamond Hill in a semi-pro league against teams from Harmony, South Statesville, Beavers Store, Scotts and Union Grove, among others. The Diamond Hill team was short on pitchers and so he volunteered to take that position. After playing for Diamond Hill, he pitched for the old Phoenix Mills team in the summer of 1948.

"When they start the game, they don't yell, 'Work ball.' They say, 'Play ball.' "
-Willie Stargell

After two years at Mitchell, he went to Catawba College in Salisbury, where he pitched two years for the Indians. The Catawba Indians played against V.P.I., Wofford, East Carolina, Appalachian, High Point and other colleges. Brendle was proficient enough at pitching to be named to the All North State Conference Baseball Team in 1950, and chose to sign with the Statesville Owls that same year in order to stay near home.

He is one of the few who played for the old Mooresville Moors and for the Statesville Owls in the heyday of the old North

Carolina State League. He was a pitcher for the Cincinatti Reds-affiliated Owls in 1950 and 1951, hurled for the Mooresville Moors in 1952, and then returned to Statesville (by then the "Statesville Sports") in 1953. When the Statesville team folded mid-season, he finished the season with the Hickory Rebels. He also pitched and was a utility man for the Dartmouth Arrows Baseball Club in Nova Scotia, Canada, for five seasons, giving him a nine year career in professional baseball.

"A hot dog at the ballgame beats roast beef at the Ritz."
-Humphrey Bogart

He has no favorite baseball movie or a particular favorite team. Brendle says he greatly admired the Braves when they were a Boston team and he himself was pitching. After his star pupil Herman Starrette went pro, he always rooted for whichever team "Herm" was on.

He married Shirley Rogers, a Statesville lady, in 1960 and the couple have two sons, Ronnie and Paul Jr., who goes by "Pete." Pete played baseball under his father's coaching at North Iredell and then at South Iredell High after his father transferred there.

"Hitting is timing. Pitching is upsetting timing."
-Warren Spahn

"What do I look for in a baseball game? I like to see how a guy, particularly a pitcher, handles himself. From being a coach

I look for mistakes in games, like over-throwing, the players not talking among themselves and not backing up fellow players. Professional baseball has changed from when I was a pitcher. I used to pitch for nine innings by myself. Today they drag the game out, changing pitchers. They have an opening pitcher, a specialist in throwing to south paws and a closing pitcher. Still, I love the game."

"The way a team plays as a whole determines its success. You may have the greatest bunch of individual stars in the world, but if they don't play together, the club won't be worth a dime."
                                                                -Babe Ruth

To view Paul Brendle just as an athlete would be to seriously short-change the man, as he dabbles in wine-making and has been a serious collector of Native American artifacts and a student of their culture for many years. His other passions/hobbies include camping, hunting and fishing. He also collects and makes fishing lures.

"Baseball is like a poker game. Nobody wants to quit when he's losing; nobody wants you to quit when you're ahead."
                                                          -Jackie Robinson

When Brendle wasn't playing, he was coaching. From 1950 to 1966 he coached baseball and basketball at his alma mater, Cool Spring High School. He also coached girls basketball and some 8-man football. Following consolidation of the small high schools into North and South High, Brendle was the first baseball coach at North Iredell High when it opened its doors in 1966. He held that position through 1972 and then coached the same sport at South Iredell High from 1976 to 1983. In his spare time, he taught driver's education for 38 years.

In many ways the consolidation of the small rural high schools that dotted Iredell County into the giant high schools was a good thing, he pointed out, but also it was not so good in certain respects, for where you had had five basketball or baseball teams, now you had but one. In essence, fewer schools meant fewer teams and so fewer players. Also, he pointed out, where he had known the families of the boys he coached at Cool Spring, when he coached at North Iredell there were boys from Harmony, Union Grove and so forth that he didn't know.

He took a four-year hiatus from education to try being a salesman with the Trailblazer-Winchester Co. in Statesville, but missed the classroom and students and the baseball diamond.

"You spend a good piece of your life gripping a baseball and in the end it turns out that it was the other way around all the time."

-Jim Bouton

Brendle was honored on June 1, 2010, when he was asked to be one of three former Owls—with Jerry Fox and "Squirrel" Thomas—to throw out the ceremonial opening pitch for the new Statesville Owls team of the Southern Collegiate Baseball League. But instead of going to sit in the dugout, where he could be found for about 40 years, he then sat in the bleachers with friends and former students, including "Herm" Starrette, Jerry

Fox and and Bobby Stevenson. Brendle said it was the first time he had ever seen a baseball game from the bleachers.

"Baseball is an allegorical play about America, a poetic, complex, and subtle play of courage, fear, good luck, mistakes, patience about fate, and sober self-esteem."

-Saul Steinberg

Interviewed by sports writer Mike Owens of the *Record & Landmark* upon his retirement from teaching in June of 1983, Brendle reflected on a career that had occupied most of his adult life. "Looking back, I don't think if I had the chance to do things over I would change very much. I've always been disappointed a little more each year by the fact that the players are becoming less and less dedicated to the sport of baseball. I remember the days when you could take a drive around the community and the young boys were out throwing a baseball. Every weekend there was a 'big' game somewhere in the area....The kids nowadays have a chance to get their own cars and spend a lot of their time working to maintain those cars.... No doubt, the priorities have changed...but the attitude change has been the biggest, I think."

"Don't tell me about the world. Not today. It's springtime and they're knocking baseballs around fields where the grass is damp and green in the morning and the kids are trying to hit the curve ball."

-Pete Hamill

Brendle's attitudes about life and baseball have not changed substantially since that 1983 interview and write-up.

"Having played baseball for some 16 years as a pitcher and as a coach for 30 years, I have noted some parallels between the National Pastime and The Game of Life.

"First, both have rules to play by and rules to live by. You must go by the rules. Next, both have bumps in the road, highs and lows. As a player or coach you must learn to deal with it. Also, you must be observant as a player, a coach, or in life: There are a lot of details you must take care of. In baseball, it's repeating the fundamentals until they become habits. And finally, you must play the game to win, but know that you might not. Everyone is not gifted, but you can show good sportsmanship, win or loose, which shows the character of a player. I'd say that if you can handle the pressures of a tight ball game, you can probably handle the pressures of life."

Coach Brendle conservatively estimates that he has played in 1,200 to 1,300 games and has coached some 600 baseball games: at North Iredell, at South Iredell and as a coach for the Statesville Recreation Department and for American Legion teams.

"I think seeing the kids I coached develop makes it all worthwhile. A lot of my best friends are former ball players I coached."

"A life is not important except in the impact it has on other lives."

-Jackie Robinson

L. B. Bristol

Reminders of our common past are all around us, just awaiting rediscovery. A case in point involves an email received in 2007 by David Bradley of the Greater Statesville Chamber of Commerce from a lady in Nashville, Tennessee.

The lady explained that she worked for a group that sponsors two Bible colleges in Nigeria. The group had received a donation of books, mostly religious in nature, and were going through the volumes to see if any might be suitable for sending to the colleges in Africa. Apparently, while examining them, a small piece of paper, perhaps used as a bookmark, was dislodged and floated to the floor.

The paper turned out to be a 1927 ginnery ticket from the L. B. Bristol Cotton Ginning Company of Statesville, N.C.

As the lady explained, "We do not know from which book it fell, so we do not know whom to contact to see if they want it back." She thought the receipt might have some historical value and contacted the chamber. David Bradley contacted Tim Dearman, publisher of the *Record & Landmark*, and Tim passed it on to me.

So, here back home 80 years later, is a piece of Statesville's past, measuring 3 3/4 by 4 1/2 inches, dated October 7, 1927. It directly leads to two subjects: Mr. L. B. Bristol and the importance of cotton to Iredell County in 1927.

Besides running a cotton gin, Lee Berts Bristol was the popular mayor of Statesville at that time; his portrait can be viewed on a wall in City Hall. I think he looks somewhat like President Theodore Roosevelt.

Born in Burke County in 1869, Bristol came to Statesville in 1889 to work for the Wallace Brothers. By 1911, he was elected an alderman (town commissioner).

Although his formal education ended in the eighth grade, L. B. Bristol is remembered as one of Statesville's most progressive and interesting leaders. His administration was a long one—1917 to 1927—and encompassed the acceptance of the automobile. While it is true that there were automobiles on the streets of Statesville fully a decade before Bristol became mayor, it was during his tenure that the auto became a common sight.

Among other projects, Mayor Bristol promoted the paving of streets, the construction of sidewalks and the installation of stoplights. He also vigorously supported the municipal fire department.

His Honor was also a dapper dresser who preferred to be chauffeured around rather than to drive himself. He had varied business interests; besides his cotton gin, which stood in the area of The Farm and Garden Services, 202 Light Street, he owned farms on what is now Bristol Drive. In addition, Bristol served the state as quartermaster general of the North Carolina National Guard under Governor Locke Craig.

Bristol is said to have been able to greet, by name, every citizen, black or white, that he met. He seems to have loved being mayor and was loved by the town in return.

A man who had labored to improve his station in life, Bristol was almost ruined by the Great Depression.

"Bert" Bristol died of a heart attack at his home on the corner of West Broad and Meeting streets in 1935; he was 65 years old. He was survived by his wife, the former Mary C. Cowles, and four children. He is buried in Oakwood Cemetery.

The old post office and courthouse was built on the site of the Bristol home. It is interesting that Mayor Garland Shelton died there in 1940 during the dedication of that building.

Back to the ginnery ticket. The ticket was made out to what looks like "John Turner," but the surname may not be correct. John's bale of cotton weighed 479 pounds and he apparently was paid 18.75 cents per pound, meaning that he got $89.91 for this bale.

Mike Miller of the Iredell County Agricultural Extension Agency noted that October 7th would have been at the very beginning of the cotton harvesting season.

By and large, cotton fields are becoming increasingly rare in Iredell County. Cotton, both before and after the Civil War, was a vital part of Iredell's economy. Agent Miller said that in 2005 Iredell had 1,000 acres planted and a yield of 1,099 pounds of raw cotton per harvested acre. That sounds like a very large amount of cotton.

However, in 1927, the year of the ginnery ticket, Iredell had 35,100 acres planted in the stuff with a yield of 270 bales per acre and a total production of 18,920 bales.

Cotton, if not king then, was still minor royalty.

An anonymous tribute to Mayor Bristol found in the archives of the genealogical society revealed something of the style and flair of the man: "The familiar figure of Mayor L. B. Bristol astride a spirited horse, riding through the streets of Statesville early mornings or late in the evening, is one of the real hallmarks of this community."

The ginnery ticket, signed by the mayor, is a bit of local Americana that came very close to having been shipped to Africa, and had it not been for a concerned individual, it very well could have been gone from us forever. Instead, it is going to Mayor Bristol's great-grandson, Cowles Bristol, Jr.

Hopefully, something of the spirit of Bert Bristol, astride a charger, may still be found on the streets of Statesville today.

STAN BROOKSHIRE

Stanford Raynold "Stan" Brookshire, of Troutman, was mayor of Charlotte for four two-year terms, from 1961 to 1969, and at the time of his service, was the longest-serving mayor in the city's history.

Stan was born in Troutman on July 22, 1905, one of nine children of James C. and Effie Perry Brookshire. The Kerr Drug store at 522 North Main Street, Troutman, occupies the site of the old Brookshire homeplace.

After graduating from Trinity College of Duke University in 1927, Brookshire came to Charlotte to work on the *Charlotte Observer.*

He was elected president of the Charlotte Chamber of Commerce in 1960 before being elected mayor.

Although he did not face the problems fellow Iredell-born Mayor Ben Douglas faced during the Great Depression, when Brookshire, a Democrat, took the mayoral reins in hand, there were potentially difficult times for the Queen City.

Due in part because of Brookshire's leadership, Charlotte peacefully integrated its gargantuan school system and public accommodations in the 1960s and largely avoided much of the violence that saw parts of large cities like Los Angeles and Detroit burn following the assassination of Dr. Martin Luther King Jr. in April of 1969.

Brookshire founded the Charlotte-Mecklenburg Community Relations Committee. Lake Norman, North Carolina's "Inland Sea," was developed by Duke Power Company during Brookshire's mayorship, becoming the state's largest man-made lake.

Mayor Brookshire championed urban renewal and beautification and, like Mayor Ben Douglas, realized the importance of transportation to the city's future, resulting in the planned automotive expressway that bears his name.

Stan Brookshire died in Charlotte on October 10, 1990, at the age of 85. He was buried in Evergreen Cemetery in Charlotte.

He was survived by his wife Edith, a son, a daughter and eight grandchildren.

The next time you're going down I-77 and see the exit sign for the Brookshire Freeway, remember that Stan Brookshire was a son of Iredell County.

J. P. CALDWELL

Born in Statesville on June 16, 1853, Joseph Pearson "J.P." Caldwell had the same name as his father, who had been a state senator in 1833 and 1834, a member of the state house of commons—later called the state house of representatives—from 1838—1844, and had served two terms, 1849-50 and 1851-52, as a Whig in the U.S. House of Representatives. The elder J. P. Caldwell (1808-1853) passed away at the age of 45, when young J. P. was less than a month old.

J.P. the younger was principally educated at home by an older sister and attended some night school but never darkened the door of any college. However, years later he was awarded an honorary degree from Erskine College in South Carolina. He began his career in journalism at the age of 14 on *The Statesville American*. When the publisher of that paper announced it was changing into a Republican newspaper, Caldwell went to work for *The Statesville Intelligencer*, a Democratic publication. Caldwell subsequently worked for papers in Charlotte and Raleigh, each time being promoted to positions of more responsibility.

In 1880 Caldwell purchased *The Landmark* from J. S. Ramsey, who had purchased it from John Hussey. Caldwell stayed at the helm of *The Landmark* for a dozen years, and then became editor of *The Charlotte Chronicle,* whose name he changed to *The Charlotte Observer* in 1892. He sold half interest in the Statesville paper to Rufus Reid Clark, from south Iredell, who assumed the editorship of *The Landmark.* Caldwell continued to make contributions to *The Landmark* through 1906, at which time he sold the rest of his interest in the paper to Mr. Clark.

Caldwell initially opposed a tax for the establishment of the Statesville City Schools, arguing that the common man was already taxed to his limit. Homer Keever, in his *Iredell: Piedmont County*, states that the editor "felt that anything more than learning to read and write was a luxury and tax money should not be used for it." Later Caldwell changed his mind on this issue and became a great supporter of the public schools.

Along with Rev. Dr. Wood of First Presbyterian Church, Caldwell welcomed Jewish families to Statesville and influenced the community into accepting them. He would put small news items into *The Landmark*, just as he did for the Christian denominations, such community items as "The Hebrew ladies will hold a bake sale...," the same as if it had been the women of the Presbyterian Church holding the sale.

Politically he was a strong Democrat and his paper reflected his views in his editorials. Caldwell's newspaper was the primary source of news for a large part of Iredell and surrounding counties. There was no radio, television or Internet competition, and although there were some other newspapers that sprung up from time to time, none of them had the scope, staying power and influence of *The Landmark*.

Besides having a strong sense of what was news, J. P. Caldwell had a subtle sense of humor. From time to time he published news items from "Cabinsville," a fictitious community located somewhere in northern Iredell. Some readers knew that "correspondence" from Cabinsville's mayor was an exercise in tongue-in-cheek journalism, while others read these reports as factual local news.

Caldwell also gets credit for the creation of that mythical beastie, the "santer," later called the "wampus." Some have maintained that there was some sort of chicken-eating varmint roaming these parts that was the factual basis for Caldwell's santer stories, which premiered on August 28, 1890, during a slack news period.

In addition to putting out *The Landmark*, Caldwell also found time to be mayor of Statesville (1886 to 1889). His administration was notable in prodding the town to install electric lights in the business district. Caldwell had his fingers in several other pies. He was vice president of an enterprise called The Statesville Land Development and Manufacturing Company, a director of the First Building and Loan Association and was an early investor in the Statesville Cotton Mill. He had also served as president of the town's first Chamber of Commerce, which was organized in May of 1889.

Even after he moved to Charlotte, Caldwell continued to maintain a home in Statesville.

J. P. Caldwell died on November 22, 1911, at the age of 58, and is buried in Statesville's Oakwood Cemetery. Caldwell's first wife, the former Maggie Spratt, and two of their children preceded him in death. He married a second time, to a fellow *Observer* writer, Adelaide "Addie" Williams, and there was a daughter by this union. As a mark of respect, Statesville's mayor issued a proclamation that all town businesses be closed at the hour of Caldwell's funeral at First Presbyterian Church.

Iredell historian W. N. "Red" Watt commented that Caldwell's funeral drew the largest number of influential men to Statesville in its history. A North Carolina Highway Historical Marker was erected in his memory in 1949 at the corner of West Front and Mulberry streets, reading: "J. P. Caldwell, Editor of Statesville 'Landmark' 1880-92, Charlotte 'Observer' (1882-1909). His home was two blocks north."

MILTON CAMPBELL

With the approach of fall the school year resumes in Iredell County. The big yellow buses will again be on the road. Children, who had gotten used to sleeping to eight or nine a.m., will again be roused out of bed at an early hour.

"Who is responsible for all this education at the expense of the tax-paying public?" you may ask. Do not look to the Superintendent of the Mooresville Graded School District or to the Superintendent of the Iredell-Statesville Schools; they are merely continuing in positions that others had vacated.

The name of the man most responsible for our public schools, the largest employer in Iredell County, was a fellow named Milton Campbell who lived near Trinity Methodist Church on NC 115 north of Statesville. Milton Campbell had been the first postmaster of the New Hope Post office when it was established in 1832.

Mr. Campbell was appointed chairman of the board of superintendents of the Iredell County public schools in 1841 and performed the duties of county superintendent for almost twenty years, until his death in 1860 at the age of 67 years, 2 months and 3 days.

True, there were schools in Iredell before 1841: Crowfield Academy near Mount Mourne, the Ebenezer Academy near Bethany Church, Clio's Nursery between Snow Creek and the Yadkin all come to mind. These and others, however, were private schools; parents paid tuition to have their children—usually just the boys—educated at these venerable institutions. Public schools would educate the farmer's son, the daughter of the clerk at the store, the laborer's children.

Part of an 1853 letter from Mr. Campbell to North Carolina's first Superintendent of Public Instruction, Calvin H. Wiley, has survived. Then, as now, funding was a major concern:

"Our court[s] has not laid the amount of taxes the law contemplates, but what they have done aids the funds considerably. We give the teachers from $12 to $29 per month, they boarding themselves. The districts generally do not have a public school every year. Some do. The others have a subscription [private] school for the winter they have no publick school."

There is one other thing to remember Milton Campbell for. After the Civil War when Iredell County adopted townships, the basis for the 16 townships was the maps of school districts Mr. Campbell had drawn, each township being made of four to six school districts being "lumped" together. The number of school districts was calculated so the children would be within a reasonable walking distance of a school.

The schools of the day were usually of log construction, with a single teacher being paid a dollar a day for 10 to 12 weeks of teaching. The children were mostly taught during the winter when they were not needed as much to work in the fields.

Sometimes schools started in the summer and ran for several weeks and then closed down again to allow the children to help harvest crops.

There might be 20 to 50 scholars per teacher, the children ranging in age from 5 to 20. Formal education normally ended at the seventh grade. There were no computers, no cafeterias, no state-provided textbooks, no PTOs, no Friday night football games, no marching bands and no big yellow buses.

Mr. Campbell's remains rest in the cemetery of Snow Creek Methodist Church. No school within the county bears his name, and no portrait of Mr. Campbell hangs on the wall of any school building. But if you seek his monument, look around you. Mighty oaks from tiny acorns grow.

"Uncle Martin" Campbell

Beginning in the 1860s the Rev. Horatio Alger Jr. (1832-1899), of Massachusetts, wrote more than 100 novels about young boys who, although born in poverty, through hard work, perseverance and occasional good luck, rose out of poverty and achieved honor and a degree of prosperity, i.e. "the American Dream." Alger's novels were about as predictable as hot weather in August, but they were not written for literary critics; they were written for young boys, and for all we know, some less-fortunate boys may have been inspired to live a life like a character in Alger's stories, provided of course, they could have afforded the purchase price of one of the books.

Mooresville had a young black man who began in poor circumstances and lived a life of respectability and even was largely responsible for the organization of two churches. One might characterize his life as a true local variation of a "Horatio Alger story."

* * *

When Martin Evans Campbell died on Tuesday afternoon, Sept. 19, 1944, many people who read his obituary in the old Mooresville *Enterprise* probably didn't believe it, for those townspeople with some age on them remembered him as an old man when they were children. Known to most everyone as "Uncle Martin," the subject of the obituary was, at the time of his death, possibly 106 years old. And at that time he was reckoned as the oldest person in Mooresville and probably in Iredell County as well.

Martin Campbell is believed to have been born on Christmas Day, 1837, a son of slave parents in the Eufola community in northwestern Iredell County. According to one account of his early life, he left his home in 1852 at about the age of 15 and came to what would become Mooresville and spent the remaining years of his life in his adopted town. Several printed interviews over the years present some contradictions, as you will find below.

Mr. Campbell claimed that before the War Between the States he had belonged to a Colonel Campbell who had sold him to a Mr. Dick Johnston, both of whom lived above Statesville. According to an *Enterprise* interview in 1937, after the War he stayed with the Johnstons. "They thought a lot of me and told me I could do a turn better than most, so I stayed for a years. Then I come down here to visit the rest of the colored folks who had left and settled here. After that I just couldn't go back. You see, I loved Marse [Master] Johnston, but these was my own folks, and I been here ever since."

There is no question that he remained active until near the time of his passing, doing manual work for the public. His first work in Mooresville may have been for Isaac Harris, sawing and hauling logs to make lumber for the construction of homes. Isaac Harris is remembered as Mooresville's first elected mayor.

As Martin worked at whatever task he was performing, he was known to sing a favorite old hymn.

Mooresville's *Enterprise*, predecessor of *The Tribune*, did a piece on him in November of 1937, just before his 100th birthday if he was born in 1837. Here follows part:

"'The Old Time Religion' in true shouting tempo may be heard almost any Saturday afternoon along Main street as old Uncle Martin Campbell ambles along with his walking stick, his gray hair and beard glistening in the sunshine, and in his dim old eyes the light of many things remembered and perhaps the glory of things to come 'In the Sweet Bye and Bye,' another of his favorite songs. When asked who taught him to sing, the aged Negro said, 'I reckon the Lord did, and so I always sing the Lord's songs. Sometimes folks asks me why I sing along the street and I tell them the truth. It's the ways I makes my change for the church on Sunday—the Baptist church. Yes, ma'am, I am a Baptist. Why, I bought the lot and built the church house for the first Baptist church us colored folks had in this town.

"Martin has been a landmark of Mooresville for the past half century or more. He says he is 93 years old. For many years he did the hog killing for the people of the town, taking their hogs on his little one-mule cart to Troutman's furniture factory, where he slaughtered them and brought them back to their owners. Those hog-killing days were Martin's singing days, and many are those who as children can recall following him along the street and listening to the almost weird notes of his melodramatic voice, interspersed with pleading to his old mule to 'go 'long' and an occasional look over his shoulder at the fine load of 'hog meat.'"

Martin Campbell's grandson, the late James L. Campbell, published a small, interesting book about his family in December of 2000, titled, *From Slavery to the 21st Century as Seen Through the*

Eyes of a Grandson. In it, James said this about his grandfather, "After he raised his six children, he decided he wanted to be on his own; he was tired of white people telling him every move to make. He bought an old mule and a wagon and started hauling trash or anything you wanted moved. He plowed gardens, slaughtered hogs and was a cattle doctor before there were any in Mooresville...."

In another *Enterprise* article published in 1941, a week before his 100th—or 104th—birthday, it was recounted that for a number of years he had owned the Baptist church for blacks [Jones Chapel Baptist Church] in Mooresville's West End community. "However," stated the article, "when the old building began to rot and fall away, he set about to build a substantial brick church through public subscription and finally succeeded through contributions of his many white friends throughout the country and through his own people and efforts. He is a deacon in the church and practically controls its work, which is one of the leading colored churches of the community."

According to grandson James Campbell, the church begun by his grandfather split in 1997, with part of its members forming into what is today called Campbell Missionary Baptist Church, located on West McLelland Avenue.

In May of 1942, two years before his passing, Martin Campbell brought to town's newspaper a little advertisement. *The Enterprise* reported, "Martin Campbell, colored, lives in Mooresville, N.C., and is writing for a wife 85, not over 90, that is a Christian woman that can make him happy and comfortable. I'll give her plenty to eat and a nice place to rest. I haven't been hungry in my life. I am 104 years old. I own a church. I am known everywhere. I am not a preacher but I am a delegate."

It is unknown how many inquiries he received about this.

* * *

Whatever his exact age, at the time of his death Martin Campbell had outlived three wives: the former Helen Phifer, Martha Henderson and Minerva Redfear. He had outlived the six children he had by his first wife. He was survived by six sons by his wife Martha, all regarded as upright and respected citizens by the town: Frank, Odell, Oates, Isaac, Dock, and Eli Campbell. He was also survived by a brother.

As of his 100th birthday celebrated in 1941, he was reckoned to have had 30 grandchildren, 22 great-grandchildren and two great-great-grandchildren. Indeed he had "pulled himself up by his own bootstraps" and had become the respected patriarch of a great, growing clan.

BUCK CLAYWELL

The late W. A. "Buck" Claywell Jr., of Kentwood Road, Statesville, was witness to an event that happened in the closing days of World War II. Although I spoke with him in 2007, more than 60 years after the event, he remembered it like it had happened yesterday.

In August of 1945 Claywell was a 24-year-old petty officer and a member of the 186-man crew of the *USS Cecil J. Doyle* (DE-368), a destroyer escort ship on duty in the Pacific. August of 1945 was the last month of World War II, although no one knew it at that time. Parts of an atomic device nicknamed "Little Boy" had been delivered to the island of Tinian, at that time a U.S. airbase within bombing range of the Japanese home islands. "Little Boy" had been delivered by the heavy cruiser *USS Indianapolis* (CA-35), the flagship of the U.S. Fifth Fleet. The ship, called "*The Indy*" by her crew of 1,196 officers and men, had completed the delivery of the atomic device from San Francisco to Tinian, a top secret mission, in record time.

The whole mission was to deliver and assemble parts of atomic weapons on Tinian and from there drop atomic bombs on Japan by air. This mission was one of the two most important U.S. secrets of World War II, the other being the time and place of the invasion of Europe from England (D-Day).

In fact, the *Indy's* mission was so secret that its departure time, destination, mission, expected time of arrival and expected time of return were not posted anywhere. When the ship left port, it was as if it had vanished from the sea.

After delivering the bomb parts to Tinian and following a hasty stop at Guam, *Indianapolis* was heading for Leyte in the Philippines when she was hit by two of four torpedoes fired by the Japanese submarine I-58 at 12:15 a.m. on July 30, 1945.

Indianapolis capsized and sank in 12 minutes. An estimated 300 men died in the attack, leaving some 900 sailors to go into the tropical water at night. The ship had sunk so quickly that many of the men were not fully dressed, about a third did not have life jackets and no life rafts had been deployed. Some of the men were burned or otherwise injured and many of them were soon covered by fuel oil.

The *Indy*'s failure to appear for her next assignment was not immediately noticed; no report was made that the cruiser was overdue. It would be four days in hell for the survivors before help appeared.

On the morning of August 2nd, a Navy PV-1 Ventura bomber on routine patrol for enemy submarines spotted an oil slick, debris and a large number of men in the water. Ships and aircraft were immediately notified and were dispatched to the area. No one knew yet what ship had sunk.

Many of the sailors of the *Indianapolis* perished from a number of causes, such as the lack of food and water, exposure resulting in the loss of skin, and sunstroke. Many succumbed to thirst and drank seawater, resulting in salt poisoning and madness.

Many others died from shark attacks. This incident is believed to have been the most ferocious shark attack on humans in recorded history.

The first U.S. Navy ship to arrive on the scene was the *Cecil J. Doyle*, with Petty Officer Claywell aboard. The *Doyle* was commanded by Graham Claytor Jr., who didn't wait on orders, but on his own initiative pushed his vessel at flank speed to the location radioed-in by the patrol plane. An hour and a half after the *USS Doyle* got underway, she received official orders to go to the scene. Years later Captain Claytor would become Secretary of the Navy.

What was it like for the men in the water?

One survivor, a doctor, related his memories years later in "The Search for the *USS Indianapolis*," a TV program which aired on The Discovery Channel.

Dr. Lewis Haynes said, "We had no food, we had no water. We had nothing. All I did was become a coroner. I would pronounce them dead.

"And we tried to keep them from drinking salt water. They'd yell at me, 'Doc, come over here. Is this guy dead?' and I'd paddle over and I'd look in his eyes and if his pupil was dilated and I put my finger in his pupil, and if he didn't blink, I'd declare him dead and then we would laboriously take his life jacket off because we needed every...life jacket we could get our hands on.

"And that was hard work, getting an oil-soaked life jacket off. And then we'd say the Lord's Prayer and then let him go....

"I don't go to church anymore," said Haynes. "Not that I'm not a Christian, and I believe there is a God, but they always say the Lord's Prayer, I'm crying, and I can't do that. And I must have known 100 men on that ship very well. And many of my friends died in my arms...."

The *Doyle* was steaming as fast as she could with "Buck" Claywell aboard her. Petty Officer Claywell was born and raised in Iredell County and attended Statesville High School when it was "D. Matt Thompson High" on West Front Street. Before the war he and his dad ran Claywell's Super Duper Mart on Armfield Street.

Claywell went into the Navy in 1944 and was assigned to the brand–new destroyer escort, *Cecil J. Doyle*. The ship's usual duty was to patrol and to retrieve crews of downed aircraft.

"My bunk was in the chow hall of the *Doyle*," he recalled. "They'd raise the bunk up against the bulkhead [wall] during the day. When we got the message about a large number of men in the water, we didn't know what it was [that had sunk] and it was some 300 miles away.

"We were used to picking up survivors from plane crashes. I was a member of the detail that helped get survivors out of the water.

"We came in slowly and turned the flood lights on. You should have heard them rejoicing when we pulled in! Rejoicing! They had been in the water a long time; it hadn't rained a drop. They had oil all over them.

"The salt water made some of them crazy. I heard that on the night before we got there, one of them, a young ensign who had drunk sea water, said that there was fresh, cool water just under the surface, that the *Indianapolis* was there and you could just swim up to a drinking fountain and drink all you wanted, and some believed him and swum down. They weren't seen again.

"What we did was we threw a rope net over the side of our ship and also let down lines. They put the lines around them under their shoulders and then we pulled them up to the deck a little bit at a time.

"It was something else! We gave up our bunks for the boys to sleep in. The survivors were in bad shape. There was only one boy I saw that was what you'd call 'clean.' He had been near the bow of the *Indianapolis*, and when the torpedo hit, the explosion threw him clear out into the sea, like a bird through the air, away from the oil.

"Later, after all the survivors had been picked up, we had to clean the water of debris and bodies. We collected their dog tags to turn in, and we wrapped the bodies up in mattress covers, put in scrap metal for weight, and sewed up the bags. Then we had burials at sea.

"After handling the bodies, I couldn't eat for a week. You could see where the fish ate on them, and there was a terrible smell.

"This was the only time I ever heard about our Navy handing out liquor rations, but they did to the enlisted men who handled those bodies.

"We came back to the U.S. at San Francisco after duty off the coast of Japan after the surrender. It was 1946, and we passed under the Golden Gate Bridge. There was a saying, 'The Golden Gate by '48.' Well, we beat that by a couple of years."

The Navy terminated search and rescue operations for *Indianapolis* survivors on August 8, 1945, after more than a dozen ships and many aircraft combed more than 30,000 square miles of ocean.

Of about 900 men who went into the water, only 321 came out alive, and five of those died soon afterwards.

The sinking of the *USS Indianapolis* is considered by many authorities to have been the greatest tragedy in the history of the United States Navy.

The *USS Doyle* had a proud record. She was not only the first U.S. ship on the scene, she was also the last U.S. ship to leave the scene. Altogether the *Doyle*'s crew rescued 93 men and recovered the bodies and gave final burial rites to 21 others. She also was the first ship to identify the survivors and report this information up the chain of command.

"Buck" Claywell was honorably discharged and returned to his wife and his job at the market with his father. He then worked for the J. C. Penny Company and then did 12 years as a gospel music DJ for radio station WFMX in Statesville. He finished his business career selling life and health insurance.

Mr. Claywell was on the mailing list of the *USS Indianapolis* Survivors Association and regularly received newsletters from that organization. To the dwindling of survivors, the *Indy* is "Still at Sea."

Buck Claywell summed his experiences of so long ago:

"Those boys were forever grateful to us for picking them up. They couldn't thank us enough. I'll tell you, I was young then, I could take it. I couldn't do it now at 86."

HARRY P. DEATON

If I were asked to name the one person most responsible for Mooresville becoming the community it is today, it would not be John Franklin Moore, for whom the town is named.

While it is true that Mr. Moore donated the land for the depot, a school and several churches, and the town is rightly named in his honor and he was a big man in our history in more ways than one. But Mr. Moore, from what we know, did little with the town once it was established. He died at the relatively young age of 55 in 1877. Had he lived longer, he probably would have done more.

If it can be said that Mr. Moore gave the village birth, he did not live to raise the village to a town. That task fell to a man from Cabarrus County named Harry Preston Deaton, editor of the *Mooresville Enterprise.*

Mr. Deaton was born in Concord on February 2, 1872, the son of Pinkney Stuart and his wife Mary Grissian Alexander Deaton. Harry Deaton was a veteran, having volunteered and served in Company "L" of the 1st North Carolina Infantry Regiment during the short-lived Spanish-American War, and was justifiably proud of his military service.

In the obituaries that *The Enterprise* carried, Harry consistently made it a point to identify veterans. His own military service left him with a permanent hearing disability.

He married Miss Minna Blanche McNeely of Mooresville in 1902. From this union two daughters were born: Mary Moore and Catherine.

Before coming to Mooresville he had worked after school on a paper in Concord, then worked on the *Charlotte Democrat* and later on the *Charlotte Chronicle.* He then worked on the *Concord Daily Standard.* It is reported that he also had worked briefly on papers in Washington, D. C., Richmond, Memphis, Charleston, Atlanta and Birmingham, Alabama.

In 1899 he came to Mooresville, which a contemporary once described as "a wide place in the road with a few stores... with the mud hub deep on Main Street."

Mooresville had had several short-lived newspapers before Harry got here. The *Mooresville Record-Times* had just gone "busted" and Harry tried to revive it. The *Record-Times* had very little advertising and a subscription list of only 228 people paying a modest 50 cents a year. When Town Magistrate C. V. Voils strapped Harry with the *Record-Times'* unpaid bills, Harry changed the name of the paper to *"The Mooresville Enterprise,"* and *The Enterprise* it was to be for more than 40 years.

The premiere issue of *The Enterprise* rolled off the presses on September 8, 1899. It was to be solely Harry's paper with the exception of a four-year period, August, 1906, to October, 1910. At that time Harry sold the paper to a Mr. J. Bailey Robeson, left Mooresville, and returned to Concord to help run the *Concord Tribune,* and also to be nearer his ailing widowed mother.

The Enterprise office was first located over the old Miller Drug Store in what was known as the Leazar Building on South Broad, which later would be the site of the first town hall, police station and fire department. Later the paper moved to a site which is now the parking lot of the Mooresville Chevrolet dealership.

Following his mother's death, Harry came back to Mooresville, bought the newspaper back from Mr. Robeson, and took the reins in his hands again. He ran the paper until his death. In 1921 Harry took Frank B. Freeze, a local man, as a partner and co-owner.

Harry poked and prodded and praised the town. He reported what was good and through his editorials pointed out what needed fixing. For a man whose job it was to report on those around him, he remained a very private person. He wrote little about himself in the pages of the paper; you literally have to read between the lines to get to know him.

One of the most appealing facets of the man was his dry sense of humor.

A good example of this can be seen in the "Local Briefs" section from a December, 1919, *Enterprise*.

"It is said that some local astronomers have predicted the world to be burned up on or about the 17th of this month. If such a thing should happen, our next issue of *The Enterprise* will not reach you. In any event, about the greatest disaster to be visited upon this community to our knowledge is that Sheriff Alexander is due here on the 16th and 17th with the tax books."

Harry passed away on October 25, 1945, aged 73, after an illness of several months. He was buried beside his wife of 38 years in Mooresville's Willow Valley Cemetery.

He had led a full life: he had been a member of the First Presbyterian Church, a Knight of Pythias, a Mason, a charter member of the Mooresville Rotary Club, a member of the town volunteer fire department, and a member of the North Carolina Press Association.

In addition, he had served as a town commissioner for a number of years. He was proud to have been a Southerner and was a life-long Democrat.

Following Harry's death the paper continued under Frank Freeze for about a year, but Frank died in November, 1946. *The Enterprise* continued until February 27, 1947, when the estates of the two deceased partners sold the business to a Mr. L. M. Williams of Kannapolis.

All told, *The Enterprise* had published a run of some 2,470 issues. Tom McKnight's *Mooresville Tribune* agreed to take over all of *The Enterprise*'s unexpired subscriptions.

In June of 1949 Harry's daughters donated bound copies of *The Enterprise*, covering the years 1904 through 1947, to the Mooresville Public Library. These papers were later copied onto microfilm and they can be viewed today by anyone with the time and interest to do so.

Unfortunately, the issues of *The Enterprise* from its start in 1899 through 1904 are missing, as are scattered issues here and there. But even so, much of the early history of Mooresville and the surrounding area has been preserved in its pages.

The motto under the masthead of *The Enterprise* could well serve as Harry's epitaph: "Devoted to the Upbuilding of Our Town and the Best Interests of the Community."

SYDNEY L. DIXON

Iredell County has had, and continues to have, its quota of people one might describe as "characters." Occasionally you run across such a person when reading old issues of the local papers. Case in point: Sydney LeRoy Dixon, poet.

Mr. Dixon, whose first name was also sometimes spelled "Sidney," lived in this area and occasionally contributed columns and poems to the old *Landmark*. As far as is known, no one has yet attempted a compilation of his works.

Sydney was blessed by the Muse of Poetry, if not by the gods of commerce. Unable to support himself with verse alone, he often took to the country roads of the day as a peddler, or in the terms of the day, a "drummer" of small dry goods in Barringer and Coddle Creek townships.

The Rev. J. I. Goodman, writing back to Mooresville from Colorado in the 1930s, recalled Mr. Dixon, whom he had befriended, and Dixon's gift for rhyme. Said Rev. Goodman, "His life was simple. At first he drove a stack of bones called a roan mare [hitched] to a one-horse wagon, which was a home to him, and in which he carried numerous items of trade. These items included garden seed, needles, pins, thimbles, etc., which he exchanged for chickens and eggs with the housewives. He was square in his dealings, polite to customers, but so shaggy and unkempt that many women would have nothing to do with him."

His horse, it was said, was so well trained that when Dixon, wrapped up in a blanket on cold days, left this hack to walk several hundred yards to an isolated farm house with his wares, his horse would proceed to the next house, stop and wait for him.

In January of 1886 Dixon opened a general merchandise store in the Spring Grove community near Prospect Presbyterian Church, but this did not apparently last long, as he did not sell whiskey.

"His mind was well educated and given to the poetic," continued Rev. Goodman. "He might have been a real poet but for some early hindrances. Indeed, he did write lyric verse, some of which was worthy to be called poetry. His effusions were printed by the Statesville *Landmark* when he would permit.

"One night he and I were talking across the counter when I told him of a ridiculous episode in the life of one of our citizens, and suggested that he put it to verse.

"After a few moments thought, he rolled his quid of tobacco to one side of his mouth and out flowed the rhythms, verse after verse. Spontaneous? Absolutely so."

Dixon was supposedly born in or near Huntersville and was a Davidson College graduate, although the college has no record of him in its archives of either attending or graduating. Perhaps he attended a country school in the vicinity of Davidson. *Mooresville Tribune* founder, editor and publisher Tom McKnight thought that Dixon was a Davidson College graduate and stated that he was a brother of Thomas Dixon, Jr., author of "*The Clansman*," which was made into the famous D. W. Griffith movie, *The Birth of a Nation*. Research has not bourne this out, but Sydney could have been the brother of the Rev. Thomas Dixon Sr., a Baptist minister.

Robert A. Lowrance of the Prospect neighborhood re-membered Dixon in the 1930s. Lowrance believed that shortly after his supposed college days Dixon had been disappointed in an affair of the heart "and rapidly degenerated into a tramp, ut-terly indifferent to his personal appearance." Dixon, Lowrance said, first came into Iredell and Rowan selling cotton planting machinery manufactured in Huntersville. "As an old man," wrote Lowrance, "with tobacco juice running out of both corners of his mouth, he was vain about pretty girls, and any pretty girl who would kiss him could have a dress free."

Dixon supplemented his meager income by occasion-ally working as a poet-for-hire, dashing off verse for young men to send to their sweethearts, and it is his verse that has kept Mr. Dixon in memory. Regrettably, much of his opus has been lost.

His greatest work, at least if greatness can be equated with length, was a 66-verse poem entitled, "A Sketch of the Life of Smiley J. Brown, the South Iredell Swindler." It seems that Poet Dixon and Mr. Brown had become arch-enemies, probably be-cause of a debt owed by Brown to Dixon. It is believed that 100 copies of the 66-verse slanderous poem were printed, with the result that Brown took Dixon to court for libel.

The October 30, 1890, *Landmark* told more: "It is well known to our readers that S. L. Dixon, as poet laureate of Barringer township, has a grievance against the truly good Smiley J. Brown, formerly of Mooresville but now of Charlotte, and that he took his pen in hand some time ago and blew a blast of about 50 verses which shook Smiley up for the first time in his life.

"The poet had his production printed in pamphlet form and circulated it. Smiley claimed that some of the transaction with which he is charged in rhyme took place before he was con-verted and on these, he pleaded the statute of limitation. He denied his guilt of other of the charges and indicted Mr. Dixon in the criminal court of Mecklenburg County.

"The trail came off week before last and *The Charlotte News* says that the defendant [Dixon] submitted, defendant took the insolvent debtor's oath and was discharged. He was warned by Judge Meares that if he repeated the offense he would be put on the chain gang."

Tribune editor McKnight admitted that he had sought a copy of the (in)famous poem for 15 years and when he finally located a complete copy, he printed the entire work in his "Community Chaff" column of the *Mooresville Tribune* in February, 1956. As McKnight explained, "But not until last week have we ever had any success in getting our hands on anything written by Dixon. Fred Gray Deaton of Statesville knew a man in Charlotte who had once possessed a copy of Dixon's famous poem on Smiley Jetson Brown. Sure enough, the man had it and sent it to Mr. Deaton."

The poem is much too long to print here, but as a sample, near the end of the poem are found these four verses, constituting a dialogue between Smiley J. Brown and Mr. Joyner, the Iredell County jailer, in whose care Mr. Brown (Dixon hoped) would find himself:

Now, Mr. Joyner, if you please,
Give me a bed to take my ease.
I am a man of high renown;
My name is Smiley Jetson Brown.

I know you are a man of fame
And I will treat you as the same;
I always treat my patrons well
And you can take that empty cell.

The old jail blanket down he spread
And put his coat beneath his head;
His prayer he said, the words were thus:
'O Lord, do please old Hedrick cuss.'

Now I lay me down to sleep,
These strong brick walls me safe will keep.
If I should die before I wake
Instead of me, old Hedrick take."

A shorter work of Mr. Dixon was published in the old *Landmark* of February 21, 1891, that perhaps presages Iredell's annual hot air balloon festival, here given with a few editorial changes:

THE AIRSHIP

An airship I would wish to see,
But do not care to ride.
For it will sail too high for me
To suit my lowly pride.

Old terra firma suits me best,
Without aerial fame,
By railroad I would feel more blessed
And get there just the same.

I know I would uneasy feel
And when the ship did stop,
She surely then would smash her keel
And strike the ground, "Kerplop!"

And when we pass the cotton fields
Where farmers hoe the crop
They fast would run, take to their heels,
And where, then, would they stop?

The farmer would quickly drop his hoe
And then would throw his hat.
And then would halloo,"Don't you go
And leave me with this brat!"

The horses, too, would run away,
The mules would kick for home,
The tenants, too, would run and say
"Old Nick has surely come!"

The old bell cow would see the sight
And with the herd would sail
Then round the field would take her flight
With lofty head and tail.

The buzzard bird away would fly
And then for food would lack.
And when a hog or horse will die
They never will come back.

The men below, upon the ground,
Will look like they are tricked,
For there, quite low, they all are found
And when they walked, they kicked.

I once was in a steeple high,
High Trinity, you know-
And it was pleasing to the eye
To see the things below.

The forest trees with fringe appear
With limbs spread on the ground,
While everything, both far and near,
So strangely will be found.

The growing wheat and growing corn
Will spread their carpets green
And clover fields help to adorn
To make a pleasant scene.

Oh, who would walk upon the deck
When they are sailing high,
And if the ship perchance did wreck,
Oh, whither could we fly?

Mr. Dixon, "The Bard of Coddle Creek," passed to his reward while a resident of the state Confederate Soldier's Home in Raleigh on March 23, 1902, aged 80 years. He served during the Civil War as a private in Company "K" of the 30th North Carolina State Regiment. He is buried in Raleigh's Oakwood Cemetery.

MARTHA HOLLAND DOBSON

Many Americans were watching their TVs on January 28, 1986, some glued to their sets, as the space shuttle *Challenger* lifted off its launch pad at Cape Canaveral and began climbing into the infinite blue of the Florida sky.

Everything looked good until 73 seconds after lift-off, when the shuttle and the rocket it was attached to became a fireball nine miles in the air.

Americans, by and large, had become somewhat complacent about these launches, almost believing the space shuttle launches were no more dangerous than starting the family sedan and driving to the supermarket.

For one local woman, however, the thought that went through her head as she watched the TV screen was: "That could have been me in that shuttle!"

And it could have been.

Martha Holland Dobson, then a teacher of French at Troutman and Brawley Middle schools, had been in the final five of North Carolina teacher candidates trying for a seat aboard the *Challenger*. Each state was responsible for choosing a teacher representative to become a "mission specialist" on NASA's *Challenger* flight, which was a chance to be America's first "Teacher in Space."

Dobson, a Statesville native who lives in north Iredell recalled, "(Sharon Christa) McAuliffe and I have the exact same birthday, September 2, 1948. Ben and I were on our honeymoon at Hilton Head and were watching the TV when we saw the *Challenger* explode. I think about the *Challenger* and its crew every year, as it's near our anniversary and Ben's birthday."

The *Challenger* shuttle had become "Old Reliable" to NASA. The craft first flew in 1983 and had completed nine missions without a major problem. During that time, the spacecraft had been a temporary home to 60 astronauts, had been in space for 62 days, had orbited our planet 995 times and had traveled a total of almost 26,000,000 miles.

Originally scheduled to be launched at 3:43 p.m. on January 23, the launch was delayed and rescheduled at least six times due to weather and technical problems.

Instead of Martha Dobson, America's first teacher in space aboard the *Challenger* was Christa McAuliffe, a Boston-born, New Hampshire social studies teacher.

Understandably, McAuliffe had been excited about her selection from more than 11,000 applicants from the education profession. "I watched the Space Age being born and I would like to participate," McAuliffe once said.

Besides McAuliffe, the *Challenger* crew consisted of mission commander Francis R. Scobee; pilot Michael J. Smith; mission specialists Ronald E. McNair, Ellison S. Onizuka and Judith A. Resnik; and payload specialist Gregory B. Jarvis. McAuliffe was also listed as a payload specialist.

The Rogers Commission was appointed by President Ronald Reagan to determine the cause of the tragedy. A faulty O-ring seal has been blamed for the multi-million dollar, seven-life disaster, the O-ring supposedly deformed by the unseasonable cold weather that allowed hot gases to burn through and ignite an external fuel tank.

Dobson graduated from Statesville High School in 1966, attended St. Andrew's Presbyterian College in Laurinburg for two years and graduated from UNC-Chapel Hill with a degree in French Education in 1970. She also completed a six-week French immersion class at McGill University in Montreal, Canada.

"For the space shuttle program I had to prepare a portfolio, write essays and come up with a proposed project to be partly done aboard the shuttle," remembered Dobson. "I had to supply references and was interviewed by the Department of Public Instruction in Raleigh.

"I grew up in the Space Age, saw Neil Armstrong walk on the moon in 1969. I've always been a risk-taker, an out-of-the-way traveler. I think that to go into space, to see Earth from that vantage point, would be an awesome experience.

"Besides, who knows what I could use in a classroom later? That kind of experience would make a difference in my life, and had I been chosen, perhaps a difference in the world. It was an honor to have made it as far as I did in the selection process."

Dobson had already done a bit of traveling on old Terra Firma at ground level. Employed by ARAMCO Oil Company in Saudi Arabia for three years, she had taught French to the children of Americans working there and English to Saudi men.

She had already been in school in Canada, had visited most of the countries in Europe and had been to Egypt, Pakistan, Iran, Bahrain, Thailand, Singapore and Hong Kong. Having a background in other languages and having international experience probably helped her in being considered for the Astronaut Corps, she said.

Dobson isn't sad that she wasn't chosen, even if the *Challenger* mission had been successful.

"I met many talented, interesting people as a result of being considered for the program and have gained a lot by networking and sharing," she confided. "A lot of doors opened to me because of my involvement in the Teacher in Space program, even though I didn't make the final cut.

"As a result of being among the North Carolina finalists, I became a Christa McAuliffe Fellow in 1989, a program of the federal department of education which worked with Christa McAuliffe's mother. The fellowship gave a grant of $15,000 to $20,000 to complete a project within a year. My project was to develop ways to teach a foreign language to dyslexic children, and some of the information I found and developed works well in teaching students who are not dyslexic or for students for whom English is a foreign language.

"I used some of my McAuliffe Fellowship research in pilot programs at Pressley Elementary School in Statesville and with students in Forsyth County. I also use it in Yadkin County where I currently teach."

Had she ever considered the possibility of disaster when she applied to be the first teacher in space?

"Not really," she replied. "I should have thought about it, but I'm a risk-taker. People said I was crazy to travel in the Middle East as a single female. If you think about all that can go wrong, you won't do anything."

If offered another chance to ride the shuttle, would she take it?

Dobson paused for a moment and then said, "Well, I've always had an itchy foot; I love to travel. I'd have to think about it."

She can't control the widening grin on her face.

BEN DOUGLAS

The study of local history is a funny thing. You discover that sometimes people flower in home soil, but sometimes they bloom in a distant garden.

An example of this can be found in the lives of three Iredell County men you might not be familiar with, but who have likely affected your life; all were mayors of Charlotte, the largest city in North or South Carolina.

You have probably departed from or picked up someone arriving at Charlotte Douglas International Airport. Douglas Airport was named in honor of Mayor Ben Douglas of Iredell County's Scotts community. Although all times have their difficulties, Ben Douglas served Charlotte during especially trying times, and served that metropolis well.

* * *

Ben Elbert Douglas Sr., of Scotts, was the first Charlotte mayor to serve three two-year terms, 1935 through 1941. A Democrat, he was also noted as being the first Charlotte mayor elected directly by the voters. Previously, the city's mayors had been appointed. Because of his accomplishments in office, Douglas has been called "The Builder of Modern-Day Charlotte."

Born in 1894 in Iredell County, Douglas was raised in Gastonia and served as a lieutenant in the U.S. Army during World War I. Moving to the Queen City in 1926, he owned Douglas Furs, located at the corner of Elizabeth Avenue and Independence Boulevard. Douglas' administration came during the last half of the Great Depression. Douglas was successful in applying for and receiving federal funds for the Queen City during those desperate times.

The Charlotte Airport is the project that is most often associated with Mayor Douglas and rightly so. The proposal to build a modern facility for the city was met with skepticism by many, and Douglas devoted his considerable skills in promoting the airport.

By receiving funding from President Roosevelt's Works Progress Administration, the airport in Charlotte became the WPA's largest recipient of funds at the time in North Carolina. This provided many local jobs.

The ground breaking ceremony was held in 1935 and the facility was dedicated as "Douglas Municipal Airport" on April 21, 1941. Douglas later called this event "the proudest day of my life."

Besides his involvement with air travel, Mayor Douglas also helped get funding for the Mint Museum of Art, which opened October 22, 1936. He was also instrumental in having the first public housing erected while he was in office.

The American Legion Memorial Stadium, not far from his place of business, was opened while Douglas was mayor. The stadium was the site of the first annual Shrine Bowl Game of the Carolinas between some of the best high school athletes in North and South Carolina. Due in no small part to advances the city made during Ben Douglas' administration in recruiting industry and jobs, by 1940 Charlotte had become the state's largest city.

After serving as mayor, Douglas continued in public service as the state Director of Civilian Defense during World War II was a member of the North Carolina Highway and Public Works Commission. Furthermore, he was instrumental in bringing in new industry and in improving state parks while he was chief of the state's Department of Conservation and Development in the 1950s.

Ben Douglas died on July 27, 1981, at the age of 86, and is buried in Charlotte's Elmwood Cemetery.

Rev. J. H. Fesperman

While doing research for the 75th anniversary of Holy Trinity Lutheran Church in Troutman, a small book surfaced which is believed to have once been part of the personal library of Augustus Davidson Troutman, better remembered as "Uncle Gus." The book was written by a former pastor of one of the two small Lutheran churches which merged to form Holy Trinity Church.

The volume was entitled, *The Life of a Sufferer: An Autobiography,* and was written by the Reverend Joseph Hamilton Fesperman, who had been pastor at St. Michael's Lutheran Church in the 1870s. The congregations of St. Michael's and St. Martin's churches merged in 1924 to form Holy Trinity Lutheran Church (ELCA).

Rev. Fesperman's life had all the elements of a good story, although in some respects it was the story of Job.

Joseph Fesperman was born on July 7, 1841, in Salisbury, North Carolina, the son of Michael and Cynthia Gardner Fesperman. When he was thirteen, a throw from a horse caused him to have a leg broken in two places which resulted in his being bed-ridden for six weeks.

"The first night after I was hurt I gave myself, body and soul, to God in prayer," he later wrote. This was his first step in deciding to become a minister. An early impediment to his plan was the death of his father who died when Joseph was still young, leaving him and his mother in very poor circumstances.

Basically self-educated, Joseph acquired more knowledge by intensive reading and listening carefully to "well-informed men" whenever possible: "I had no pecuniary means with which to educate myself," he wrote, "but studied with all my faculties, concentrated on one subject—entrance into the regular ministry of the church.

"I studied some theological books, and my desire to preach became more intensified. I retired to bed thinking about preaching, I dreamed of it, talked in my sleep concerning it, and when I awoke it was the first thought to enter my mind.

"I was invited sometimes to speak in Methodist churches, and at camp meetings, where I had abundant opportunity for the exercise of mind and tongue," he wrote.

At one such camp meeting he was asked to preach and he later gave an account of the occasion. "While I was in the midst of my discourse some aged men and women commenced clapping their hands and shouting, and one young man ran to the pulpit praising God."

Fesperman had the ability to sway his listeners even if he didn't have the official credentials of a preacher.

He entered into the Lutheran ministry in 1858, and he had a church in Rowan County when the Civil War interrupted his life's work. Although he was fulfilling the functions of a minister, he still had no "official papers" from the church.

"When the war between the north and the south was precipitated and entrance into the army became unavoidable, I packed *Schmucker's Popular Theology*, Gregory's *Evidences of*

Christianity, Porter's *Homiletics, The Lives of Ancient Philosophers,* my Bible and Hymn Book into my knapsack, and went into the service of the Confederacy against all my inclinations, but thank God my mind was not warped by prejudice, and my heart was not debased by ill will."

He enlisted in Statesville on August 8, 1862, for the duration of the War. He was mustered in as a Private in the Fifth North Carolina Infantry Regiment, and was promoted to Sergeant on 1 January, 1863.

In his 1892 autobiography Rev. Fesperman tells more about the life of the soldier: "I endured many privations in the army, but I was not guilty of taking any article of food or clothing. I refused to eat stolen rations. License or no license, I intended to preach, and many times exercised the talents I possessed in exhorting the soldiers to become Christ's followers, and live consistent and blameless lives. Some preferred cards to these services, but not a few gave me their cards to burn and manifested a disposition to join me in praying for their salvation."

On May 3, 1863, at the Battle of Chancellorsville, he was captured by Federal troops. He was taken to Clifton Barracks in Washington, D.C., and, characteristically, he preached to the other men confined there on the very night of his arrival.

As he finished this impromptu worship service he was approached by two Union officers, one of whom identified himself as the commander of the prison barracks, a Colonel Alexander, who offered Fesperman "...lucrative railroad positions, superior educational facilities... under the written seal of the President of the United States" if he would take the Oath of Allegiance.

These were, as Fesperman states it, "terms, however, that I could not consciously accept."

According to official records he did not stay at Clifton Barracks for more than a dozen days, as he was received at City

Point, Virginia, on May 13, 1863, for exchange. In his autobiography, however, he states "After several months of prison life in Washington City, I was exchanged, came home, and then returned to the 5th North Carolina Regiment, and on account of general debility, was detailed as a clerk in a Confederate States Arsenal, located in Salisbury, N.C."

Through official records we learn that he was reduced to ranks—no information is given as to the reason— prior to April 2, 1864, but was a sergeant again by 1865.

Fesperman was captured in Salisbury on April 12, 1865, by units of Union General George Stoneman's cavalry. As Rev. Fesperman wrote, the Union soldiers "...came through the country, set fire to the Arsenal, the flames reached my room and consumed books, clothing, and all that I possessed.

"I was taken a prisoner and conveyed on foot through the mountains of North Carolina to [Nashville] Tennessee, and from thence by railroad to Camp Chase, Ohio [arriving May 2, 1865], where I suffered many great privations until several months after the War closed.

"There were twelve ministers confined in Camp Chase, and we held interesting services every Sunday. I prayed for the prisoners and preached to them, but my heart yearned for my home and for proper authority to proclaim God's Word."

He was released from Camp Chase on June 13, 1865, after taking the Oath of Allegiance to the United States government.

"I came from prison to my mother's home at length, sick and penniless, and found myself in the midst of a face to face, hand to hand, inch by inch, conflict with unfortunate circumstances, and I was not allowed to choose my foes, my battle fields, my ammunition or my generals."

Through sheer perseverance he resumed an active ministry. He was officially licensed to preach in 1868 and was finally ordained at Salem Lutheran Church in Rowan County in 1871.

Rev. Fesperman's professional career was brief, but intensive. He was minister at Beth Eden Lutheran Church in Newton from 1870 to 1872; he organized and was first pastor of Providence Lutheran Church in Rowan from 1871 to 1876; and was pastor of St. Paul's Lutheran Church in Iredell from 1871 to 1874.

These over-lapping dates probably indicate that Rev. Fesperman was a circuit-riding minister, preaching at one church one Sunday and at a different church the next, until he had made the rounds of a circuit.

His last church was St. Michael's Lutheran Church, in Iredell County, of which he was minister from 1871 to 1877. In 1877 a leg injury, perhaps the same one he received when thirteen years old, caused him to retire from the active ministry.

He moved to Statesville around 1910, where he still occasionally performed marriage ceremonies and baptisms.

Besides his autobiography, *The Life of a Sufferer*, from which the above quotations are taken, Rev. Fesperman was the author of *A Sick Man's View of Christ and the Scriptures*. According to his obituary in *The Landmark*, these two volumes "attracted considerable notice and were widely read."

Rev. Fesperman died from tuberculosis on April 26, 1917. Three ministers conducted his funeral service, and he was laid to rest in St. Michael's Burying Ground, south of Troutman.

He was twice married. His first wife was Crissie Ann Lentz, who was the mother of his children, four of whom survived their father. His second wife, Mattie E. Witt, also survived him.

Peace to his ashes.

Miss Cora Freeze

Once upon a time in this country there was a special breed of person who became a school teacher and stayed in that profession for his or her entire life. It usually was a woman who never married. Many communities had an "old maid school mar'm" who was affectionately remembered by generations of children. Such a teacher was Mooresville's Cora Levinia Freeze. "Miss Cora" was my seventh grade reading teacher in school year 1960-61 at the old Mooresville Junior High on West Moore Avenue across the street from Central Methodist Church. She had also been my father's teacher. In addition, she was a distant cousin on my mother's side.

* * *

"Monday Memorial Service for Cora Freeze, Teacher" was the headline for the obituary printed in the *Mooresville Tribune* of November 11, 1987. Cora L. Freeze, 85, had died the previous Tuesday, Nov. 5, at her home on South Main Street. Truly, the word "Teacher" was all the obituary she needed.

Miss Cora came into the world on May 22, 1902, born in the house at 228 South Main she was to live in all her life. One of five children, Cora was the sole daughter of Rufus Wilburn Freeze and Sallie Templeton Freeze. Miss Cora's mother, Sallie, had been a graduate of Statesville Female College—now Mitchell Community College. Miss Cora's maternal grandfather, Joseph Templeton, had been one of the signers of the charter for the town of Mooresville.

Mr. R. W. Freeze, her father, had had a general store in Mooresville and at the time of his death at age 63 in 1920, was a director in each of the city's two banks, but the Great Depression hit the Freeze family hard.

Educated in the Mooresville Graded School District established just three years after her birth in 1905, she later graduated from Salem College and also took classes at Davidson and at Carolina. Miss Cora began her 40-year teaching career in 1926 in the old South Elementary School on Church Street, and laid her chalk down at the close of the 1965/66 school year. The only grade she ever taught was the seventh grade. When she began teaching South School had no library and she made the founding of a school library her first goal. She initiated a series of successful fund-raising activities, including selling popcorn on the town streets as well as selling live chickens, and by serving dinners to the town's civic clubs.

In 1976 she recalled, "For the library project we raised $1,000 in one month's time. The library was born and I'll never forget buying a ham and we sold chances on it." This raffle—viewed by some as a form of gambling—brought the disapproval of then-Superintendent H. C. Miller and the town school board.

"After quite an argument," she recalled, "our so-called 'gambling devices' stopped, but our point was won, because from then on the school board appropriated money for the library. It wasn't long until I realized that working with youngsters was very hard, but very rewarding. I loved it and them."

Older generations of her students will recall her class trips to Charlotte to the Ford factory and to the *Charlotte Observer* Building to see newspapers being printed. The students went to Ivey's and Efird's department stores and rode the escalators and then went to the Hotel Charlotte for lunch, followed by a movie in a big theater. She even started a harmonica band at South School.

After the current Mooresville High School was constructed, the old Central High building became the system's junior high for white students. It was there Miss Cora finished her career under the principalship of Mr. Belus V. Smawley—in the same building she had attended as a first-grader in 1907 and had graduated from in 1921. While she was in high school, she and five or six close friends made up a basketball team that took on all comers and could have gone pro.

Retirement was a tough decision to make for Miss Cora.

"In 1966 I didn't want to retire, but I thought I should. I swore Mr. Smawley and [Superintendent] Dr. Morgan to secrecy. I thought perhaps I'd change my mind, but old arthritis was beginning to get me. I had finished, or was about to complete my 40th year. My good friend Mr. Smawley always assured me if I wanted to return, he would get me a contract."

I remember Miss Cora, her freshly coiffed hair in tight ringlets with a hint of blue rinse. Miss Cora occasionally told us how she had worked to restore her home. I think she took in some boarders. She also sold *World Book Encyclopedias* and our family bought a set, as did many others. She even sold plots in the then-new Glenwood Cemetery when it opened.

She had us—her reading class I was in—memorize the long poem, "America" by Ruth Tooze, and that golden oldie "Thanatopsis" by William Cullen Bryant. I still remember parts of the latter, 50 years later. Memorization was not a dirty word in 1960. Miss Freeze collected wise sayings, maxims and mottoes and forcibly shared them with us.

She encouraged us to eat crackers **with** our school vegetable soup, rather than crumbled up **in** the soup, as many of us did. She told us that table manners—all manners, really—were important and said a lot about a person and related a story she herself knew to be true, about a local man who didn't get a great job with General Electric because he did not exhibit proper table manners.

Miss Freeze collected the old "Blue Horse" labels from packets of paper and notebooks and had accumulated enough to get a portable TV. Her class regularly beat the other 7th grade homerooms in about anything we competed in.

Miss Freeze knew all the important people in town on a first-name basis; she had either taught them or their siblings or their parents. She knew who you and your family were. Her name was the one you wanted as a reference for a job or for college.

Cora Freeze was an active member of First Presbyterian Church her entire life, and since 1990 Mooresville's First Presbyterian Church has been awarding the "Cora L. Freeze Scholarship" to college-bound students. First preference is given to those majoring in education.

Never one to waste anything, Miss Cora donated her body to science, so her headstone in Mooresville's Willow Valley is only a marker.

Miss Cora Freeze never married, unless you count her 40-year marriage to her job. Still, one could say that she had hundreds of children. I am proud that I was one.

Dr. Shelley Frontis

If you do much reading in local history you will almost certainly meet some characters you would like to have known personally. Shelley Frontis is one such person, and even though he died six years before I was born, I feel that I know something of the man.

Dr. Shelley Frontis was one of the most gifted men to ever call Mooresville home. By profession he was a dentist, but he also wore the hats of a historian, a mayor, an after-dinner speaker and a poet.

This is not surprising, considering his family roots.

His grandfather, Stephen Frontis, was a native of France who had come to America in 1810. Here he was converted to the Presbyterian denomination and eventually became a Presbyterian minister. He accepted a pastoral call to Bethany Presbyterian Church in northern Iredell County and was installed as pastor of Bethany and neighboring Tabor Church in May of 1830. While at Bethany he compiled the history of that congregation, and is credited with establishing the county's first temperance movement.

It was during his Bethany pastorate that Rev. Frontis was named to a "Committee of Eight" to draw up plans for the organization of Davidson College.

Rev. Frontis served as the regular pastor or as stated supply to many of the Presbyterian churches in the area. He was pastor to the First Presbyterian Church in Salisbury, and at Centre Church in Mount Mourne and at Prospect, east of Mooresville, where he eventually made his home. Rev. Frontis also taught French at Davidson College. The current sanctuary of Centre Church was constructed while Rev. Frontis was the minister.

Shelley's father was Professor Stephen Frontis, Jr., (1838 - August 4, 1892) who, with his brother-in-law Augustus Leazar, moved to Mooresville in 1874 from the Prospect community and started the Mooresville Academy, a private school which was the forerunner of the present-day Mooresville Graded School District.

The Frontis family was among the nineteen Prospect members who formed the core of the town's newly-established First Presbyterian Church. "Professor Frontis," as he was called, was unanimously elected presiding elder of the new church.

The Mooresville Academy operated for about thirty years. Professor Frontis continued as its head after Shelley's Uncle Augustus left education to enter politics.

Shelley was born on April 6, 1870, on the Frontis farm in the Prospect community, but moved to the village of Mooresville at an early age and grew up with the town.

Recalling the town's early years, Shelley once recollected: "When I moved to Mooresville, there were no streets, just a big road that followed the railroad, and a few paths that led from the big road to the houses you could count on your fingers. There were three stores and a little school house known as North Bend. There was no church nor were there any preachers. My, but we did have a good time for about a year."

He later matriculated from nearby Davidson College, the alma mater of both his father and his Uncle Augustus, and then graduated at the head of the Class of 1899 of the Baltimore College of Dental Surgery. He returned home to become Mooresville's first professionally-trained dentist.

Shelley married Lillian Frances Williams of Freemont, North Carolina, in 1902. They were the parents of five children: Shelley Jr., Irving, Stephen, Mary Celeste and Borel. The children's escapades sometimes served as material for Dr. Frontis' verses.

Like his father, Shelley was an elder of Mooresville's First Presbyterian Church and was Clerk of the Session. While serving in this capacity, Shelley and two other gentlemen compiled the church's history for its fiftieth anniversary celebration.

Shelley also served as Mooresville's mayor from 1913 through 1917, and was a member of the town's school board.

A very gifted speaker, Dr. Frontis was often in demand at civic functions and as an after dinner speaker to the various fraternal and patriotic organizations that were so popular around the turn of the century. His words, it is said, were always spoken fast and very audibly and came from his lips with ease. "His audience, no matter whether at church or social gathering, was very attentive."

His speeches were laced with scriptural references, bits of his own and others' poetry, amusing anecdotes and humor. Even though he was a Presbyterian elder himself, he once described a Presbyterian as "a man who religiously kept the Ten Commandments and every other God-blessed thing he got his hands on."

It was during the 1920s that Shelley began submitting his poetry to Harry P. Deaton's weekly *Mooresville Enterprise*. Deaton published about a dozen of Shelley's poems in his newspaper.

Frontis' poems are about commonplace things. One tells of the adventures of his youngest son, Borel. In another he humorously describes his efforts to rid himself of an aggravating case of eczema and tells of the cures suggested by so-called friends.

Herewith are transcriptions of two of Dr. Frontis' poems.

While Dr. Frontis' meter and rhyme may show room for improvement, it is the feel of Shelley's poetry that is important: the aroma of simple foods prepared with love, the feel of a warm kitchen.

Shelley lived the biblical allotment three score and ten years, dying at his home at the age of seventy in 1941 after a year of declining health. His remains rest in Willow Valley Cemetery.

* * *

MUSH AND HAM

You may talk about your grapefruit,
Corn flakes and shredded wheat,
Buckwheat cakes and syrup
And other things you eat,
Or brag about your veal chops
That bear some famous brand,
But for a good square breakfast
They can't beat mush and ham.

A spoonful of oat toasties
And one thin breakfast strip,
Preceded by a grapefruit
After it's been split;
These followed by a piece of toast,
Some butter and some jam,
Have not that inward influence
Of good old mush and ham.

Such dishes may at last fulfill
The Epicurean's dream,
When all these shredded somethings
Float in the richest cream;
But for these newfangled dishes
I would not give a d——,

When I could have served up to me
Good old mush and ham.

It seems to be the style now days
To serve an honored guest
A breakfast that sits lightly
Just beneath the vest.
But all these stylish dishes
Served up for show and sham
Fail to appease the inner man
Like good old mush and ham.

Have you never breathed the fragrance,
As down the stairs you came,
That brought the water to your mouth,
A thrill clear through your frame,
And reminded you of days gone by
When you were wont to cram
Your stomach full of gravy
And good old mush and ham?

Times have changed and so have breakfasts,
But the good old days of yore
Will forever linger with me,
And be cherished evermore;
And the oilcloth-covered table,
And Mother's frying pan
Will not fail to remind me
Of good old mush and ham.

Yes, my thoughts turn backward now
To the days of long ago

When breakfasts were real breakfasts
And not vain and empty show;
And I hunger, yes, I hunger
In a way that is no sham
For that steaming cup of coffee
And a plate of mush and ham.

DINNER IN THE GROVE

Our old country churches-
Many of us can recall,
Were wont to have a meeting
In the spring and in the fall,
When there'd gather saints and sinners
In a hallelujah band,
On the Saturdays and Sundays
Through which the meeting ran.

With crowds that gathered on those days
The church would overflow,
For then it was they always served
A dinner in the grove.
And I've wondered if the people
Attending in great droves
Were looking for salvation,
Or the fishes and the loaves.

Now if it was the dinner
That attracted some to church
'Twere better that they thus be caught

Than be left in the lurch.
For had they not been thus enticed
And brought within the fold,
They'd have missed both their salvation
And dinner in the grove.

I must confess that dinner,
When it's served out in the grove,
Makes an appeal that many folks
Don't generally ignore;
And the fellowship engendered
About the festive board
May yield a harvest later on
Of more'n a hundred fold.

For when we mix ourselves all up
Around a table spread,
The poorest and the humblest
Mingle with the thoroughbred,
And no fellowship is lacking
As amongst the throng we move
When rich and poor alike partake
Of dinner in the grove.

Our Sunday school conventions,
Homecomings and picnics,
The reunions of old families
Away out in the sticks,
Ne'er fail to get a gathering,
Because out in the grove
They always serve a feed to please
All comers, young and old.

The stomach answers to appeals
Much quicker than the heart,
And dinner on the program
Much interest doth impart;
And it isn't only laymen
Or laywomen that respond,
But preachers too, you may depend,
Will turn out good and strong.

I hope these dinners in the grove
Will not go out of style,
For here a fellow eats his fill
Of chicken, ham, and pie,
And if he licks his fingers off
And wipes them on his pants
There're others who'd the same thing do
If they dared take the chance.

The general good feeling
That prevails at every feast
Bespeaks a kindly fellowship
That nowhere else you'll meet.
Here we elbow one another
And from restraint feel free.
O, yes, these dinners in the grove
Always appealed to me!

Rev. Stephen Frontis

It is rare when one family, over the span of several generations, profoundly influences the religious, educational and political fiber of an area, but such is the story of the Frontis family. The pater familis was the Reverend Stephen Frontis.

Stephen Frontis, patriarch of the Frontis clan in America, was born in Cognac, France, in 1792 to a Roman Catholic father and a Protestant mother. He grew up in Switzerland and was trained as a cabinetmaker. He came to the United States in 1810 and by 1817 had moved to North Carolina and was an assistant to a Presbyterian minister who also was the headmaster of an academy in Oxford.

About a year later, Frontis moved to Raleigh, where he took a job teaching French. In October, 1820, he enrolled in the Presbyterian Seminary at Princeton, New Jersey. He was licensed to preach in October, 1823, was ordained the next month, and became a naturalized American citizen the following June.

November of 1824 found Rev. Frontis doing missionary work in the eastern North Carolina towns of Greenville, Plymouth, Tarboro and Washington. He next moved to the then-territory of Michigan, preaching in Detroit and in Canada, where he spread the Gospel in English and in French.

Leaving the Michigan area in October, 1825, he spent a brief time in Pennsylvania, Delaware and eastern Maryland.

In the spring of 1828, Frontis accepted a pastoral call to Bethany Presbyterian Church in northern Iredell County. He was received into the local Presbytery of Concord on April 1, 1829, and installed as the minister of Bethany and nearby Tabor congregations the following month.

Frontis is credited with establishing Iredell's first temperance movement, which opposed the "consumption of spirituous liquors" and their manufacture, a cottage industry in this area from its first settlement in the late 1740s. Shortly after his arrival in Iredell, Frontis succeeded in getting 25 signatures on a temperance pledge, most of the signatories being heads-of-household, but northern Iredell, in particular, had long been a stronghold for the production of fruit brandy and corn whiskey.

In 1830 while at Bethany, Rev. Frontis married Martha Dews. The couple had four children—three daughters and a son. According to Iredell historian Homer Keever, by the 1830s the Rev. Frontis—in addition to his ministerial duties and his work in the temperance movement—was also operating a two-teacher school for young ladies, a school that emphasized instruction of the French language.

It was also while Rev. Frontis was pastor at Bethany and Tabor that he was named to the "Committee of Eight" that met at Prospect Presbyterian Church, just over the Rowan County line from Iredell, to draw up plans for the establishment of a Presbyterian school that would prepare young men for the ministry and other "learned professions."

A site was soon selected in northwestern Mecklenburg County on lands owned by William Lee Davidson Jr., son of the local Revolutionary War hero. The Committee of Eight went on to establish the institution as Davidson College and so it remains today, although a majority of the students are now young ladies.

Rev. Frontis resigned his positions at Bethany and Tabor in March, 1836, but one of his most important contributions while at Bethany was his compilation of that church's early history, which he wrote in the front of a session book.

His next appointment was to the Salisbury Presbyterian Church in September, 1837. During this period he served as supply pastor for Thyatira Church and Franklin Church, both in Rowan County. Frontis' wife, Martha, assisted him in conducting a school in their Salisbury home.

In the fall of 1844 Rev. Frontis was named to a church committee which was to "prepare and report [on] some plan for the instruction of negroes." This was a rather risky undertaking in the years following the slave rebellion led by Nat Turner in southern Virginia in 1831.

By the time Rev. Frontis decided to leave Salisbury in June of 1845, he had delivered about 1,370 sermons in nine years.

In 1846, the pastor was back in Iredell County as the supply minister at Centre Presbyterian Church in Mount Mourne, as well as being the stated supply pastor at Thyatira Church from 1846 to 1851. His duties were confined solely to Centre Church after the spring of 1851. Three years later, at the time that Centre's present sanctuary was constructed, Rev. Frontis was named to the Board of Trustees of the newly-formed Concord Female Presbyterian College at Statesville, an institution better known today as Mitchell Community College.

After the death of his wife about 1856, Rev. Frontis left the active ministry and retired to his farm in the Prospect community. He was succeeded at Centre by the Rev. William Walter Pharr, who was to be that congregation's pastor for the next half century.

Rev. Frontis married again, to Rachel Beaty, and they had one child, David, who became a physician.

Rev. Frontis did not remain retired long. He returned to the pulpit to serve as supply pastor for Prospect Church for six months between the ministries of the Rev. E. D. Junkin and the Rev. Winslow Watt. He also served as the superintendent of that church's Sunday school. Rev. Frontis took on no further duties as a regular pastor, but still led 71 worship services after his supposed retirement. In addition, in 1860 and 1861, he was acting professor of French at Davidson College.

Rev. Stephen Frontis died from "disease of the heart" on April 12, 1867, at the age of 76. He is buried in the Prospect Presbyterian Church's cemetery. According to a 1924 history of Prospect Church by J. C. Jamison, "Mr. Frontis was a man of great piety, and was deeply interested in everything that pertained to the advancement of the Redeemer's Kingdom."

His headstone at Prospect is interesting. The inscription reads: "His works follow him," and carved on the stone above the words is a hand, the index finger pointing heavenward.

PROF. STEPHEN FRONTIS, JR.

The Reverend Stephen Frontis' son, Stephen Jr., was born in 1838, while his father was the minister at the Salisbury Presbyterian Church. When Stephen Jr. was about eight years old, the family moved back to Iredell County, where his father assumed the pastorate of Centre Presbyterian Church in Mount Mourne.

The Frontis farm near Prospect Presbyterian Church on the Iredell-Rowan line, where the elder Frontis served off and on as pastor, was home to young Stephen Jr. He attended Davidson College, which his father had helped organize.

Stephen Jr. married the former Julia Celeste Leazar, from the Prospect Community, on September 24, 1859, and the couple moved to Mooresville in 1874—the year after the town was incorporated. The couple was among the nineteen Prospect Church members who left that congregation to form the nucleus for Mooresville's First Presbyterian Church in November of 1875.

Stephen Jr. was unanimously elected and ordained as a ruling elder of the new congregation. He also served for a time as the church's clerk of session.

It is in his relationship to his brother-in-law, Augustus Leazar, that Stephen Jr. is best known. The duo established the first classical school in Mooresville, a preparatory academy that may be regarded as the genesis of today's Mooresville Graded School District.

Begun about 1874, the Academy, also known as Frontis and Leazar's School, operated for about thirty years and offered the classics in its curriculum, including French, music and geometry.

In 1892 Professor Leazar left his career in education to pursue a career in public service, and Professor Frontis continued with the school. Accord to Professor Frontis' son, Shelley, this school was the town's main drawing card during its early years, predating the establishment of the Mooresville Cotton Mill.

Stephen Jr. and Julia were the parents of three daughters, in addition to their son Shelley.

Stephen Jr. died in 1892; his wife survived him by thirty-three years. They are both buried in Mooresville's Willow Valley Cemetery.

JAMES GAY

James Gay, of Iredell County, is recognized as the very first North Carolinian to have a book of his poetry published. Mr. Gay liked to write patriotic verse and was prevailed upon by some friends to give an impromptu recitation at a barbecue being held in Statesville during a big 4th of July celebrations held about two centuries ago. These Independence Day celebrations included oratory, barbecue and presumably, many toasts to the Constitution, the President, the Congress, Independence and so on. This was a major event in those early days of the Republic and being asked to say a few words on the occasion was considered a great honor.

Mr. Gay began recitations on Independence Day in 1805 and seems to have continued with his yearly orations through 1809. In 1805 his recitation followed a large barbecue meal and numerous toasts.

His efforts were appreciated to such an extent that the committee in charge of the festivities began to plan to have him have more verse ready for the next year and the next. Unfortunately, political differences caused the big celebrations in Statesville to come to an end around 1809.

Mr. Gay's verses were collected and published in Raleigh in 1810 by William Boyles. The full title of the book bears knowing: *A collection of various pieces of poetry, chiefly patriotic, published at the earnest request of a number of good citizens for the improvement of patriotic minds.*

As Richard Walser of the Department of English at North Carolina State University points out in his introduction to the 1963 reprinting of Gay's book, we know a good bit about the poet from a nine-page autobiography included in the book of poems. Another source for information about James Gay and his family comes from research by Iredell historian Homer Keever and genealogical work by a great-grandson of Mr. Gay who published *A Story of a Gay Family* in 1920.

We know that Mr. Gay was born in Northern Ireland in March of 1744. He was apprenticed to a carpenter in a town near Belfast, later moved to Scotland, but returned to Northern Ireland after two years. In May of 1765, he headed for America. He was soon in Philadelphia where he found himself a wife in 1768 and to James and Margaret Mitchel Gay was born a son.

Eager to have land of his own, he, the Mrs. and the baby headed south along the "Great Wagon Road" and ended up on the banks of Fourth Creek in then-Rowan County in 1771. He settled in the Oak Forest community some 10 miles east of Statesville near what is now New Salem Methodist Church, just inside the Iredell County line.

Although records are sketchy, James appears to have served for most of the War for Independence and saw action in several battles. After the war he returned to family and farming and even became a constable. James did all right for himself and his family; by 1800 he had acquired over 1,500 acres of land, owned a store and a still house.

The area where he settled had something of an unsavory reputation. Homer Keever says of the neighborhood, "Tradition is insistent that the movement for a church in the community came because the muster ground, race track and grog shop [tavern] nearby had given the place such a name for drinking and gambling and rowdyism in general that it was called 'Rowdytown' or 'Scuffletown.'"

Mr. Gay donated land for the building of a church. The church was a union chapel and was used equally by the three prominent denominations in the area, the Methodists, the Baptists and the Presbyterians. The Presbyterians organized Fifth Creek Presbyterian Church in the late 1840s and gradually stopped attending the union church. Mr. Keever tells us that the Methodists also started going elsewhere to worship around 1872, when they organized New Salem, which left the Baptists at what had been a union church.

Mr. Gay passed to his reward on February 4, 1819. He is buried in the cemetery of Third Creek Presbyterian Church in Rowan County. He and Mrs. Gay had two sons and a daughter and there were also some grandchildren.

The church, for which Mr. Gay donated land, was first known as "Gay's Chapel," but later the name was changed to "Union Chapel Baptist Church," and it is known by that name today.

A FOURTH OF JULY POEM
BY JAMES GAY

The day we hail that gave us birth,
Among the nations of the earth;
The Fourth of July, may it be
Remembered still that we are free,

In seventeen hundred seventy-six;
Our Independence we did fix;
That we in after days might see
The benefits of being free.

And now my brethren we arrive,
At eighteen hundred and five;
May we still join with all our might,
To keep the chain of freedom bright.

May sons unborn to sons still show,
How Independence strong may grow;
May honour, peace and love declare,
That we united brethren are.

"Mac" Gray

Many roads, buildings, parks, schools and even towns in Iredell County are named for people. There's Huskins Library at Mitchell Community College, Anderson Park, Wilson Lee Boulevard, N. B. Mills School, the town of Mooresville, Celeste Henkel School, and Free Nancy Branch, just to name a few. There's Iredell County, too, named for James Iredell.

And then there's Mac Gray Auditorium at Statesville High School. Just who was Mac Gray, anyway? If you had suspected that he had something to do with the schools, you would be right. Robert McAuley Gray was the second superintendent of Statesville City Schools, following Professor D. Matt. Thompson in that position.

Professor Thompson was struck by an automobile in December of 1920 while crossing the street in front of what was then called the Federal Building (now Statesville City Hall) and while he did survive the accident, injuries left him unable to continue the duties of superintendent.

"Mac" Gray, as he was called, is very possibly the only educator to have held prominent positions in the Mooresville City, Iredell County and Statesville City school systems.

Born about two miles east of Mooresville in 1879, Gray came from good stock. His father was a prosperous yeoman farmer who had served as a county commissioner; his mother, a McAuley, was from Statesville and had graduated from what was to become Mitchell Community College.

Gray's first schooling came at the old Mooresville Academy, followed by Erskine College. Gray furthered his education with a variety of courses, including at least one at Columbia University in New York City.

His initial experience as a teacher came in 1901 at the Coddle Creek Academy near the church of the same name in southern Iredell. He singlehandedly taught about 50 young scholars, first grade to college preparatory, in one room.

Next he taught at Bain Academy in Mecklenburg County for five years and then was employed as a principal in Huntersville. He returned to Mooresville and was principal of the Mooresville Academy, his alma mater, in its last year before it became part of the newly-formed Mooresville Graded School District.

Gray next taught at a private boys' school in Charlotte, then moved to Statesville, where he and his brother, Polk C. Gray, operated a drug store on the square.

After this sabbatical, he re-entered education when he was elected superintendent of the Iredell County Schools in 1912, serving in that capacity for five years.

In the school year 1917-18, Gray headed the Dunn, N.C., Public Schools. With our nation's entry into World War I, Gray went to work for the YMCA at Fort Oglethorpe, Ga., teaching illiterate soldiers to read and write.

Returning to Statesville in 1920, he was working in the private sector when Professor Thompson's accident occurred. The city board of education, knowing Gray's qualifications and educational background, offered him the position of superintendent, a position he would hold for more than 20 years, assuming the superintendency on January 1, 1921.

Under Gray's leadership the Statesville city school system flourished. Statesville City School's enrollment grew and new facilities were built.

Probably the last major project with which Superintendent Gray was involved was the construction of a new high school on North Center Street, today's Statesville High School.

Gray's health began to fail him in the late 1930s, but he always rallied. Finally, he tendered his resignation because of ill health on April 8, 1941, but agreed to remain superintendent until June 30, after which the board would recognize him as "Superintendent Emeritus."

The front page of the *Statesville Daily* of July 12, 1941, reported his passing in these words:

"Mr. R. M. Gray, superintendent of the Statesville public schools for nearly twenty-one years, died suddenly Friday afternoon about 6 o'clock at his residence on West End Avenue. Mr. Gray was sitting on the front porch, talking with Mrs. Gray, when he slumped in his chair and expired suddenly following a heart attack."

"Mac" Gray was survived by his wife, the former Miss Nancy McDonald of Mecklenburg County, and by three sons, one of whom was at the time the principal of Harmony High School.

The main building of what we now know as Statesville High School was officially opened on November 9, 1942, although the building had probably been in use since the opening of that school year. It cost $142,000 and housed the 10th, 11th and 12th grades.

The old high school, "D. Matt Thompson," became a junior high school, Statesville's first.

For some time, the auditorium of the D. Matt Thompson building on West Front Street had been inadequate to handle indoor graduation ceremonies and the Playhouse Theater on East Broad Street was often used for this function. This building and grounds later became Mitchell Community College's Continuing Education Center.

In the spring of 1943 the auditorium, "modernistic and with a seating capacity of 1,152," at Statesville High School was completed and used for graduation ceremonies for the first time. *The Landmark* reported, "This was the 52nd commencement in the history of the Statesville Schools and for the first time in recent years, there was room for all who came."

Five years later, the school board decided that it would be a nice gesture to name the facility after the late superintendent. The board so ordered and it officially became "Mac" Gray (not "MacGray") Auditorium in 1948.

The Landmark further reported there would be a formal dedication ceremony in the near future. Your writer has closely examined the old newspapers on microfilm in the county library in search of the dedication ceremony but with no success. The summer and fall of 1948 was the height of the nation-wide polio epidemic. The re-opening of school was delayed several times because of this and it just may be that the dedication ceremony for the auditorium never took place.

There was, however, a dedication ceremony for the re-modeled Mac Gray Auditorium at Statesville High School on Saturday, November 17, 2007.

Mac Gray would be proud of the school system's growth and achievements and Statesville High School graduates, in particular, should know who he was.

REV. DR. JAMES HALL

Although not born in Iredell County—it hadn't been created at the time—one of the most important people to be associated with Iredell County was the Reverend Dr. James Hall, a Presbyterian minister from our county's early days.

Hall was born in Carlisle, Pennsylvania, in 1744. In 1751, 7-year-old James and his parents, James Sr. and Prudence Roddy Hall, made the arduous, bone-jarring trip down the Great Wagon Road from Pennsylvania to what was then still Anson County and settled near the fourth creek west of Salisbury, at a settlement called the Fourth Creek community. That place is today called "Statesville."

Mr. and Mrs. Hall had come to Pennsylvania from Scotland. This part of North Carolina was settled by many people like the Halls, who had come from Scotland or from Northern Ireland who were called "Scots-Irish." They were a frugal people who were said to have "short arms and deep pockets" and they wanted several things: They wanted their own land, they wanted to be left alone by the government and they wanted to worship God in their own manner.

Son James decided to become a minister at an early age, but his father's poor health caused him to shoulder the responsibilities of being the bread-winner of the family for some years.

As soon as he was able, he attended the College of New Jersey at Princeton, graduating in 1774. He was such a good student that he was offered a professorship in mathematics there, an appointment he turned down to pursue his calling to the Lord's service. He is also said to have broken off an engagement to a young lady because the responsibilities of being a family man would have interfered with his calling.

He was called to Fourth Creek Meeting House—now First Presbyterian Church, Statesville—was ordained and became pastor of the congregations of Fourth Creek Meeting House (established around 1757), and the meeting houses of Concord in the Loray community and Bethany, about seven miles north of Fourth Creek community.

As trouble between the British government and Britain's provinces in America grew, the Rev. Mr. Hall, rather than remaining neutral, took an active part on the rebel side. He helped organize militia companies. In 1776 he was elected captain of a militia cavalry unit and led men from this area in joining with General Griffith Rutherford in the two-month campaign against the pro-British Cherokees in Georgia. Besides being a military captain, Rev. Hall was also appointed chaplain of the regiment. Hall County, Georgia, is said to have been named for him.

At least two more times the Rev. Mr. Hall became Captain Hall. In 1779 he led local troops against the British in northwestern South Carolina.

There is a great story about Rev. Hall that is probably true. When General Cornwallis and his redcoats made ready to cross the Catawba, hot on the heels of the American Army of the South, Militia General William Lee Davidson sent out couriers to raise the militia. One rider is said to have arrived on a lathered horse at Fourth Creek Meeting House on a Sunday morning during worship services.

The rider dismounted, went into the church and handed Rev. Hall the message from Gen. Davidson calling out the militia. Rev. Hall read the note, quickly concluded the worship service and turned the meeting into a recruiting depot, reminding the men in the pews of their Scots and Scots-Irish, freedom-seeking heritage. A goodly number of the congregation joined the cause and went home to get their muskets and gear.

Again Rev. Hall was unanimously elected captain of the unit. He was a fighting parson, backing up his words with deeds. It is believed that he was at Gen. Davidson's side when Gen.

Davidson was shot and killed on the eastern bank of the Catawba River as the Redcoats made good their crossing at Cowan's Ford. Hall was offered, but declined Gen. Davidson's command after Davidson was killed.

Following Independence, Hall was instrumental in organizing the Synod of the Carolinas in 1788 at Centre Presbyterian Church, Mount Mourne. He was also involved in the formation of the American Bible Society and was the first president of the North Carolina Bible Society.

At the age of 49, he relinquished his pastorates at Fourth Creek and Concord churches so he could do missionary work, establishing the first Protestant mission in the lower Mississippi Valley in 1800 during one of his fourteen extensive expeditions. He also made numerous shorter missionary excursions.

Rev. Hall authored two books. One was a collection of his published letters describing his westward mission treks, the other a description of his work during the frontier camp meeting revivals.

There was a great debate among ministers of all denominations concerning these revivals, whether they were the work of the Holy Spirit or if they might be attributed to other spirits. Hall was a supporter of the revivals, even though arguments about them sometimes split congregations.

Had this been all that Hall accomplished, his reputation as a patriot and as a man of the cloth would be secure. But it was not enough for James Hall.

He established the famous Clio's Nursery of Arts and Sciences in 1788, an early classical school in Iredell County. Hall also founded what he called the "Academy of Sciences" near Bethany Church. This academy operated out of Rev. Hall's home and before the establishment of the University of North Carolina, was considered by many to be the finest scientific school in the state. In fact, it may have been the very first school in the state to teach science.

These two institutions, Clio's and the Academy, provided education for many men who later became prominent in law, education, in medicine and in the pulpit.

Hall was awarded honorary Doctor of Divinity degrees by his alma mater, Princeton, and by the University of North Carolina. Hall never married.

In his later years, he was often beset by bouts of depression, sometimes doubting his salvation by a Lord to whom he had dedicated his life.

It is said that a church elder once symbolically exorcised a "deaf-and-dumb" demon from him after he had refused to preach for a year and a half.

The Rev. Dr. James Hall went to his reward on July 25, 1826, and is buried in the cemetery of Bethany Presbyterian Church. His parents, James Sr. and Prudence, are interred in Fourth Creek Burying Ground in Statesville, across the street from First Presbyterian Church, their son's first church.

Leonard Ham

I *interviewed Leonard Milton Ham Sr. in Pat's Coffee Shop in Mooresville in early August of 2005. World War II had been over for 60 years that very month. Mr. Ham was a complex, interesting individual. He was an artist and a musician and had been a member, along with my father, of the very first Mooresville High School Band.*

* * *

LH: "I volunteered for the Army Air Corps. I didn't want to be going into the Navy," says Leonard M. Ham, of Mooresville. I was a pipe fitter by trade and if I'd gone into the Navy as a pipe fitter, you know where I'd have ended up? I'd have been down in the boiler room. Brother, I didn't want that. In fact, I started to enlist in the Navy but when I said 'pipe fitter,' the recruiter got this big smile on his face. I thought, 'Uh-Oh.' I'd never have seen daylight."

R&L: Why the Air Corps then?

LH: "My brother Robert and Lonnie Cox had a J-3 (small civilian airplane) here in Mooresville. I didn't have a pilot's license at that time, but I rode in planes a lot; I used to sell tickets out there at Jim Blackwelder's field. I'd say, 'million-dollar thrill for a one dollar bill.' That's how I'd sell tickets.

"I just wanted to be in the Air Corps—thought I was better suited to that than to be in the infantry, and I was married then. I thought about being a pilot, but my wife said, 'Being a pilot? Absolutely not!' Of course, you've got to do what the wife says. We got married in September of 1941. Pearl Harbor was in December of '41 and I went into the service in '42.

166

"I went in at Bowman Field, Kentucky. Next I went to Fort Logan in Denver, Colorado. Next, they sent me to Jefferson Barracks, Missouri. That was overseas training. I was stationed at Wheeler Field [Hawaii] first, then went to Hickam Field [Hawaii] after that.

R&L: Where else did you go?

LH: "I was on Okinawa, in the Pacific, when the war ended. I had been on flying status for a while, but they sent some of us down under to Tarawa. They assigned me to Bomber Command in the intelligence department and had me doing bomb-plot charts.

"We had several airplanes that could take stereo pictures. They would follow the bombing runs, take pictures and bring them back. Then we would examine the photos and hunt out gun emplacements, warehouses, anti-aircraft positions and such down in the islands. I started out on Tarawa in the Gilbert Islands, then we went to Kwajalein, which is in the Marshall Islands, then we went to Eniwetok, then to Saipan, which was in the Marianas.

"Next, we started bombing Iwo Jima and some of the neighboring islands around there. That's when we started bringing in the B-29 Superfortresses and we started bombing Japan proper, the main islands, but we were in Okinawa when the war ended. I flew quite a bit, but I never flew over Japan proper during the fighting.

"When I was a crew member, before they put me in intelligence, I was a waist gunner on twin 50-calibers on a B-24 Liberator bomber, but they took me off that when they found out I could draw. That's when they put me in Bomber Command in the intelligence department. That was around the first part of 1943.

R&L: What was it like to be a waist gunner on a B-24?

LH: "It wasn't good; it was no good at all. Take-offs and landings on small islands are not good...short runways. You back up as far as you can, get the four engines going as fast as they can go, you take off and you're over water instantly and that was no good for a land-based airplane. Same thing goes for landings.

"At that time we were losing a lot of planes on 12-hour bomber missions—six hours out and six hours back. We got up about four in the morning, had breakfast, briefings, and the Red Cross would be sitting out there with coffee and donuts, flew at about 180 knots an hour to places like Truk.

R&L: Do you remember when you heard about Hiroshima?

LH: When we dropped the atomic bomb [on Hiroshima] we got the news right after it happened. I mean we were close there in Okinawa, and we could see the B-29s. We knew right then that it was the end of the war.

"I've got pictures taken right after we dropped the bomb on Hiroshima. A while later some of the Japanese came down there, and they called for an escort for one of their "Bettys" [a Japanese medium bomber] to come in and land so they could talk peace terms, and I've got pictures of that, of the Betty coming in to land. These high Japanese officers that came in there, they wanted to talk peace.

"And then we dropped the second bomb on Nagasaki. They surrendered then, the formal surrender. I was discharged in late October and got home in November of 1945. I forget the exact date, but it was just before Thanksgiving. I had my 125 points—you had to have a certain number of points to get out— and I had mine. Then I was processed and took all these tests and all these interviews. They asked me to re-up [re-enlist], but I had a wife at home.

R&L: Have you had further thoughts about the war?

LH: Eight years ago I took a course in the Japanese language and culture. I'm studying the Japanese language right now. I've got all kinds of books, tapes and all sorts of things like that. I have Japanese friends—some up at NGK [Ceramics in Mooresville]. I have no qualms with that. When a war is over, your enemy becomes a friend. Does that sound logical?

"The times I've talked to Japanese friends—I get cards and letters from Japan now—I don't mention World War II; I don't want to hurt anybody's feelings. From after the war on up to now, I have felt—to me—they're some of the smartest people in the world.

"Every once in a while I remember when we were strafed [shot at] on Saipan. We were strafed several times in daylight raids, and that comes back to me. I wake up at night. That'll never leave me. When you're out there and you see a fighter coming at you, spitting fire, and you see bullets hitting right down at your feet and you're trying to dig a hole like a rat, you don't forget.

"When I first got on the ship to go overseas, I looked at our flag on the back of the ship while it was still in port and I said to myself, 'I hope some day I'll be back.'

"I love that flag as much as I do my own life."

* * *

Leonard Milton Ham passed away in April of 2010. His obituary in the *Mooresville Tribune* mentioned that he had been a founding member of the Mooresville Artists Guild and a charter member of the Carolina Accordion Players Association.

His daughter, Suzanne Ham Cornelius, mentioned that during the memorial service held at Mooresville's First Baptist Church, where Mr. Ham had been a life-long member and a deacon, the minister stated that Mr. Ham, while 89 ½ years old, had been coming to services at First Baptist for more than 90 years—his mother attended services there when she was pregnant with him.

Mr. Ham loved all types of art, literature and music and took accordion lessons at an age when most people become couch potatoes.

He was survived by his children, grandchildren and great-grandchildren.

EDWARD HARRIS

James Coleman, a retired public school history teacher and now (2009) the principal and history teacher at Antioch Christian Academy in Lumberton, emailed us at the *Record & Landmark* and his email found its way to your writer.

It seems that Mr. Coleman and his students had chanced upon a large—5 feet tall—ornate headstone in the Meadowbrook Cemetery in Lumberton. Mr. Coleman and his charges were impressed both by the stone's size and its epitaph, which he says, "generated more questions than answers."

The stone reads as follows: "Beneath this Tablet are deposited the mortal remains of The Honourable Edward Harris, one of the Judges of the Supreme Court of this State who, while engaged at this village in the discharge of the duties of his station, was unexpectedly summoned to appear before the Throne of the Almighty Judge of the Living & the Dead. A grateful county will cherish the memory of a firm and able Magistrate. Long will friends and relatives remember his ardour of attachment and fidelity of service and never can his bereaved wife cease to dwell on the mournful yet soothing recollection of his tenderness & worth. He died March 29th 1813 in the 50th year of his age."

Boy! They don't write epitaphs like that anymore.

In comparison, most headstones today just give the name, birth and death dates, and maybe a small epitaph, such as "Loving Mother," "Father," or "Rest in Peace."

In days past there was a kind of status thing going on in most cemeteries: The taller and more ornate the headstone and the lengthier the inscription and the more intricate the carvings, the more important, presumably, was the person buried below the marker. Based on this information, Judge Harris was a person of wealth and importance.

Mr. Coleman did some research on Judge Harris on the Internet, learned the judge hailed from Iredell County and wanted to know if anyone here could tell him more.

A quick look into William C. Powell's *Dictionary of North Carolina Biography* provided more information, as did a monograph by the late Judge David Furches.

Edward Harris was born in 1763 in that part of Rowan County which in 1788 became Iredell County. His father, James Harris, had come over from England with two brothers and their father—Edward's grandfather—in the early part of the 17th century, arriving in New York.

After the father died, the three sons moved to Pennsylvania and settled at Harrisburg. Some historians maintain that their family gave the place its name. Later the three went south along the Great Wagon Road and settled in North Carolina, first in the Poplar Tent community in what today is Cabarrus County.

Later, James moved westward and started a farm about six miles west of Fourth Creek community [Statesville] in the Loray community.

James Harris was "a strong man, a justice of the peace, a leading citizen in his section in both Church and State and an elder in the Presbyterian church."

His son, Edward, whose grave is in Lumberton, was educated by the Rev. James Hall, who was the first minister to the Fourth Creek Congregation, now better known as First Presbyterian Church, Statesville. The Rev. Hall also organized Iredell's Bethany Presbyterian Church and is buried in the churchyard there.

After finishing his education at the Clio Academy, Edward Harris went to Princeton. Following graduation, he returned to Iredell where he studied law under lawyer William "Billy" Sharpe.

Sharpe is best remembered for his map of the Fourth Creek Congregation, a gold mine for genealogists and historians.

Young Mr. Harris went to seek his fortune on the coast of North Carolina and settled in New Bern to practice law. He later was chosen to fill a seat on the bench of the North Carolina State Superior Court. He represented New Bern and then Craven County in the state legislature and was also a trustee of the University of North Carolina. In addition, he briefly served on the bench of the United States Court for the Fifth Judicial District.

Harris' first wife was Sarah Roulhac of Orange County. Following her death, Squire Harris married another Sarah, this one from New Jersey. There were no offspring from either marriage.

The part of his epitaph that says he was "engaged in the discharge of the duties of his station...summoned to appear before the Almighty Judge..." means just what it says—Judge Harris died on the bench during a trial.

Whether he was successful at defending his life and character and was judged worthy of admission to the Highest Court, we do not know. But we do know where the mortal remains of this son of Iredell County rest.

KEN HARRIS

Kenneth Rhyne Harris, of Harmony, was mayor of Charlotte from 1977-79. Born in Statesville on May 16, 1935, Ken was one of four children of Roy Lee Harris and Beulah Barker Harris. He grew up in a house that stood near Rose Chapel United Methodist Church on U.S. 21 and graduated from Harmony High School, Class of 1953. He demonstrated leadership qualities early, as quarterback of Harmony's six-man football squad, and as pitcher for the Harmony baseball team. He also drove a school bus.

Harris joined the Civil Air Patrol in Statesville, eventually becoming a licensed pilot and a North Carolina Air National Guard officer, retiring from the Air Guard with the rank of major in 1973. After he retired he continued to fly a small Cessna for a number of years.

Harris graduated from Charlotte College (now UNC Charlotte) in 1957 and did further study at UNC Chapel Hill, receiving a Business Administration degree there in 1959. He later worked for North Carolina National Bank for ten years and then entered the insurance field and had his own agency.

His experience in Charlotte government prior to being mayor consisted of a term on the city council from 1973-75.

Mayor Harris gets into the history books as Charlotte's first Republican mayor. His election to the Queen City's highest post was regarded as one of the biggest political upsets in the city's history. Ken Harris was also the first Queen City mayor to preside over Charlotte City Council with representatives elected from districts as well as those with an at-large representation.

Mayor Harris supported a mass transit system for the city and strongly supported a multimillion dollar bond referendum for additional construction and renovation of Charlotte-Douglas International Airport, although the work was completed during the administration of his successor, Eddie Knox. Douglas Airport had been named in honor of Ben Douglas, also a son of Iredell County. Harris' overseeing of the passage of the bonds for the new Charlotte-Douglas Airport was, reportedly, his proudest achievement.

As mayor, Harris was also heavily involved in arrangements for a statue of the Rev. Dr. Martin Luther King Jr. to be placed in Marshall Park. Eventually, Dr. Selma Burke, a Mooresville native, was selected to do the statue.

After completing his term as mayor, he successfully ran for a seat in the state senate, serving there from 1982-1984.

Following service in the legislature, Harris became a member of the State Board of Education, serving in that capacity from 1988-94 and was chairman of that body from 1992-94. He was also president of the Charlotte Rotary Club from 1995 to 1996 and was active in the UNC Charlotte Foundation. Harris had also been a member of the board of trustees for Johnson C. Smith University.

Son Ken Harris Jr. related that his father, "loved the ACC and his Tarheels—especially basketball—and the Panthers." He loved to read, especially the newspapers, and smoked a pipe and read the papers to relax."

Former Mayor Harris died on January 17, 2009, at a Charlotte nursing home. He was 73 and had been battling Alzheimer's for some time. Married again after the death of his first wife, Jean Helms Harris, he was survived by his second wife, Sally Harris, six children and three stepchildren, as well as by eighteen grandchildren.

Those who knew him well described him as "dependable," "amiable," "low-key" and "just a good person."

Sarah Heinzerling

You never know what you will find when you go through old files. Recently, while trying to find some information in the vertical files of the county library, I chanced across a 46-page booklet, *Songs of Iredell*, by Sarah A. Heinzerling. It was printed by Brady Printing Company in Statesville in 1934.

The booklet was a collection of sixty-two of Mrs. Heinzerling's poems, rather than a collection of songs, as the title might suggest.

More than anything, Mrs. Heinzerling's poems reminded me of verses we memorized in the seventh grade at Mooresville Junior High School under teachers Dan Woody and Miss Cora Freeze. Under Mr. Woody, a Statesville resident, I remember learning two manly poems, Tennyson's "Charge of the Light Brigade" and Rudyard Kipling's "If."

Under Miss Cora—a Mooresville institution if there ever was one—I memorized "America" by Ruth Tooze and "Thanatopsis" by William Cullen Bryant. If you ever have trouble falling asleep, I recommend these two poems as a possible solution. Mrs. Heinzerling's verses seem to be of the same genre as these last two poems; Miss Freeze would have loved them, bless her soul.

I found some information on the poet from her obituary, which was printed on the first page of *The Landmark* of March 12, 1954, under the headline, "Poetess Dies at Home Here."

Born in Reidsville in 1862, she and her husband, John E. Heinzerling, moved to Statesville in 1911. She was active in community affairs, being a member of the local United Daughters of the Confederacy and the Statesville Woman's Club. She was also active in state and national literary organizations, including the North Carolina Poetry Society and the National League of American Pen Women.

Songs of Iredell was her second book of poems, her first being *The Pines of Rockingham*, also published in 1934. Her obituary further stated that she was the author of three volumes of poetry and that she had also published a magazine, *The Pioneer*, which suspended publication in 1928.

According to a biographical note in the front of *Songs of Iredell*, her works had previously been published in *The N.C. Poetry Review*, *The Home Department Magazine* and *The Charlotte Observer*, as well as in the old *Statesville Daily*.

She published a third book of poems, *The Call*, in 1936. In it, Mr. Heinzerling gave her definition of poetry: "Poetry is thought expressed in language so perfectly measured it pleases the ear; so beautiful in phrasing it charms the eye; so tender in sentiment it stirs the heart; so lofty in appeal it inspires the mind and exalts the soul."

In one of her poems she gives a warning to would-be poets: "Who follows Shakespeare's lead should be prepared for adverse winds of ridicule...."

Most of her poems were concerned with nature, beauty, religion or patriotism, with titles such as "Appeal to Poesy," "Ode to an Ancient Oak" and "The Reign of Queen October," and might be considered a bit too florid for today's tastes. While I make no claims to being a poetry critic, there were several I came across that might be well received today.

The following abridged poem was inspired, I think, by the calling out of the Iredell Blues, the local militia company, in 1916 to go to the Mexican border during the time of troubles with Pancho Villa. This was just before The Blues were inducted into national service and sent to Europe to fight in the First World War. Perhaps Mrs. Heinzerling was among the crowd at the depot when the troop train departed for El Paso, Texas.

THE STATE GUARDS

They're calling out the State Guards,
But not for dress parade
Before admiring people
Who cheer each fresh brigade;
They mobilize for service where
New heroes will be made.

They're calling out the State Guards,
And gallantly they'll go
Defend our Southern border
Against a treacherous foe;
Alas! They will not return
Who enter Mexico!

They're calling out the State Guards;
We bid them all, God speed,"
Wherever duty calls them
In this, their country's need;
Their heritage demands no less,
Though hearts may break and bleed.

They're calling out the State Guards,
They answer, near and far;
That answer means to many,
"Sunset and evening star,"

Dear God, keep very close to those
Who soon must "cross the bar!"

Mrs. Heinzerling, who had resided at 113 North Tradd Street, was 91 at the time of her passing, and was buried beside her husband in Statesville's Oakwood Cemetery. Mr. Heinzerling died in 1941. She was survived by two daughters and two sons.

Joel Reese, local history librarian at the Iredell County Library, would welcome any copies of *The Pines of Rockingham*, or Mrs. Heinzerling's third book (title unknown) or any copies of *The Pioneer* magazine, either to keep or to copy for the library's files.

MARY C. HOLLIDAY

When someone says "pioneer," we usually think of people crossing the Great Plains as part of a covered wagon train, or folks following someone like Daniel Boone through the Cumberland Gap. Of course we also use "pioneer" to describe anyone making discoveries or advancements, such as the Wright Brothers, "Pioneers in Flight," or Thomas Edison, "Pioneer in Electricity."

Today's subject was a pioneer if there ever was one, a woman who blazed a path for others to follow. Her name was Mary Charlton Holliday.

Born in Pulaski, Virginia, in 1891 and a 1911 honors graduate of Hampton Institute, in Hampton, Virginia, Mary Charlton was supervisor of the schools for black children for four years in Columbus County before coming to Iredell County in 1915 to be our county system's first supervisor of Negro schools—sometimes referred to as the Jeanes Supervisor—a position she held for more than 40 years.

The Jeans Fund's actual name was "The Fund for Rudimentary Schools for Southern Negroes," a million-dollar benevolence established in 1907 by Anna T. Jeans, a wealthy Philadelphia Quaker, "devoted to the sole purpose of assisting in the Southern United States, community, country and rural schools for the great class of Negroes to whom the small rural and community schools are alone available."

The Iredell County Board of Education approved the hiring of a "supervisor for the colored schools" in July, 1915, by appropriating $150 of county funds. "By doing this the county will receive from outside funds $300 for this purpose," recorded the Board.

According to an article in the October 26, 1915, *Landmark*, Miss Charlton's duties were "to give domestic science and industrial training in the schools and have general supervision of their conduct." The article went on to say that cooking and industrial classes would be organized in some of the schools. "The pupils of the classes will be taught how to prepare wholesome food economically and will receive instruction in the making of shuck mats, split baskets, brooms, etc.," wrote *The Landmark.*

In 1915 there were about 40 one-room, one-teacher schools for black children in Iredell County. They were little more than shacks and had almost no educational materials. To be honest, the rural schools for white children were often little better.

By November of 1918 the county began investigating using of the Rosenwald Fund, another source for assistance in building new schools for black students with matching funds to come from the county. Julius Rosenwald, then-president of Sears, Roebuck & Co., established the fund that bears his name in 1917 for "the well-being of mankind." Some Rosenwald schools built in Iredell County were Amity, Chestnut Grove, Houstonville, Scotts-Rosenwald and Unity—later enlarged to become a full high school. These schools initially had two classrooms and a kitchen, where the domestic arts might be taught. Altogether, the Rosenwald Fund was responsible for the construction of more than 5,000 schools for black children nationwide. The school buildings were designed by architects at Tuskegee Institute.

In September of 1918 Mary Charlton married Dr. Robert Sumner Holliday, a general practitioner and Statesville resident since 1908. Dr. Holliday was a native of Cumberland County, was educated at Raleigh's Shaw University and earned his medical degree at Lincoln University in Pennsylvania. Dr. Holliday came to Statesville from Fayetteville and quickly became a leader in Iredell's black community. He held clinics for new mothers on infant care, as well as clinics for black schoolchildren. The couple resided in Statesville at 241 Garfield Street. They had no children of their own.

Under the leadership of Mrs. Holliday, by about 1920 the schools for black children had been consolidated into 11 schools.

Mrs. Holliday's salary primarily came from two sources, county school funds and the Jeanes Foundation. When she was initially hired, she received $150 from the county, $150 from the state and $200 from the Jeans Fund, for a total salary of $500 a year. By 1931 she was being paid a salary of $1,300; $700 from the county and the remainder from the Jeans Fund and state funds.

Mrs. Holliday was instrumental in securing funding for building black schools through the Rosenwald Foundation. In November of 1929, she and a Dr. Davis of the State Department of Instruction appeared before the county school board "in the interest of securing aid from the Rosenwald Fund for transporting colored children to school. The Rosenwald Fund would give $500 on purchase [of a school bus] and would pay half the operating costs."

In November of 1922 *The Landmark* reported that around $3,500 had come to Iredell from the Rosenwald Fund. The article went on to state that a fifth Rosenwald school, the Neilltown School, was to be built in the Davidson township at a cost of $1,800 and further stated that so far there were other Rosenwald schools at Belmont, Troutman, Elmwood and Shinnville. "The Negroes of a community are required to raise a certain amount before the Rosenwald Foundation will agree to assist," stated *The Landmark*.

Mrs. Holliday's contributions to Iredell County youth went far beyond her job description, as she ceaselessly struggled for more equitable funding for black students, teachers and schools. She also sought to improve the lives of the black community through the organization of Better Homes Clubs and promoted participation in local parent-teacher associations. She also encouraged black farmers to seek help from the county agricultural extension service.

As a supervisor, she needed to know what type of instruction was being carried out and what particular needs a school might have. Often Mrs. Holliday would take a train from Statesville to Mooresville, walk from the Mooresville depot out to the rural black schools, perhaps spending a whole day at one school, then walk back to the depot to take the train back to her home in Statesville.

Mrs. Holliday received a master's degree in education from Columbia University in May of 1943. In the summers she sometimes was on the faculty of Tuskegee Institute.

After 41 years of labor in the field of education she retired from Iredell County Schools for reasons of health on May 21, 1956. Mrs. Holliday passed away on April 8, 1968, in a Goldsboro hospital and is buried beside her husband in Fayetteville. Dr. Holliday had died in Statesville in March of 1966 at the age of 90. Locally, a memorial service for Mary C. Holliday was held in the gymnasium of Unity High School.

Mooresville-born sculptress Selma Burke made a bronze bas relief plaque of Mrs. Holliday for the "Colored Parent Teacher Association" of the county, which was unveiled in March of 1946 at the A.M.E. Zion Church in Statesville. Dr. Mary McLeod Bethune was in attendance and spoke during the ceremony. For many years the plaque hung in the county system's only black high school, Unity High School, but today it may been seen in the James Iredell Room of the Iredell County Library.

* * *

In this writer's opinion, it is past time that Iredell County honored Mary Charlton Holliday's memory and the pioneering work she did here by naming a school after her. Although she may be known as having been a driving force behind the construction of newer, better schools for black children, she and her husband made a tremendous impact on the black community and she, in particular, shared what she had learned with local black teachers, thereby increasing the quality of instruction. Mrs. Holliday is quoted as saying, "I've seen big things from little acorns grow, and during that time I've realized that it is not the building that is most important, but what goes on inside."

MORDECAI HYAMS

Mordecai Elisha Hyams (1819 - 1891) called Statesville home, but he is better known in scientific circles than locally, which is a shame; he was an interesting, intelligent man.

Hyams was born in Charleston, South Carolina, and was a graduate of the University of South Carolina at Columbia. He was a 30-year old school teacher living in Magnolia, Florida, when he married Caroline Frederika Smith in 1848 or 1849. Altogether he and Mrs. Hyams had seven children, six boys and a girl.

In spite of his growing family, at the outbreak of the Civil War he enlisted as a member of Company E, "The Davis Guards," of the 2nd Regiment Florida Volunteers. Because of his knowledge of plants, he was discharged from the Confederate Army on April 20, 1862, and was sent to Charlotte, N.C., to the Carolina Military Institute—which was located where the main YMCA now stands on East Morehead—where large quantities of roots and herbs and barks had been stockpiled for the manufacture of medicines.

As an agent of the Confederate government, Hyams' work would be to identify and purchase plants to be converted into medicines. Before the war, almost all medicines were produced in the North even though many of the plants the medicines were made from could readily be found in the South. Hyams continued with this work throughout the war.

After the war Mr. Hyams moved to Statesville, his home for the remainder of his life, and became the purchasing agent for the Wallace Brothers. Their 44,000 square foot herbarium—40 by 100 feet and 2 1/2 stories high—was located in Statesville where the Plaza Apartments Building now stands behind the old court house. The herbarium is reputed to have been the largest such botanical depot in the United States, if not the world.

Two of Mordecai's sons, Charles W. and George, often accompanied their father on his expeditions into the foothills and mountains of western North Carolina to locate ginseng and other valuable plants. In addition, Hyams taught locals how to identify plants the Wallaces wanted and established a barter system with the people, their rural stores and the Wallaces, to the benefit of all.

In the process of these trips, the elder Hyams chanced upon hitherto unknown floral species. Hyams is credited with discovering 166 new plant species or varieties in our state.

He retired from working for the Wallace Brothers in the late 1880s and for a time was botanist for Louis Pinkus, who also did business in the crude medicinal drug trade. Mr. Pinkus' herb house was located close to the Statesville depot.

M. E. Hyams' chief claim to fame was the re-discovery of a rare plant, the *Shortia galacifolia*, along the banks of the Catawba River in McDowell County in 1878. Experts in botany have referred to the search for this plant, also known as "Oconee Bells," as "the botanical equivalent of the Holy Grail." This small flowering plant had been discovered by the renowned French botanist Andre Michaux in 1788 during an expedition into North Carolina's mountains. Michaux brought part of a plant back with him to Paris and it was there, fifty years later as a pressed and dried specimen—a few leaves and a single seed pod—that Asa Gray, of Harvard, saw it when he was touring continental herbaria. This small, dried plant was the elusive object of rediscovery for the better part of ninety years. Gray described the plant for fellow botanists and wanted to know where, exactly, it had come from in the mountains.

The first part of the plant's scientific name, *Shortia galacifolia*, comes from the name of a Louisville, Kentucky, botanist, Charles W. Short, who died before the plant was named in his honor. The second part of its name means that its leaves resemble those of the galax plant.

Hyams described how the flower was rediscovered in May of 1877. "We were passing along the road," he wrote, "and my attention was called to an elevated hillside that I could not ascend as being at the time rather exhausted, being sixty years old, so I requested [his teenage son, George] to ascend and bring whatever was in flower."

Hyams did not immediately recognize the flower for what it was and subsequently sent the specimen to a botanist in Rhode Island who forwarded it to Professor Asa Gray at Harvard who recognized it for what it was, the *Shortia galacifolia*. Gray himself had been trying to find the plant for 30 years.

And so the quest had been completed. One author has described the quest for the plant as "the best story of 19th-century American botany." As *The Blooming News* has pointed out, "The story of this legendary plant abounds with ironies. Shortia was discovered by a man who didn't name it, named for a man who didn't see it, by someone who didn't know where to locate it."

The plant's native range is quite small. As one source has noted, "This lovely flower, a member of the Diapensia family, is native to only seven counties in the mountains of western North Carolina, South Carolina and Georgia." The South Carolina plants grow near the headwaters of the Keowee River.

Furthermore, Hyams was the author of *The Crude Drug Industry of the South* and saw the book published in four languages during his lifetime. He also listed all the forest trees then known to grow in North Carolina for the U.S. Census Bureau. Hyams rubbed shoulders with the elite of his profession and it was he who personally oversaw the Wallace Brothers' exhibits at the Philadelphia Centennial Exposition of 1876 and at the Paris Exposition of 1878—occasions in which his exhibits won medals.

Further, he was elected as a delegate to the prestigious National Forestry Congress and the American Forestry

Association Congress which met at Cincinnati in 1882. He also was an honorary member of the Elisha Mitchell Scientific Society of the University of North Carolina. He was a great correspondent with fellow botanists of his time and frequently shared specimens with them.

Although "Professor" Hyams, as he was called, was born into a Jewish family, at the time of his death he was a member of Statesville's First Presbyterian Church. After a long illness, Hyams died on May 16, 1891, and is buried in the non-Jewish part of Statesville's Oakwood Cemetery. His funeral was largely attended.

According to one source, Hyams was a first cousin to Judah P. Benjamin, Treasurer of the Confederate States of America. As his obituary in *The Landmark* stated it, "He was quite a remarkable man—a man of greater gifts than many of his acquaintances were aware.... A scientist of fine ability and a lover of Nature, he never lost sight of the truth that there is a God higher and mightier than Nature."

WILLIE AND DOTTIE JOLLY

Dottie Jolly (left) and Willie Jolly

After I was honorably discharged from the Navy in 1975 I took a job as safety officer with the Iredell County Schools Maintenance Department for a year. I resumed my teaching career at Central School on the Wilkesboro Highway in the fall of 1976. My wife, son and I were then living in Mooresville, and it was quite a drive to get up to Central School.

Beside Central School was an old fashioned mom-and-pops country store/gas station. I had heard some of the school's faculty refer to it as "Jollysville," but hadn't thought much about it. One day I went into the store to get some cheese crackers and a soda. A clerk was behind the counter. I told him what I wanted and he went to get my drink from a cooler.

On the wall behind the counter I noticed a number of newspaper clippings and photos of two attractive young women in Western costumes. The clippings informed me that those in the photographs were the "Jolly Sisters."

The man returned with my ice-cold soda.

"The Jolly Sisters," I said, pointing to the clippings, "I haven't heard of them in quite a while." The truth was that I hadn't heard of them at all, but was just trying to make conversation.

The fellow lit up with a smile like you had plugged him in. "Gracey," he called out, "this young fellow here says he remembers Willie and Dottie."

Gracey, it turned out, was the mother of the two young ladies. We talked pleasantly for a few minutes and then I went back over to the school.

The next school year I transferred to Brawley Middle School west of Mooresville where I spent the majority of my teaching career. It was a lot closer to home than Central School. I always wondered about the Jolly Sisters and what became of them.

Recently, thanks to Steve Hill and Mrs. Ethel Campbell, a first cousin of the sisters, I found out more.

* * *

"Willie" was Wilma Grace Jolly, born in March of 1927, and "Dottie" was Dorothy Dean Jolly, born in March of 1934. The duo were the daughters of Grady Houston Jolly and wife Gracey Mae Mason Jolly. The Jolly Sisters performed as a hillbilly song and dance duo back in the 1940s and 1950s. That is what people called it before country and western music became mainstream, they called it "hillbilly" music.

There were many brother and sister acts on radio and television at that time, such as the Ames Brothers, the Andrews Sisters, the King Sisters, the McGuire Sisters, the Lennon Sisters on the Lawrence Welk Show, to name a few.

While looking for other things in the old Mooresville and Statesville newspapers, every once in a while I would come across references and from these scraps, outlines of their careers as entertainers can be suggested. We know, for example, that they were singing as early as 1945 when they performed for the Statesville Lions Club, but made their big, public debut at the Fiddlers Convention in Union Grove.

By 1949 they regularly sang on Statesville's radio station WSIC-AM, 7:15 to 7:30 Tuesday evenings, and for the North Wilkesboro radio station, WKBC-AM, as "The Southern Cowgirls." For the appearance in North Wilkesboro, the sisters were in the habit of getting up at 3:30 a.m. "so they can get to North Wilkesboro for a couple of appearances each week."

They sang on WBT-FM in Charlotte in August of 1950 and continued to sing on radio for five years. They later appeared on WBTV on the "Arthur Smith Show." In September of 1950 the two were part of the cast of a Civitan Club play, "Trippin' Around," performed at Mac Gray Auditorium. They sang two numbers, "Way Out There" and "Quicksilver" in the fifth scene of the production.

Willie and Dottie sang at Shatley Springs in July, 1951, and appeared at the Carolina Theatre in Greenwood, S.C., with Charlie Slate of the Smoky Mountain Hayride Show in 1952.

More than 30 short articles about the girls appeared in the *Statesville Daily Record* between 1945 and 1955. They sang at Fraley's Food Fair, at two local Democratic conventions, at the Playhouse Theater, at benefits for the Oteen VA Hospital and for the new hospital in Alexander County. According to *The Daily Record*, "The Jolly sisters, radio performers of Statesville, were both generous and tireless with their help [with the hospital]. They sold doughnuts, sandwiches, pies and hamburgers, as well as delighting the crowd with their songs."

Dottie and Willie sang at Fourth of July picnics and at dinner dances at the Statesville Country Club. On May 12, 1952, they performed in Mooresville at the old Moor Baseball Park on South Main Street. "The Jolly Sisters of television and radio fame," reported the *Mooresville Tribune*, "will be present as an added attraction at the baseball game between the Moors and Salisbury here Monday night. A public address system will be set up so that everyone present can hear these entertainers."

* * *

Driving from the Central School community to sing for a baseball game in Mooresville might have seemed like a long trip to the sisters at one time, but a drive to the other end of the county would soon seem like a stroll to the mailbox.

In 1954, just after Dottie graduated from Central School, the sisters went on a six-week tour with a Charlotte vaudeville troupe touring the Carolinas, Georgia and Tennessee. Previously they had performed mostly at local venues; now they were ready to do some traveling and they began to meet other acts who were doing Western and country music circuits.

In October of the following year the *Record & Landmark* carried a professional publicity photo of the girls with a short article stating that a song on a 45 rpm record they had cut with the noted steel guitarist Cecil Campbell and his Tennessee Ramblers was due to be released that month on the MGM label. The song the girls were on was titled, "Steel Guitar Waltz."

"This recording by the Jolly Sisters," wrote the R&L, "who began their climb to a popular Western and hillbilly songs career at the Fiddlers Convention at Union Grove School, is their first time on the national recording level."

At the time of the recording they had been singing regularly on WBTV for about a year and a half. Willie and Dottie also recorded at least two other songs that Willie wrote, "Ocean of Tears That I Shed Yesterday" and "Since You Came Along."

According to Willie's son Robert, Willie composed many songs she and Dottie performed. Willie, a guitarist as well as a singer, could listen to a song on the radio while they were driving to a performance and figure out the chords before they got to the job. Dottie would write down the words and they'd soon have a new song they could perform.

The two girls got some of their talent from their parents. Their mom wrote songs and performed with her brothers at local parties and dances when she was young and their father played the banjo in a string band with his brother and a friend.

At the time the MGM recording was made, Dottie and Willie were touring army camps in the Washington, D.C., and Maryland area. Usually appearing as part of a larger ensemble, the girls worked with recording and film stars Tex Ritter, Audie Murphy, Tim Holt and Wild Bill Cody, among others.

The two eventually performed in the old Ryman Auditorium in Nashville on the "Grand Ole Opry," known by some as "the Mother Church of Country Music."

To an outsider the life of a traveling musician can sound glamorous, but the reality of that life causes many to abandon their dreams at the stage door. All-night bus or car rides to another city, low pay for jobs while you wait to be "discovered" by a top-of-the-line agent and the separation from family and friends, all add to the tough life of a novice entertainer trying to break into the big time ranks.

Willie married Robert G. "Bob" Carney of Lexington, in 1957. Bob, a World War II veteran, was with the United States Forest Service. Their first son was named Mike, and Willie left the act soon after the birth of her second son, Robert. Willie briefly returned to the spotlight in 1969, appearing on the Cecil Campbell TV show on WSOC in Charlotte. At that time she was living in Shelby with her husband and two sons.

Dottie, who was seven years Willie's junior, married Michael Parker in 1962. She met him when he was a trumpet player in a U.S. Army band in Florida. Parker was from upstate New York.

In a 1961 interview in the *Greensboro Daily News*, Dottie, who was then doing a solo act, revealed that she had wanted to be a singer since she was six years old.

At that time she had entertained audiences in 30 states and as a hobby, had collected charms of each state she had performed in for a bracelet. She was preparing for a 9-week tour of U.S. Army and Air Force installations in Kansas, Oklahoma, New Mexico, Texas and Wyoming. Just prior to this she had toured New England, performing in a number of Boston hotels and supper clubs. She estimated she had traveled over 80,000 miles the previous year.

Dottie was doing what in show business is called a "novelty act," which incorporated singing, dancing, dramatic bits and some comedy. To prepare for this she had taken dance training in New York City and was planning on studying dramatics in the Big Apple when she had the chance.

She was proud of having sung with the Tommy Dorsey Orchestra when it was directed by Warren Covington following Dorsey's death. "I was made for show business—there's never a dull moment," she was quoted as saying.

* * *

Today Willie is not in the best of health. She lives in an assisted living center in Shelby near her younger son, Robert. Her husband died early in 2002. Her older son, Mike, lives in Cary, North Carolina. After she and her sister broke up their act she continued to work local jobs booked through the Musicians Union, and also worked some at a local department store.

Sister Dottie lives with husband Mike, who also plays guitar, in a suburb of Chicago. The two of them still perform a little in people's homes, at small conventions and in church. Dottie stated that in her career with her sister and as a solo act she performed in 39 states and three foreign countries—Canada, Iceland and Greenland—much of it working for the government doing USO shows.

I spoke with Dottie recently on the telephone. She said she has not been South in four or five years, but said she frequently talks to her sister on the telephone.

Their father, known to many as "Grade," who was also an ordained Baptist missionary minister, passed away in 1971 at the age of 78. Mrs. Gracey Jolly passed away in 1996 at the age of 102.

The house near Central School where the Jolly family lived was razed a few years ago, as was the Jollysville store, where one could get a pack of cheese crackers, a cold soft drink and look at photos and clippings of two lovely young ladies on the wall above the counter.

HOMER KEEVER

April 12th is an anniversary of sorts, a notable date in Iredell County history. It was on this date in 1950 that Homer Maxwell Keever, a school teacher and Methodist minister, had his first historical piece published in the old *Statesville Daily Record*. His premiere article was entitled, "Old Census Records Provide Interesting Iredell History."

Keever had perused the 1860 census records for Iredell and was delighted to share some of his discoveries with a wider classroom than was available to him at school. In this first historical piece he told readers about Iredell's forty-nine manufacturing establishments, which included twenty-seven small grain mills, three blacksmith shops and the two cotton mills in the northern part of the county. He found out the names and ages of the workers in these two mills, one of which was located in Eagle Mills and the other on Hunting Creek.

In concluding this first piece Homer wrote, "With these details the ante-bellum textile industry of this county begins to take on flesh and blood. Most of the workers were girls, one of them as young as nine years old, a few more just over ten, but most of them one side or the other of twenty. In the families which lived in the mill village several of the boys...were given jobs along with their sisters, and besides the overseer there was one full-grown man in each of the two mills. It was, however, primarily, an employment for young, unmarried girls and women, and evidently offered an especial chance for a living to a widow with a large brood to be taken care of."

There is continuity at work here. In putting our history into printed form, Homer Keever was following in the footsteps of previous historians such as the Reverend Dr. E. F. Rockwell and Dr. P. F. Laugenour. Besides having Keever and Rockwell and Laugenour, we in Iredell have been blessed by a variety of other writers who have also have made contributions in preserving our collective past. A short list would include John M. Sharpe, Minnie Hampton Eliason, Rev. J. I. Goodman, Ralph Sloan, W. N. "Red" Watt, Mildred Miller, Gene Krider and others.

Homer Keever would keep writing for the next quarter of a century about his first loves, Iredell's schools and churches, and, most of all, its interesting people. He continued to have a large following after *The Record* merged with *The Landmark* in May of 1954.

A writer of versatility, Keever occasionally wrote of events in the classroom. He taught for eight years at Union Grove and had taken the Union Grove girls debate team to a state championship. He taught at Barium Springs for three years, at Central for 17 years and at Cool Spring for three. He had also been a noted basketball coach.

Homer's personal knowledge of the game came in handy when he covered the highly competitive county basketball games for *The Daily Record* while sportswriter Jerry Josey was in service during the Korean War. He even did some travelogues.

Keever really hit his stride in the late 1950s and early 1960s. All told, he wrote some 450 pieces for *The Record* or *Record & Landmark*, but occasionally he also had pieces in *The State* magazine and in the *North Carolina Journal of Education*, as well as other publications. He had thirteen entries in Dr. Bill Powell's definitive *Dictionary of North Carolina Biography*. At the time of his death, he was the archivist of the Western North Carolina Conference of the United Methodist Church.

Although an ordained Methodist minister for 48 years, he never was a regular preacher at a church, although he did broadcasts of Sunday school lessons at local radio stations and substituted in the pulpit for local ministers from time to time.

Homer Keever's masterwork, *Iredell, Piedmont County*, published during our nation's bicentennial, is long out of print and is highly collectable, particularly by those engaged in genealogy. It is a work praised for both its scholarship and its readability. It takes talent to weave the threads of historical fact into a cloth that is both interesting and smooth. Homer Keever was a skilled weaver of words.

A complete bibliography of printed works of Homer Keever runs to over 500 titles. Keever returned sometimes to topics that interested him, incorporating new findings into his work.

For example, his last "regular" column was published in the *Record & Landmark* of August 14, 1975, and was entitled "Andrew Baggerly: Dreamer Ahead of His Time?" This is very similar to his fourth published article, found in the old *Record* dated May 2, 1950, which had the title, "Baggerly, Eagle Mills Dreamer, Was 50 Years Ahead of His Time."

Homer Keever died on September 12, 1979, and is buried beside his wife, Alta, in Statesville's Oakwood Cemetery. Mrs. Keever, who passed away in June of 1989, was also a public school teacher. When the two retired from their teaching careers in 1968, they had 60 years in the classroom between them.

Some of Homer Keever's articles are available in printed form in the James Iredell Room of the county public library, while others are still available only on microfilm copies of the old newspapers.

DR. P. F. LAUGENOUR

Iredell County is fortunate to have had a number of people who have given of their time to research and record our county's past. Second, in my opinion, in importance of those who have documented Iredell County's history, after the late Homer Keever, is Dr. Philip Fletcher Laugenour, who was a Statesville dentist.

Born in November of 1852 in Little Yadkin township, Wilkes County, he was the son of Andrew L. and Eliza Ledford Laugenour. Dr. Laugenour was a graduate of Catawba College when it was located at Newton and then of the Baltimore College of Dental Surgery. Beginning in 1882, Dr. Laugenour practiced his profession in Newton before moving his practice and family to Statesville in the fall of 1893. He soon became interested in Iredell's history and interviewed older residents, many of whom were his patients. In addition, he became thoroughly familiar with the pioneering historical works of the Rev. Dr. E. F. Rockwell.

From April 16, 1914, through September 28, 1916, the old Statesville *Sentinel* newspaper published a series of Dr. Laugenour's articles. In addition, some of his articles were published from time to time in *The Landmark*.

In a belated introduction to the 1914-1916 series, the editor of *The Sentinel* remarked, "The author has devoted years of labor and thought and the result is matter of great value not only to Iredell County but to our state. The articles will be found highly entertaining and we venture the suggestion that they are well worth being filed away. One of these days all who are in any way familiar with most of these facts, whether by personal knowledge or by tradition, will have passed away."

Dr. Laugenour was interested in the genealogies of Iredell's first families, particularly the Allison, Bell, Byers, Caldwell, Carson, Chambers, Dent, Ewing, Gill, Gray, Hall,

Harris, Hill, Houston, Lazenby, Locke, Matthews, Morrison, Ramsey, Sloan, Steele, Stevenson, Summers, White, Wilson and Young families. He is regarded by some as being the county's first genealogist and also was a founding member of an early county historical society.

Although he himself was a Methodist, he preserved a good deal of the history of the area's Presbyterian churches, including Bethany, Centre, Fourth Creek (now First Presbyterian Church, Statesville) and Tabor, which were among the first to be organized here.

Dr. Laugenour was involved in an attempt to settle one of this area's most famous mysteries: The true identity of the man buried at Third Creek Presbyterian Church in Rowan County. There are some who believe it is the grave of Marshal Michel Ney, one of Napoleon's favorite generals. Others say that is the grave of an imposer, a man who called himself Peter Stuart Ney but claimed to be the French marshal when "in his cups" and on his deathbed, and that the real Marshal Ney is buried in France. Dr. Laugenour was a member of a select team that excavated the grave in the Cleveland community in May of 1887. Alas, the jury is still out on the Marshal Ney identity question.

In addition to his historical interests, Dr. Laugenour was a member of several of the town's fraternal organizations, including the Odd Fellows, the Woodmen of the World, the Masons and the Shriners. He was also a member of the Board of Directors of the Statesville Cotton Mill and a stockholder and member of the board of the Statesville Telephone Company. In addition, he held stock in the Sterling Flour Mill and the Statesville Furniture Company.

Dr. Laugenour died on Sunday, February 16, 1916, at the age of 63. He and his wife and several of his children are buried in Statesville's Oakwood Cemetery.

In his obituary printed in *The Landmark*, it was stated that "he had done more for the preservation of Iredell history than any citizen of the county and at the time of his death was probably better informed about local history than any citizen of the county."

An editorial in the Statesville *Sentinel* held similar sentiments, adding that, "He left a monument to himself in his history of Iredell county..... It can be safely said that the history is the most complete ever gotten together, of Iredell county and this territory generally."

It went on to say something of the man: "Dr. Laugenour was a good citizen, a good man. He was simple and direct as a child with a heart as big as a mountain. Such men are few and far between."

A good obituary for a good man.

AUGUSTUS LEAZAR

"Hon. Augustus Leazar died at his home at this place last Saturday morning, February 18, a few minutes past 10 o'clock, after lingering since last August, suffering a very aggravated case of diabetes."

So began the obituary in the *Mooresville Enterprise* of February 24, 1905, which attempted to summarize the life and varied careers of one of the most outstanding men to ever call Iredell County home.

Augustus was one of five known children of John Leazar (October 13, 1804-June 15, 1887) and his wife, the former Isabella Jamison (May 4, 1810-May 29, 1897) and was born on the 27th of March, 1843, on the Leazarwell plantation six miles southeast of Mooresville in the Prospect Church community of Rowan County.

Augustus took top honors of the Class of 1860 at nearby Davidson College when he graduated at the age of 17. Shortly after the beginning of the Civil War he organized a group of men that would become Company "G" of the 42nd North Carolina Infantry Regiment and was commissioned 1st Lieutenant of the unit when he was 19, a position he would hold through the War.

Augustus was with his regiment, a component of General Robert F. Hoke's Brigade, at the battles of New Bern, Richmond, Cold Harbor, Petersburg, Fort Fisher, Kinston, and Bentonville. He was paroled on May 2, 1865, and returned to his home to marry his childhood sweetheart, Miss Cornelia Frances McCorkle (January 16, 1842-September 4, 1873), daughter of William B. and Mary Marshall McCorkle.

Augustus and Cornelia had three children, two boys and a girl, but only the daughter, Carrie Augusta Leazar (September 22, 1866-January 22, 1915), lived to reach maturity. Carrie would later organize and serve as the first president of the Battle of

Bentonville Chapter of the United Daughters of the Confederacy in Mooresville.

As Bentonville is in no way close to Mooresville, the town's UDC chapter was probably given its name at the suggestion of Miss Leazar, as it was the biggest battle her father participated in.

After his wife died at the age of thirty-one, Augustus remarried in 1888 to the young Clara Fowler (November 20, 1868-August 21, 1895), the daughter of "Captain" William G. and Margaret Alexander Fowler. By this marriage there was one child, a son, Augustus Leazar, Jr., who would also become a Davidson College man. "Gus," as younger Mr. Leazar was known, became a barnstormer pilot and an early auto racing enthusiast and one of the first commercial vintners in North Carolina.

Back in his native community in 1866, Augustus Sr. embarked on the first of his careers: education. He taught at the Prospect Academy which stood adjacent to the Presbyterian Church of the same name. In 1967 there was a N.C. Historical Highway Marker erected to Mr. Leazar on the church grounds. Leazar later taught at the Poplar Grove Academy near Coddle Creek Presbyterian Church before coming to the newly-chartered town of Mooresville in 1873 to pursue the same profession.

It was here that Leazar, with his brother-in-law Stephen Frontis, Jr. (1838-1892), operated the academy that was the ancestor of the present-day Mooresville Graded School District. Known as both "Frontis and Leazar's School" and as "The Mooresville Academy," this institution was begun in 1872 by Prof. Frontis and proved to be a great drawing card for the new town. According to one source, "Many students came to this new school from the surrounding country because under the supervision of Mr. Frontis and Mr. Leazar it soon gained the reputation of being the best in this part of the country." It is said that Professor Frontis usually taught the lower grades, while Professor Leazar led the upper.

This was not a public, tax-supported school, but was a private academy and boarding school which charged one dollar per month's instruction in the primary department and an additional dollar per month as one advanced into the intermediate, higher intermediate, and classical departments.

The top fee was $4.50 per month for a college-bound student taking Latin, Greek, and higher mathematics.

In 1880 the school had an advertised capacity of one hundred pupils. The school was located (appropriately) where the education building of Mooresville's First Baptist Church now stands.

Mr. Leazar, in association with a Mr. Goodman, was, for part of this same time, an editor and co-owner of the *Iredell Gazette*, a weekly newspaper that began publication in Mooresville around June of 1878 and lasted until about 1894. As far as is known, only two issues of the *Gazette* have survived (both from 1880); both are on microfilm at the Iredell County Public Library.

In 1882, after being in education and newspapering for 17 years, Mr. Leazar left both occupations to begin a career in public service. It was politics that was to be the major focus of the remainder of his life.

Elected as a Democrat to four terms in the N.C. State House of Representatives (1892-1890), Leazar was chosen as Speaker of the House in his last term. It was during his career as a law-maker that he was involved in several pieces of legislation that were to mark him for the remainder of his career and life.

The most notable of these was an act to establish a state agricultural and mechanical college. Leazar, as chairman of the Committee on Education, and in league with a like-minded group of progressive young men known as the "Watauga Club," introduced legislation for this college which was passed in March of 1885. It was necessary, however, to do this again with a bill co-authored by Leazar and Dr. Charles William Dabney which was passed in 1887. That college is known today as North Carolina State University, and if any man deserves the title "Father of N.C. State," it is Augustus Leazar. When the college opened in 1889, Leazar was appointed to its first Board of Trustees.

Another piece of legislation associated with Mr. Leazar, while not authored by him but strongly pushed through the House by him, was the 1885 bill which separated the county schools from the county commissioners, putting them under separate county boards of education. While in the House he also "led the successful fight that ended the giving of convict labor to build railroads for private corporations."

The final piece of legislation associated with Leazar was of a more controversial nature than these others. This was the 1887 proposition for the creation of a new county, to be named "Lillington," that would have had Mooresville as its county seat.

This new county was to be composed of Iredell's two southernmost townships, the Coddle Creek and Davidson townships, as well as parts of Iredell's Fallstown and Barringer townships, plus the northern third or so of Mecklenburg and western parts of Rowan and Cabarrus. The Lillington bill aroused the ire of both Statesvillians and the citizens of the other counties involved.

In his defense it has been said that Mr. Leazar did not personally support this bill, but introduced it into the legislature in accordance with the wishes of his constituency.

Whatever the case, the Lillington bill "died a-borning" and caused Mr. Leazar much loss of face with the majority of Iredell County. The albatross of Lillington around his neck probably caused Leazar's defeat when he challenged incumbent conservative Democrat John Steele Henderson for a seat in the United States House of Representatives in 1890 and 1892.

The people of Mooresville did not completely give up on the idea of a new county with Mooresville as its county seat and as late as April of 1923, were still discussing the idea.

Leazar was out of the public eye temporarily following this debacle, although he continued to serve as a trustee for State A. and M. College, the University of North Carolina, and his alma mater, Davidson College, as well as being a member of the North Carolina Board of Agriculture.

He returned to active public service in 1893 with his appointment as superintendent of the State Penitentiary. While in this capacity (1893-1896) he became the first superintendent of that institution to put it on a self-supporting basis instead of a taxpayer liability by starting a system of state prison farms. Indeed, the system yielded a surplus of over $91,000 in 1896, which was no small sum.

Leazar is also remembered for his advocacy of humane treatment of prisoners. He recommended the separation of young prisoners from "older and more hardened inmates," and he favored commutation of prison sentences for good behavior.

As Mr. Leazar's health declined he retired to more sedentary pursuits, such as supervision of his large farm which was located just within Rowan County. He resumed residence in Mooresville and continued to serve the local community as a forty-year elder in Mooresville's First Presbyterian Church and as director of the Bank of Mooresville. At the time of his death on February 18, 1905, he was also a director of the proposed North Carolina Midland Railroad which was to reach from Mooresville to Winston.

Mr. Leazar's obituary in *The Enterprise* concluded, "Very beautiful tributes were paid to the memory of our distinguished deceased citizen, reference being made to his strong Christian character, his devotion to his church, his loyal and patriotic service as a soldier, his usefulness as an educator and trainer of youth, and his ability as a statesman."

Local Confederate veterans serving as honorary pall-bearers, escorted Augustus Leazar to his final resting place in Mooresville's Willow Valley Cemetery following his funeral service at the First Presbyterian Church. His gravestone is the tallest in the cemetery and is located less than a block from the site of his Mooresville Academy.

"Gus" Leazar

Gus Leazar would have liked Mooresville's calling itself "Race City, U.S.A." He also would have liked the proximity of Iredell County to the Charlotte Motor Speedway, for Gus Leazar was a speed pioneer—in the air and on land.

Augustus "Gus" Leazar, Jr. was the son of one of Mooresville's most prominent men. His father, Augustus Leazar, and Stephen Frontis, Jr. began the Mooresville Academy in the 1870s. It was the town's first industry and the predecessor of the Mooresville Graded School District.

Augustus Sr. also served four terms in the lower state house, helped establish the college that eventually became N.C. State University, was a newspaper publisher and editor, etc.

Augustus Jr. had pretty big shoes to fill had he followed in his father's footsteps, but he did not, and set out on his own course and became prominent in his own chosen fields of endeavor.

Gus was born in Mooresville in 1890, the child of Augustus Sr.'s second wife, Clara Fowler, whom the elder Leazar married in 1888. Clara Fowler Leazar died in August of 1895 at the age of 27, leaving the five-year-old Gus without a mother. Augustus Sr. died in 1905, when Gus was 15.

As a boy he showed an aptitude for things mechanical and an interest in things that moved with speed.

In 1909 he was offered an appointment to the U.S. Naval Academy, but turned it down to continue studies at his father's alma mater, Davidson College. In 1910, at the age of 20, Gus went abroad, visiting England, Scotland, France, Germany, Italy and Switzerland.

We next hear of the young man racing cars on the wide, flat sands of Daytona Beach, Florida.

There is a story that one day an airplane landed on the wide sand near Gus. He sauntered over to the aircraft, the first he had ever seen up close, and made a deal with the female pilot:

If she would take him up, he would give her a once-in-a-lifetime ride in his souped-up jalopy.

The pilot was Ruth Law, the celebrated pioneer aviatrix. In 1915 Law was flying at Daytona Beach and while there was the first pilot to "loop the loop." This may have been the occasion when she and young Gus Leazar met.

Anyway, Gus gave her a ride in his speedy car, she returned the favor and ever after that Gus dreamed of flying. He eventually got his pilot's license and was a civilian pilot when the United States entered the First World War.

Gus enlisted in the aviation branch of the Army Signal Corps, which at that time was in charge of all Army aircraft. Gus's considerable talents were recognized and he was assigned to be an instructor of new pilots at an Army base in Texas. Lt. Leazar never crossed the Atlantic to fight as a knight of the air, but instead, taught what he knew of airplanes and flying to those who did go into aerial combat. In that way he contributed in a significant manner to the success of the Army Air Corps and thus to the success of the Allied cause.

After the war Gus was stationed at Langley Field, Virginia. He made numerous flights in an aircraft he called "The Black Cat," doing public relations work. He also spent some time as a barnstormer, one of those intrepid young men said to have "more courage than common sense."

In July of 1919, less than a year after the Armistice, Leazar was successful in obtaining a civilian airplane pilot's license, his number being #809, which indicated that he was the 809th person in the United States to secure a civilian pilot's license.

It was in the same month that *The Landmark's* Mooresville correspondent gave readers an update on young Leazar's career:

"The people of his hometown," the correspondent wrote, "have watched with pleased interest the record of Lieut. 'Gus'

Leazar who has distinguished himself in the aerial service, and his numerous acquaintances in the town and county will be interested in the following taken from the Washington correspondent of *The Charlotte Observer,* of the 10th:

'Pilot Lieutenant Augustus Leazar, with Sergeant First Class Albert R. Reith, passenger, in a Curtiss JN4-H "Jenny," made a flight from Wilson, N.C., to Langley Field, 160 miles, in 1:20, at an altitude of 5,000 feet. Lieutenant Leazar, by his flight today, completed a decidedly valuable series of flights to the air service in the interest of recruiting and demonstrated the importance of aerial service.

'His flying was for a total distance of 2,450 miles at an average speed of 74 miles per hour. Stops were in 20 cities and none of them had ever been visited by an airplane. The tour covered sections of Virginia and North Carolina.'"

In 1921 Gus agreed to be the test pilot for Carr E. Booker's experimental airplane, "The Hummingbird."

"The Hummingbird" was a tiny biplane, 16-feet long with a 20-foot wingspan, and weighed only about 450 pounds. Its power plant was an 18-horsepower Harley-Davidson motor.

Booker, who was also a Tar Heel, was trying to develop an aircraft that would be to airplanes what the Ford Model-T was to automobiles: a simple vehicle that the average person could use and afford.

In its first flight Gus Leazar got the flimsy aircraft about 30 feet off the ground before trouble developed. "The Hummingbird" was repaired, modifications were made, and Leazar took it up again, this time getting to an altitude of 250 feet before the engine began spewing black smoke.

On April 23, 1921, he tried again, but again experienced erratic engine performance. He landed safely and three days later tried to put the diminutive aircraft through its paces one more time. Encountering trouble once again, he made a somersault while trying to land. Leazar knew when to stop and walked off the field and away from the aircraft while he still could.

In June, 1923, Gus married Frances Pennell Dunn, of Raleigh, who was nine years his junior. Gus was the one who gave his bride her first flying lessons. The Leazars had two children, a son and a daughter.

After leaving the military, Leazar qualified for a commercial pilot's license and was connected with the National Aeronautics Association of the United States, the official record-keepers of American aviation. Leazar carried a membership card signed by Orville Wright. Gus Leazar is remembered as the first man to ever make a night flight from the Raleigh Municipal Airport.

After holding the position of manager of Curtiss-Wright's base at the Raleigh airport since the 1920s, in November of 1930 he was sent to Atlanta to be the manager of the Curtiss-Wright base there. The *Raleigh News & Observer* complimented Gus on the job he had done in Raleigh:

"Mr. Leazar has made a record which has won repeated commendation from his superiors in the organization. At Atlanta he will take charge of a much larger organization, located in a large, lighted field, to and from which North-South and the new East-West passenger planes and the North-South and the Florida mail planes fly daily."

Later he as employed by the federal government as a civilian aviation supervisor; at the time of his retirement he was chief of the Southeastern Division, Civil Aeronautics Board.

When he retired the Leazars returned to Raleigh, and Gus became farmer. Acquiring acreage that had been in his wife's family, he began growing several things, including grapes, which he sold commercially to wineries. And so, Gus Leazar can be looked at as a pioneer in North Carolina's nascent wine industry.

Augustus Leazar, Jr. died on February 1, 1960, in Raleigh. He was 69. His body rests in Raleigh's Oakwood Cemetery beside that of his wife, Frances, who passed away in 1994.

Samuel Mascotts

There used to be a cemetery less than 50 yards north of the intersection of Broad and Center streets ("The Square") on the eastern side of Center, in downtown Statesville. The cemetery had only one grave and one grave marker and was curiously located in a grassy strip between the sidewalk and the street. If you had noticed the stone—actually it was a 2 x 3 foot slab of concrete—and had you read it, you would have read: "'SAMMY' KILLED BY AUTO 8-23-46."

This was the grave of a member of the Statesville Fire Department whose formal name, as found in the Statesville City Directory of 1944-1945, was "Samuel Mascotte," but was better known as just "Sammy," or sometimes as "Samuel Mascotts." Sammy, you see, was the beloved French terrier that was the department's mascot. Sammy had been killed by a hit and run driver while crossing The Square.

While a white and black-spotted Dalmatian is the breed of dog usually associated with firefighters, Sammy was of the lesser-known French terrier breed. Sammy's grave also marked the location of Statesville's first fire station. Today the site is occupied by a common-place parking lot.

According to the *Statesville Daily Record* of September 1, 1953, a fire station was erected on this site in 1875. The building, which also housed the city's police department, was situated some distance back from the street. Around 1912 the old station house was extensively remodeled and an addition erected closer to the street. This was about the same time that the city purchased its first gasoline-powered fire truck.

Prior to this, the trucks had been powered by hay-burning, two horse power—literally—affairs. One horse-drawn truck was retained until 1918, when the second motorized truck was purchased, bringing the era of horse-drawn fire engines to a close in the City of Progress.

The current Fire Station #1 on South Meeting Street was first occupied in April of 1953. The police department shared this building with the firefighters until their own building was completed in 1963.

In an informal history of the fire department compiled by J. D. Harris in 1983, we learn more about Sammy, the fire dog.

"The police department," wrote Harris, "received a call about a dog running cats. The police brought the dog back to the fire department. Dr. Lynch, a veterinarian, told the firemen that the dog was one year old and was a French terrier. Fire and police personnel fell in love with the dog.... Sammy's favorite food was hamburger and people would take him to Hefner's for meals."

In May of 1945 Sammy went missing for a period of ten days, but was reported to have been seen in Harmony. Then-Assistant Police Chief Rumple drove to Harmony and retrieved Sammy. The dog had been confined in a screened porch and was said to have lost weight and was said to have "suffered mental anguish" from his separation from the police and firemen. Whether Sammy had been kidnapped or had been taken in as a stray by the Harmony resident was not disclosed.

At the time this incident *The Landmark* stated that Sammy had then been a companion of the two departments for ten years.

"Sammy never rode a fire truck," remembered J. D. Harris, "but did ride in cars with W. L. Neely and other firemen. He was with the fire department for 13 years. He was killed by an automobile on August 23, 1946. P. S. West donated a hand-built casket for Sammy and the firemen dug up concrete at the old fire station on North Center Street to bury him.... [Sheriff] Charlie Rumple wrote Sammy's name in the concrete over his grave."

At the time of his death Sammy was described as being "old, blind, deaf and rheumatic," so his death, while tragic, may not have been entirely the unknown motorist's fault.

Sammy's obituary, printed on the front page of the old *Daily Record* on August 24th, tells more.

"Whoever hit Sammy," stated the article, "didn't stop to give him aid. He was trying to make it home to the fire house when killed, home to his friends, the firemen and police, who thought highly of, and cared well for Samuel Mascotts—that's how he is listed in the city directory."

Sammy, in spirit, steadfastly maintained vigil over the site of the old home of Statesville's Finest and Statesville's Bravest for more than half a century, until changes in the street, curbing and sidewalk during renovations to a nearby building and ensuing work on Statesville's streetscape project necessitated the removal of his marker. It was subsequently stored at Station #1 and then re-interred in "a revered spot" at Station #4 on Martin Lane in 2011. Sammy's actual remains are believed to still be in the original burial location, in a small casket four feet below the parking lot ramp.

Sammy is believed to have been the only canine ever put in the *Statesville City Directory*. His name can be found on page 235 of the 1944-45 *Directory*, with his occupation given as "city fireman" and his residence, 120 North Center.

Stories such as that of Sammy, the firehouse dog, are at best small footnotes in the history of Statesville, but it is such details that give the fabric of local history its texture and color.

MARY MAYO

Mary Mayo Riker was probably the most successful and best-known vocalist to ever call Iredell County home. She was born in Statesville on July 20, 1924. Under her professional name, "Mary Mayo," Riker had an interesting career. That she went into music surprised no one; she could hardly have done otherwise.

Mary's father was Franklin Wing Riker, a renowned tenor soloist and music educator. He had studied in Germany, Italy and France, and had performed in major churches in New York, Boston, Philadelphia and St. Louis. In addition he sang minor roles at the Metropolitan Opera in New York City and was also Dean of the Voice Department at Cornish Three Arts School in Seattle, Washington.

Mary's mother, the former Lois Long of the distinguished Long family of Statesville, was a daughter of Judge Benjamin Long and a sister of minister and artist Rev. MacKendree Long. Lois Long Riker was also a distinguished concert vocalist, a soprano, who had studied voice in New York City. She and her husband often appeared in concert together.

Mary Mayo Riker graduated from Statesville High School, then known as "D. Matt Thompson High," in the Class of 1940. I have my mother's 1940 high school annual, "The Trail," and there is Mary Mayo Riker's photo just below my mother's, whose maiden name was Nellie Steele Rhodes. The two must have stood together in line many times when their class was put into alphabetical order.

You would have expected to find Mary Mayo Riker's name under the Senior Superlative, "Most Talented," but that recognition went to another girl. She was, however, recognized by her classmates as "Most Courteous."

My mother was singled out by her classmates as "Biggest Flirt" in the yearbook, a dubious honor at best.

After D. Matt, Mary attended Mitchell Junior College—now Mitchell Community College—for a year, and then transferred to Peace College in Raleigh. She later graduated from the prestigious Julliard School in New York.

Mary had her own radio show on station WBT in Charlotte after World War II. Then she moved to New York where she sang at the Roxy Theater and eventually became the lead female vocalist with the Glenn Miller Orchestra when it was under the direction of Tex Beneke following Miller's death in 1945. If you don't know who Glenn Miller was, go ask you grandparents.

Mary was on Arthur Godfrey's Talent Scouts, a very popular program, and recorded a number of solo albums on the Capitol, Columbia and MGM labels. She was signed by Capitol Records first by the legendary songwriter, Johnny Mercer, and it is Mary's voice you hear "doubling the strings," on the Johnny Mathis hit, "Chances Are." She also made appearances on Jackie Gleason's and Perry Como's TV shows. Frank Sinatra, "Old Blue Eyes," chose Mary as the female vocalist on his first TV show.

Mary married Al Ham, the bass player and one of the arrangers for the Miller Band. Al Ham was also produced early hits of Johnny Mathis and Tony Bennett and a number of original Broadway cast albums. When they would go out with friends Mary and Al were sometimes introduced as "Ham with Mayo," which never failed to get a chuckle.

There was nothing funny about Mary's voice, however. She had a career that spanned more than four decades and a phenomenal vocal range that spanned more than four octaves.

In 1963 she cut a long-play album with keyboard artist Dick Hyman titled "Moon Gas," which is a top-shelf collector's item and will run you a cool $100 today on eBay if you can find a copy.

The high point of Mary's career may have been when she sang for President Nixon in 1969 at the White House in the jazz concert honoring Duke Ellington's 70th birthday. Her fellow musicians were a list of "who's who" in the music of the time: Milt Hinton, Hank Jones, Louis Bellson, Dave Brubeck, Clark Terry and Gerry Mulligan. Our own Mary Mayo was the only female performer.

Not bad for a local girl.

If you were around in December of 1971, then you have probably heard Mary Mayo's voice. She and her daughter, Lorri, were vocalists in a group known as the "Hillside Singers," who sang in one of Coca-Cola's best-remembered TV commercials. The song they sang was partly composed by Al Ham.

You probably remember it, a catchy little tune called, "I'd Like to Buy the World a Coke," later re-recorded as "I'd Like to Teach the World to Sing." This group went on to record two long-play albums.

If you listen closely, you can hear an ethereal, clear soprano voice floating above the rest. I like to think that's Statesville's Mary Mayo's angelic voice.

Mary passed away in New York City in December of 1985 at the age of 61. At her memorial service in St. Peter's Church, George Shearing played her version of "Dancing in the Dark" on Billy Strayhorn's piano, and Margaret Whiting sang, "Spring Will Be a Little Late This Year."

Carrying on the family tradition, Mary's daughter, under her professional name, Lorri Hafer, is a professional vocalist, singing big band and jazz numbers, often aboard cruise ships. I know, tough, dirty work, but someone's got to do it.

Lorri is often accompanied by her pianist husband, Mike, and by their son, Paul, who plays string bass and drums. Lorri and Mike performed in Mitchell Community College's Shearer

Hall on August 7, 2011, on the very same stage her grandparents and her mother had performed. It was this writer's distinct honor to introduce Lorri and Mike to the audience.

The musical tradition of this gifted family continues.

JOHN MCCONNELL

Many of Iredell's early colonial settlers came from either Germany or Northern Ireland. One in the latter group was John McConnell, who was born in Ireland in 1721 and came to America in 1740, when he was nineteen years old. John followed what was called the "Great Wagon Road" from Pennsylvania to the South in the late 1740s and settled in the Davidson's Creek area of what would eventually become the southwestern corner of Iredell County.

John purchased a grant of 587 acres from an agent of Lord Granville in 1752. At the time of the purchase, this tract was a part of Anson County, which was then much larger than to-day's Anson County. Anson was named for George, Lord Anson, a British admiral who had guarded the Carolina coast from pirates. Anson County had been a part of Bladen County until 1750. Anson, in turn, was divided up into smaller chunks in 1753 and the area where Mr. McConnell lived became Rowan County, named for Matthew Rowan, who had been acting governor when the county was formed.

In 1788, Rowan County itself was further divided and Mr. McConnell found himself living in the county of Iredell. Thus in less than 40 years John McConnell had lived in four different counties without ever having moved!

John and his wife Mary had nine children, which was not an unusually large family for the time: seven daughters and two sons. This area of North Carolina is still home to their many descendants.

John McConnell passed away on December 30, 1801, in his eightieth year, about six months after having made out his will. As genealogists well know, wills are very useful documents: they usually list names of children and their spouses and they often include an inventory of possessions, which give clues to the details of life long ago.

McConnell's will is here given, just as it was originally spelled and punctuated. Careful reading will reveal that the unknown scribe spelled John's surname three different ways: McConald, McConnel and McConnell. This was most likely deliberately done to demonstrate the scribe's spelling prowess.

* * *

In the name of God Amen this 12th day of may in the year of our Lord Eighteen hundred & one I John McConald Sr. of the County of Iredell in the state of North Carolina being old & stricken in years & not in a good state of health but of perfect sound mind & memory & calling to mind my mortality & that it is appointed for all once to die Do make this my Last will and Testament in the following manner & form first of recommending my soul to God who gave it my body to the Earth to be buried in Christian burial without pompt hopeing through the merits Death and portion of my Lord & Savior Jesus Christ to receive a full and free pardon of all my sins & to inherit everlasting Life & as touching such worldly estate as God hath blessed me with in this life I give and bequeath in the following manner and form.

(Viz) It is my will & I order that all my just Debts be paid & satisfied by my executors hereafter named incluesing my funeral Expenses

Item I give and bequeath to my loving wife the plantation on which I now live my dwelling house with all the furniture therein her chois of two negroes, & one horse, of her own chuseing four cows, six head of sheep, saddle and bridle, Six head of hogs at her chois all to be at her own disposal the house and land Excepted but to be peacibly possessed by her During her lifetime & at her death sd house & land be deeded to my son Benjamin both old and new tracts to them their heirs and assigns forever.

Item I give and bequeath to Jas. Davidson my daughter mary husband five shillings stearling money to be levied out of my estate to him and his heirs forever.

Item I give an bequeath to my grand sons William Andreas McRee & John Lata McConnel, David McRees son and Benjamin McConnells son five hundred acres of land in the Cumbarland to be eaqually devided between them & if either of sd boys should die before mature age of 21 their part to be at their fathers Disposal to them their heirs and assigns forever.

Item, I give and bequeath to my Loving sons John and Benjamin at my wifes decease all my books to be equally divided between them & their heirs forever.

Item, it is my will & I order that the remaining part of my estate heretofore not mentioned be put to sale Excepting my wearing apparel which I leave to my two sons equal & the sd money ariseing from the said sale to be equally divided between my Wife, Wm. Andrew McRee, my daughter Margaret, my son John, my daughter Rebkah, my daughter Ann, my daughter Sarah & my daughter Jeane & my son Benjamin to them forever.

Item, I name, nominate, constitute, & appoint my loving friend Moses Winslow & my son Benjamin, Executors of this my Last Will & Testament hereby revoking all other wills heretofore by me made by word or writing ratifying & confirming this and no other to be my last Will & Testement.

Signed, sealed & Pronounced by the said John McConald as his last will & Testement in the presence of us.

Wm. Graham, James Conner, Jas. Price, Senr.

* * *

Much of the McConnell tract is now under the waters of Lake Norman. When the lake was being formed in the late 1950s, the headstones—there would have been nothing left of the bodies due to our acidic red clay—were moved from the Bakers Graveyard and reinterred in a corner of the church-yard at Centre Presbyterian Church in Mount Mourne. John McConnell's headstone can be seen there today on the back row, but is very difficult to read.

THOMAS JEFFERSON McKINLEY

Several years ago I was looking through the microfilmed issues of the old *Landmark* newspaper and came across the following story in the January 1, 1896, issue titled, "Said He Was Born in Statesville," which I have paraphrased here below. I tried to get some follow-up information at that time, but was unsuccessful, so I printed out a photocopy of the article, filed it, and moved on to other things. Recently I came across the article again in my files and decided to try to find out more about Mr. McKinley once again. I'm glad I did.

* * *

Thomas Jefferson "Old Jeff" McKinley died in Great Barrington, Mass., on December 21, 1896. That much is certain. It is also fairly certain that he was at least 100 years old, and may have been as old as 112, making him at the time of his death perhaps the oldest man in New England.

He claimed to have been born in 1785, the slave of Mrs. Ann Hart, the owner of Hart's Tavern in Statesville. After being the property of Mrs. Hart for an unspecified number of years, he became the property of one of Mrs. Hart's sons, John, with whom he lived for three years. He next was owned by a Mr. Branard of Cabarrus County, referred to in *The Landmark* as being a "Quartermaster General." It was while he was with Mr. Branard that McKinley, at risk of his own life, rescued his owner's daughter from being killed by a bull. He was apparently rewarded with $100 in cash for his bravery.

He was next associated with the sheriff of Cabarrus County for seven years and assisted the sheriff in maintaining the county jail in Concord.

The next chapter in his life was perhaps the worst; he was with a slave speculator named "Hughsky" (Hugh Sky?) and was made the overseer of a group of 75 slaves that were being taken to New Orleans to be sold. When the group arrived in the Crescent City, to McKinley's surprise, he was sold along with the group he had escorted.

He next became the property of a Mr. Walker who was a member of the Louisiana state legislature and who was later elected governor of Louisiana. McKinley is said to have been the property of Mr. Walker for over 30 years. While with Governor Walker he married and the couple had two children. At an unspecified time during the Civil War McKinley ran away from his owner and became attached to the Union Army's 49th Massachusetts Infantry Regiment then at Port Hudson, La. He stayed with this regiment as it went to Vicksburg and Danielsonville (Donaldsonville?).

McKinley was with the veterans of the 49th Massachusetts when they returned to Berkshire County, Mass., in August of 1863. By dint of hard work he became a market gardener in the town of Great Barrington, made a good living and married a Great Barrington woman. At the time of his death in 1896—according to the article in *The Landmark*—he was a member of the local Baptist church, and despite being illiterate, owned "two unincumbered [sic] houses and lots on Church street and about $600 in cash."

* * *

Although I had no doubts as to the authenticity of the story, I wondered how much of his biography could be independently verified. There were a fair number of details mentioned in the 1896 *Landmark* article which could be checked. And after all, why would McKinley have told people in Massachusetts that he had been born in Statesville, N.C., if that had not been true?

First of all, the surname "Hart" was found in Iredell in the first U.S. Census, 1790. There were two men named Hart who were heads of Iredell households in 1790, James and Mathew. James was a militia captain and had two slaves in 1790 and six slaves in 1800. Mathew Hart owned one slave in 1790. The names of the slaves were not given in the Census. Iredell historian Homer Keever, on page 156 of his *Iredell: Piedmont County*, mentions Hart's tavern in Statesville.

In *The Heritage of Iredell County, Volume II* (2000), there is an article on the descendants of Samuel Hart by the late Charlotte Kay Hart. Ms. Hart first tells of Samuel Hart, born in Maryland and settling in what is now Iredell County sometime during the American Revolution. Samuel had a son named John. Samuel is known to have married twice; his first wife was Elizabeth Hall and his second wife's name is unknown; her name could have been "Ann." Samuel is buried in Fourth Creek Burying Ground in Statesville across from the First Presbyterian Church. So there was a Hart's tavern in Statesville and some of the Harts were slave owners.

Next I tried to find Quartermaster General Branard of Cabarrus County, but without success.

Before the Civil War it was common for slaves from this area to be taken and sold in the Deep South, so this part of this story has the ring of truth. I found that there was a Mr. Joseph Marshall Walker who was the 13th governor of Louisiana, serving as that state's chief executive from January 28, 1850, to January 18, 1853. Previously Mr. Walker had been elected to the House of Representatives of Louisiana in 1820 and was reelected in 1822, 1832 and 1836. Governor Walker died in 1856.

Now as to Mr. McKinley's claim to have been in the Union Army. The 49th Massachusetts Volunteer Infantry Regiment mustered in September 18 through October 28, 1862, at Camp Briggs, Pittsfield, Mass., for an enlistment of nine months in response to Lincoln's call for troops on August 4, 1862. After arrival in New Orleans in early 1863, the 49th was transferred to Baton Rouge and became part of the Union Army's 1st Brigade, 1st Division, 19th Corps, the Army of the Gulf, and apparently came under fire near Port Hudson, La., on March 14, 1863. At that time the town of Port Hudson was one of the final two Confederate strongholds on the Mississippi River.

On May 24th the 49th Massachusetts, with other units, made an assault on Port Hudson and lost 16 officers and men killed and 64 wounded. Port Hudson eventually surrendered to Union forces on July 9. So the 49th Massachusetts was in the Port Hudson area when McKinley said he joined up with them.

The regiment next was sent to Donaldsonville. Later that summer with their 9-month enlistments being up, the regiment embarked on a steamer in New Orleans and went up the Mississippi to Cairo, Illinois, and from there were transported by train back to Massachusetts, arriving there in August. The unit was mustered out of federal service on September 1, 1863. Mr. McKinley says he went with them.

Mr. McKinley's life story's timeline matched the history of the 49th Massachusetts. I was unable to find if McKinley was formally sworn into the Union Army, but fugitive slaves—often referred to as "contraband"—frequently served Union troops as cooks, butchers, teamsters, etc., but McKinley apparently was a musician, a flute or fife player, and his instrument has been preserved in the Great Barrington town archives. Remember that at this time Mr. McKinley was around 80 years old.

Next I consulted the Mason Library in Great Barrington and was given the name of a local historian and genealogist, Mr. Gary Leveille.

Mr. Leveille found a drawing and brief biography of "Old Jeff" McKinley (with his surname spelled "McKenley") with the following information: He was a door-to-door produce peddler who was born in Statesville, N.C., sometime prior to 1789. "He was sold and taken down river as part of a slave gang and sold to a man named Walker." In addition, McKinley "fell in with a south Berkshire company of the 49th Massachusetts Infantry at Port Hudson." He settled in Berkshire County, Mass., after the Civil War and at one time was a member of the Hope Fire Company.

"He had a good name, lived long and was upright and honest," stated the *Berkshire Courier* newspaper in McKinley's obituary of December 21, 1896. "There was a good heart packed away in that old black skin and there was also a patriotic loyalty about him that is shamefully lacking in many a white man. There is a lesson, too, which may be learned from his life, if one will but couple the fact of his remarkable longevity with what seems to have been the motto of his life, 'It is better to wear out than it is to rust.'"

Based on what I was able to find, I believe this is a true account of an Iredell County African-American who was part of the Union Army during the Civil War. Although born into slavery, he seems to have done all right by himself.

"Old Jeff" was also mentioned in a book, *The Companionship of Books and Other Papers*, by Frederic Rowland Martin, published in 1905. In his book Martin says, "'Old Jeff' was only a 'darky,' and his external life was bare of all adornment, yet I believe he was wiser and more of a gentleman than are many well-dressed sons of luxury to whom, because they have a little social and political power, men bow down. He once expressed after the following fashion his idea of what it is to be a gentleman: 'From the way a man treats me I can always tell whether he is in reality a gentleman or only a common man dressed in a gentleman's clothes. A man may lift his hat to a lady in passing her upon the street, and yet be at heart a most contemptible creature; but if he can lift his hat as cordially and speak as politely to me, a poor old colored man, as to a fine lady or a millionaire, then I am sure he is, in whatever else he may be wanting, a true gentleman.'"

If that was the complete story, it would be enough, but there is a bit more to it. As Paul Harvey used to say, "...And now for the rest of the story."

It seems that one of the lots on Church Street with a house on it that Old Jeff McKinley owned in Great Barrington was the very house in which a noted civil rights pioneer and writer was born in February, 1868. His name was William Edward Burghardt "W. E. B." Du Bois, an author, editor, historian and sociologist. A Harvard graduate—bachelor's degree cum laude in history, 1890—Du Bois is believed to have been the first African-American to earn a doctorate degree, also from Harvard, in 1895.

In 1910, Dr. Du Bois was one of the co-founders of the National Association for the Advancement of Colored People (NAACP). Although the cabin owned by "Old Jeff" McKinley was later torn down, the site of the house where W. E. B. Du Bois grew up in Great Barrington, Mass., was designated a historic landmark by the town in 1994.

PHIL MCLAUGHLIN

There's not much to tell about Phillip McLaughlin that would make you suspect he was once a movie star, but he was. He was also known as a hero: "Mooresville's Hero." But that was back in the summer of 1935, and to use an over-worked cliché, a lot of water has passed under the bridge since then.

I spoke with Phil at his home on Pine Street in Mooresville in August of 1992 about those summer days almost 60 years gone and the silent movie, "Mooresville's Hero," in which he starred.

You have to remember that 1935 was the sixth year of the Great Depression. Money was scarce, many people were unemployed, times were hard, and movies helped take peoples' minds off their worries.

"At one time we had three theaters running in Mooresville," said Phil. "People in those years, when they didn't have anything else to do, they could go to a ball game or go to a theater. You couldn't travel."

The town's newspaper, the *Mooresville Enterprise*, and one of the theaters, the Carolina, sponsored a three-man Hollywood film crew to come to Mooresville to produce a two-reel silent farce-comedy film entitled, "Mooresville's Hero." The crew was under the direction of one Colonel Don O. Newland, who was credited as being one of Max Sennett's leading directors. The studio company called itself "Consolidated Film Producers."

Phil, or "Dynamite McLaughlin" as he was known then, was the quarterback of the Mooresville High School Blue Devil football team. He was recruited for the leading part; many people in the community auditioned for the other parts. Starring, along with Phil, were: Hugh L. Sloop, Homer Brantley, Mary Neel, Sarah Louise Benfield, and Mrs. Mildred Hartness Thompson.

Phil was, of course, was cast in the major male character role, "Billy Brown," our hero. Homer Brantley acted as Phil's rival, a cub reporter, and Mr. Sloop rounded out the male characters as "Mr. Henpeck," the downtrodden husband.

Miss Benfield had the leading female part as "Baby Ethel." Mrs. Thompson provided comic relief in the part of "Katrinka," a country flapper and comedienne; "Mrs. Henpeck," the domineering wife, was originally to have featured Mrs. F. V. Fields, but sickness in her real-life family caused her to relinquish the part which would now be played by Miss Neel.

Messrs. John Lyttle, J. E. Dickinson, and Mooresville Police Chief Earl Rimmer had minor roles in the production.

Said Phil, "They interviewed and picked the people. They had more than what they used. At that time I was still in high school, playing ball. We went through a kind of rehearsal until they agreed that everything was all right."

The professional film crew used what were then state-of-the-art special effects. "The biggest feature [stunt] they had," according to Phil, "was a car wreck, right on the square at Moore and Main. It was on a Saturday afternoon and they had the town filled up with people for that. It was like there was a parade or picnic going on, there were so many people in town. That was the big thing. They took two nice automobiles, about the same models as they were gonna show in the wreck, and they pulled 'em up, nose to nose, one coming up Moore Avenue, and one on Main Street, and then they backed those cars back, filming all the time, to reverse it. Then they took the new cars out, parked 'em, brought two wrecked cars in—and I mean they wrecked 'em—in other words, it looked just like a complete wreck. They put 'em nose to nose and they shot that. Of course they had some black powder and a fuse lit to make it look just like a big impact when the powder goes off.

"Anyway, after they reversed the film, it showed them cars coming' right together, and that thing flashes and all. They put the people in it and fixed it up just like it was a wreck."

As to the plot...well, there wasn't much of one to speak of.

Phil continues, "There was a young girl, and of course two young men are after her, trying to date her and all: me and Homer Brantley. Mr. Hugh Sloop played the father of the girl; it was supposed to be in his home that all of this was taking place. He'd have a cigar in his mouth—one of those exploding cigars—and he'd get after everybody, running 'em off from his daughter. 'Izzy' Fields, as best as I can remember, she must have been the mother. Anyway, she was in the chase."

The location shots were advertised in *The Enterprise* and many people came to town to see the movie being filmed, and, of course, these same folks would very likely pay to see the finished product.

"In the theater they had it all set up," remembers Phil. "Hugh Sloop provided the furniture and made a living room on the stage of the old [Carolina] theater, and that's where all of the inside shots were taken."

Footage of the theater audience during the filming of the interior scenes was also incorporated into the finished production, thereby ensuring even more of a turnout.

"Part of this, the shooting of it, took place over at Con Johnson's home on Academy Street; the rest of it was shot around town. Also part of it was filmed in Liberty Park, down what we called 'Slicky Rock' in those days, in that open gully near where the War Memorial building is now."

Phil was not paid for his cinematic efforts. He laughs about it now. "No, there wasn't any pay back in the Depression years. It was all publicity for Mooresville and *The Enterprise*, and, of course, for the theater. It was something, back in those days."

Being the leading male character, you would think that Phil would have ended up with the girl, but such was not the case. He did, however, get to kiss her.

"Mooresville's Hero" had its world premiere on Thursday, May 30th, 1935. Were there spotlights reflecting off the Carolina Theater's marquee? Were there a chauffeured limousines to bring the stars to the grand opening?

"Heck no. Are you kidding?" replies Phil.

There had been a private screening on the previous night, attended by Mooresville Mayor Ben Houston, the cast, and a select group of other leading citizens.

As would be expected, Phil caught a lot of good-natured grief from his high school chums, and put up with a lot of ribbing for the next few years.

Phil elected not to pursue a screen career. He was more interested in performing on the gridiron than on the silver screen.

"Only thing after that, why, I was still playing ball. So I forgot all about the movies."

He graduated from Mooresville High School in 1938 and got a job at Cascade Mill where he worked for thirty-three years, about twenty of those years as the head of the preparation department. Following his retirement from what was by then Burlington Industries, he worked eleven years as the training officer for the Mooresville Fire Department.

While working at the mill he married Rachael Smith. They have a son and two grandsons, all of whom love sports, particularly football.

As to what ultimately became of the film, "Mooresville's Hero," that is a mystery.

"It was shown at the theater a number of times during the 'Thirties, but what happened to the film, I can't tell you, says Phil. "It seemed like, vaguely, I can remember that there was a copy stored in one of those theaters, but they said that it had deteriorated. That was during the War, but I can't be sure about that."

Of the original cast, only Phil and Sarah Louise Benfield, now Mrs. Richard Wright of Charlotte, are still players in the drama of life; the others have made their exits from the stage.

Wouldn't it be nice to find a copy of the movie and pay a visit to the Mooresville of 1935? President Roosevelt and fedoras, Civilian Conservation Corps boys and the blue National Recovery Act eagle, A-Model Fords and lemonade on the front porch, and a young man, grinning bashfully in his role as hero.

Our hero; Mooresville's hero.

* * *

Carl Philip McLaughlin, 95, passed away on August 18, 2011, at Brian Center in Mooresville. Besides being a supervisor at Cascade Mills for 30 years, he had been a Sunday school superintendent, an assistant athletic director of the local American Legion's baseball team and had coached football at his alma mater, Mooresville High School. He was inducted into the first class of Mooresville High's Athletic Hall of Fame.

REV. DR. ALEXANDER MEANS

This column concerns a man who excelled in several fields, though he was little known locally as many of his accomplishments were not made in North Carolina. He was a true Renaissance man.

* * *

Alexander Means (1801-1883) born in Statesville on February 6, 1801. His father was an immigrant from Tyrone County in Ulster, Northern Ireland, and his mother was a Pennsylvanian. Alexander was the couple's only child. His earliest education in reading writing and arithmetic came from his mother, though he did receive some instruction at local "old field schools" and may have been a pupil at the Ebenezer Academy, which still stands north of Statesville on Highway 21 beside Bethany Presbyterian Church.

His family lacked the resources to further his education, but young Alexander so impressed some of his local teachers that they offered to help pay for his further education. These offers, though generous, were refused by his parents and Alexander began work as a school teacher about age 17.

COUNTRY DOCTOR

After teaching a while he took a job as a store clerk and then left North Carolina for the boonies of Georgia. Under a Dr. Randolf and a Dr. Walker he received on-the-job training in medicine and became a practicing physician. He later did some academic study in medicine at Transylvania College's School of Medicine in Lexington, Kentucky, in 1825. Then it was back to Georgia where he entered into a medical partnership in Covington, Ga., with Dr. Henry Gaither.

It was about this time—late 1820s or early 1830s—that he bought a small homestead in Covington, Newton County, Georgia, and began work on a Greek Revival-style house which still stands today. Means called his home "Orna Villa," which means "Bird House." Means' portrait still hangs over the mantle in the main dining room of Orna Villa.

MINISTER

Dr. Means became a Methodist Episcopal minister in 1828. His contemporaries have described him as a "preacher of rare eloquence." Many of his sermons, speeches, reviews and scientific discussions were widely circulated and it is said that he received invitations to speak from the president of Connecticut University as well as from President Zachary Taylor.

SCIENTIST

Means became fascinated with the discoveries in the field of electricity in the 1840s. In 1851, he traveled to England where he met and became friends with two of Britain's leading scientists, Sir Michael Faraday and Sir Charles Lyell. Inspired by their work with electricity, Means began his own experiments. On June 2, 1857, Means exhibited the first incandescent light in America at Atlanta's Old City Hall. Means built a machine that produced frictional electricity causing current to pass through wires that were attached to a chunk of black carbon, which caused the material to ignite. One eyewitness account stated that "Never ... have I seen a more brilliant light. Nothing in all the phenomena of our wonderful age has ever impressed me more than this exhibition and I can never forget it as long as my memory lasts."

In recognition of his work, Means was received by the elite Royal Academy of Science in London and was also a corresponding member of the American Scientific Association. Most of his experiments were conducted in a second-floor room at Orna Villa. He also did work on a practical electric motor and a device that was the forerunner of the phonograph.

CIVIL WAR

While originally against secession, Alexander Means became caught up in the events leading up to the Civil War. In 1861, he became a member of the Georgia Secession Convention and spoke passionately against secession. When the first test vote was taken, Dr. Means and 129 other delegates voted against leaving the Union, while 165 delegates voted for it. Another test vote was taken yielding nearly the same result. As it became clear that the secessionists would carry the day, Means cast his vote with the secessionist majority when the official vote was taken because he felt it was important to "present as solid a front as possible to our enemies by swelling the majority vote."

His diary entries reveal that Dr. Means then was devoted to the Confederacy. He delivered an impassioned speech at the Covington Courthouse on January 21, 1862, calling for volunteers for the Confederate Army. One observer reported that on hearing his words, "Old men wept and young men shouted and shed tears...and volunteers came forward." At the age of 60 he was too old to serve in the Army himself, but he became Inspector of Munitions for the Confederate Army.

COLLEGE PROFESSOR

The Methodist Episcopal Georgia Conference formed a "manual labor school" (a type of vocational program) in 1834 and named Dr. Means its first rector. He was instrumental in the founding of Emory University in Oxford. When Emory University opened in 1836, he was chosen as the first chair of its physics department. He later served as president of the university in 1854 and 1855. He held simultaneous professorships at Emory University, Augusta Medical College, and Atlanta Medical School where he taught physics and chemistry. During the 1859-60 term, he delivered a twenty-six part lecture series on "A Nebular Theory of Planetary Formation."

A LIFE WELL-LIVED

As one source has stated, "Alexander Means was a man of exceptional diversity even in an age when men of many talents seem to have flourished. He was a school teacher, college professor, a pioneer of scientific education, a doctor, scientist, statesman, college president, and poet." The life of Alexander Means intersected with some very well-known figures in history. He once entertained President Millard Fillmore at Orna Villa, was received by Queen Victoria and the Prince of Wales in London. He was a house guest of Michael Faraday and Charles Lyell and he delivered the funeral oration for President Zachary Taylor in 1850.

The Rev. Dr. Means died in 1883 and is buried in the cemetery at Oxford College, Ga. Orna Villa, his elegant home in Oxford, Ga., is believed to be haunted by his ghost, while others contend it is his son Tobe's spirit that is responsible for the strange creakings and groanings that are sometimes heard.

J. P. MILLS

John Pinkney Mills was born in 1851 on a self-described "poor farm eight miles above Statesville," and was one of fourteen children of Noble Neill Mills and Amanda Melissa McLelland Mills. He moved to south Iredell around 1872, when he was sent by Mr. Pink Carlton of Statesville to run a branch of Carlton's dry goods store in Mooresville.

This was a year before the town was chartered, and in Mills' own words, "The town had four dwelling houses in it then, and rail fences bordered the railroad track."

Mills' first wife was Miss Clementine Harris, a pretty blonde school teacher who was the daughter of Isaac Harris, the town's first elected mayor, and then after Clementine's death, he married Nannie Lathan. By the first Mrs. Mills he fathered four children; by the second Mrs. Mills he had twelve.

In 1933, seven years before his death, Mills penned a short autobiography, about a third of which follows, that has been handed down through the family. At the time Mills wrote it, he was a prosperous, respected citizen of Mooresville, a town he had helped to get on its feet.

The autobiography, photos and information on J. P. Mills was shared with me by his grandson, Mr. Bob Mills, of Statesville, in 2005.

"You want to know what positions I have held in the history of the town? There wasn't anything going on that I was not into, right on up to the Cascade Mills, the pants factory and the shirt factory! I was deacon in the old Presbyterian Church, where the Baptist [church] now is, and was elected chairman of the board of deacons, and secretary and treasurer in time to collect and disburse every dollar that went into construction of the first part of the present church.

"I was a county school committeeman before we organized a graded school in Mooresville and was one of the citizens who invited Dr. Graham to come from Charlotte and speak to a mass meeting on the advantages of a graded school. The result of his visit was the beginning of the present school system, which was one of the very early graded schools in the small towns of North Carolina.

"Mr. Will Johnston held the position of chairman of the board until he resigned to become a county commissioner, when I succeeded him in office. All the present buildings were erected while I was serving on the board.

"But before that, I served on the town board and suffered, along with all the rest of the members, the penalty of non re-election for opening a street to what is now Eastern Heights [old Lowrance Hospital area]. That is Center Avenue. But people said that we were opening a street to nothing but a 'rabbit field' and wasting money to bridge a 'hollow.'

"Then there was the question of good roads. I was chairman of a local committee to send a petition to the legislature to authorize the building of sand clay roads in Coddle Creek, Barringer and Davidson townships. After much opposition on the ground of certain failure, I succeeded in getting the question submitted to the county. My brother was chairman

of the county board and I just wrote to him to bring his end of the board and come down here.

"They did come and met with the local committee, and we got Mr. [Zeb] Turlington to draft the petition and later to see it through the legislature. A county convention was called at Statesville, and by unanimous vote a bond issue of $400,000 was launched for good roads in Iredell. Sand clay was the beginning, but as the need for more lasting construction became evident, a macadam road, one of the first in the piedmont, was built from here [Mooresville] to the Catawba River [NC150, the River Road].

"When the bank was organized, in response to the needs of merchants who were forced to the inconvenience of doing their banking in Charlotte, J. E. Sherrill was the first president and C. P. McNeely was called...to take the position of cashier....

"By the way, one of the first acts of the town board at that time was to prohibit saloons within two miles of the corporation [city limits], a drastic step in those pre-prohibition days. I was a bank director in the loan and trust and the building and loan, also the telephone company.

"The first telephone system here was a private one, installed and owned by Sam Brawley. Dr. McLelland and I were the committee who bought him out, representing the predecessors of the present Mooresville Telephone Company.

"Lights, too. Mr. Donald and I were the committee from town to buy and install the first municipal light plant. We bought the Vanderbilt plant and shipped it here from Baltimore.

"I was the first man to suggest the Mooresville Cotton Mills...Mr. [Augustus] Leazar drew up the papers, and sure enough, it appealed to the citizens and $35,000 was promised, which built Mill #1. The equipment necessitated a debt, but that was paid off and the mill expanded twice before the rest of the present big plant was undertaken.

"In 82 years, a man can see many changes in the same locality."

* * *

We should sometimes think about the contributions of the founding fathers and mothers of the communities in Iredell County.

QUINCY SHARPE MILLS

Sixty-four service men from Iredell County are known to have died during what was once hopefully called, "The War to End All Wars," better remembered today as World War I. One of those killed was Quincy Sharpe Mills. Born in Statesville in 1884, Quincy was the only child of Thomas M. and Nannie R. Sharpe Mills.

Quincy was a graduate of the University of North Carolina, Class of 1906. While an undergraduate at Carolina, Mills was an editor of three student publications and was a correspondent for both the *Charlotte Observer* and for the *Richmond Times-Dispatch*. He was also initiated into Phi Beta Kappa. Had there been a school of journalism at Carolina, he would have been enrolled in it. For ten years—1907 to 1917—Mills worked for the *New York Evening Sun* as a reporter, his beat being city hall. He also wrote editorials.

After America declared war, Mills volunteered for the U.S. Army and as a second lieutenant went to France with Company "G," 168th Infantry Regiment, 42nd Infantry Division, known as the "Rainbow Division."

One of Lt. Mills' letters to his mother can be found in Norfolk, Va., at the Armed Forces Memorial on a sheet of bronze-clad aluminum. Twenty letters similar to his are scattered around the Memorial as if blown by the wind. The letters span America's wars, from the American Revolution through 1991's Operation Desert Storm, and those in charge of the Memorial are currently in the process of adding letters from our troops in Iraq and Afghanistan. The memorial, located along Town Point Park, part of Norfolk's waterfront, was dedicated on July 4, 1998.

The letter was written to his mother in Statesville on June 18, 1918, five weeks before his death. It reads:

"Dear Mother:

Even the trenches can be beautiful when they are trimmed with flowers, and the barbed wire forms a trellis for rambling vines and shelter for innumerable thrushes and other songsters-one explanation, no doubt, of why the cats have a penchant for No-Man's-Land. The birds warble all the time, even when there is considerable activity, and it seems to me that their voices never sounded so sweet before. A number of them inhabit six small trees, two birch trees and four wild cherry, which rise on the central island (entirely surrounded by trenches) of my strong point, or *groupe de combat* as the French call it. At the base of one of the birches is a flourishing wild rose bush, literally covered with blossoms, some of which I sneaked up and picked—keeping not only head but also the rest of me carefully DOWN during the process....Here are some of them for you, and also some daisies and yellow asters from the edge of one of my trenches."

Lt. Mills, then 34 years old, was killed in action at Chateau-Thierry, France, by a German artillery shell on July 26, 1918, less than four months before the Armistice. His remains are interred in the American Cemetery at Seringes-et-Nesles, Aisne, France.

The Armistice—a cease fire—went into effect at 11 a.m. on the 11th day of the 11th month, 1918, and was originally called "Armistice Day." On June 1, 1954, President Dwight D. Eisenhower signed legislation which changed the name to "Veterans Day."

It was reported that in several places that when the Armistice took effect, men from both sides came out of their trenches into what a few minutes before had been known as "No-Man's-Land" and shook hands and embraced, deliriously happy that they had survived the First World War.

A number of Mills' writings were collected by James Luby as *One Who Gave his Life: War Letters of Quincy Sharpe Mills...* (New

York: G. P. Putnam's Sons, 1923). Mr. Luby was the senior editor of the *New York Evening Sun.* There is a copy of the book in the Iredell County Public Library and the book has also been re-printed in paperback and is available through eBay and Amazon. com. A second book of his writings was published in 1930, also by Putnam's, and is titled, *Editorials, Sketches and Stories.* This book seems to be out of print, but was digitized by the University of California in 2010 and is available online.

In the book, *North Carolina: A Guide to the Old North State,* by the Federal Writers' Project, it is pointed out that Statesville was the hometown of Lt. Mills.

Lt. Mills' papers, some 750 items taking up two and a half linear feet of shelf space, can be found in the Southern Historical Collection in the Wilson Library at the University of North Carolina, Chapel Hill. They were donated by his mother in 1941.

Mills' name can be found on Iredell County's World War I Memorial Marker on the lawn of the Iredell County Hall of Justice in Statesville.

The $5,000 undergraduate Quincy Sharpe Mills Scholarships at the University of North Carolina at Chapel Hill were endowed in 1956 by the late Mrs. Nannie Sharpe Mills in memory of her son. Preference is given to minority and disad-vantaged journalism students.

HOMER MYERS, JR.

There is a scene in the 1975 Steven Spielberg movie, *Jaws,* in which grizzled shark hunter Quint (Robert Shaw) is telling Sheriff Brody (Roy Shieder) and Hooper (Richard Dreyfus) the story of the *USS Indianapolis.* His tongue loosened by liquor, Quint reveals that he was one of the crew of the *Indianapolis,* a World War II heavy cruiser, and tells how they endured four days in the water, being attacked by sharks and going mad from thirst under the relentless, hammering tropical sun. Peter Benchley's novel upon which the movie was based was fiction, but the words put into the mouth of actor Robert Shaw were close to the truth.

In the summer of 1945 the Pacific was anything but peaceful. Although Nazi Germany had surrendered, the war with Japan was not over and Japanese resistance, instead of crumbling, became more fierce as allied forces neared the Home Islands.

The heavy cruiser *USS Indianapolis* (CA-35) was under top secret orders to deliver components of the first atomic bomb, code-named "Little Boy," to the U.S. airbase on the island of Tinian. From Tinian the assembled bomb would be carried in the belly of a specially-modified B-29 Superfortress bomber, "Enola Gay," and would be dropped on the Japanese city of Hiroshima on August 6.

So secret was the whole project that the Navy did not even put the *Indianapolis'* name, mission or expected return date on the big board in the Navy's CINCPAC (Commander-in-Chief, Pacific) headquarters.

And so, after it was torpedoed by a Japanese submarine on July 30, 1945, it would be four days and nights before the "Indy" was reported overdue.

The ship was crewed by almost 1,200 officers and men.

One of the Japanese torpedoes hit near an ammunition bunker which basically split the ship in two. It sank within 12 minutes, taking about a fourth of the crew with her. About 900 men went into the waters of the Philippine Sea. About two-thirds of the 900 who survived the sinking perished due to shark attacks and salt water poisoning during those four desperate days. There were reports that some men succumbed to thirst and drank sea water and subsequently went mad.

A Navy aircraft accidently spotted the men and wreckage. When the group was finally rescued, 317 *Indianapolis* sailors remained to be pulled from the water. The fate of the "Indy" and her crew is regarded by some historians as the worst naval disaster in U.S. history.

"THE GREATEST GENERATION"

Homer "H. C." Myers, Jr. sat in the comfortable den of his home in Union Grove in October of 2004 and shared his memories of those days almost sixty years before. A successful dairy farmer, husband, father of four and grandfather of 13, his home was within sight of the steepled, white Zion Baptist Church, where he was a member and a deacon.

If you saw him sipping coffee in a cafe, you probably wouldn't have looked at him twice. But once, he was a warrior and a pilot.

Myers was part of what Tom Brokow called "The Greatest Generation"—those Americans who grew up during the Great Depression and endured the Second World War.

It was August 2, 1945. Captain Homer Myers and his B-17 crew, part of the 3rd Emergency Air/Sea Rescue Squadron, 5th Air/Sea Rescue Group, 5th U.S. Army Air Force, had flown to New Guinea to pick up a new aircraft and were taking it back to their base in the Marianas. They had been persuaded by a ground crew to stop, refuel and rest on the island of Peleliu, a place that supposedly had "the only beds with fresh sheets in the Pacific."

Myers said they arrived about 3 p.m. and were "enjoying a bit of rest when a major came running in and asked where the crew of the Air/Sea rescue plane was."

A Navy patrol aircraft had spotted a large group of men adrift in the water some 200 miles to the north.

RESCUE MISSION

Even 60 years later the memory of those events was so strong that Myers frequently had to stop his narrative to get his emotions under control.

Continuing the story, he told how they hurriedly refueled the B-17 and stuffed in three dozen big, inflatable rubber life rafts to go with the standard 26-foot plywood lifeboat that they already had aboard the rescue-equipped Flying Fortress.

Once they arrived at the location, they could see the men, now spread out over what looked like 30 square miles.

As his crew tossed the heavy rafts out of the bomb bay at 1,200 feet, Myers silently wondered if they might be doing more harm than good to the sailors in the water.

A PBY Catalina flying boat set down on the water near the men, even though it wasn't supposed to. As many men as possible crammed inside; others scrambled up on the high wing—anything to get out of the water. Circling overhead, it looked to Myers like "those men got on it like flies on a piece of bread."

The B-17 that Myers was piloting couldn't land on the water, but it circled as long as it could, wagging its wings to let the men below—spread out over a large expanse of the Pacific—know that they had been seen and that help was on the way.

By this time it was getting dark and Myers and his plane had to return to base. Rescue ships were converging on the scene, but it would be daylight before most arrived.

The next day Myers flew his plane back over the area and saw "the place covered with ships searching for survivors."

AWARDED FOR THEIR FEATS

Myers and all his crew were awarded the Air Medal for their role in the rescue of the *Indianapolis* survivors. After the war ended Myers stayed in the service and eventually retired as a major in the Air Force Reserves.

In 1992, a reunion of *USS Indianapolis* survivors was held in the city for which the ship was named. Myers was one of those who, although not part of the ship's crew, had been especially invited to attend.

One of the men who had been in the water embraced Myers and said that Myers and his crew had saved his life.

Homer C. Myers of Buck Shoals Road, Iredell County, had played a small role in a footnote to the history of World War II—small to everyone except those 317 men floating in the shark-infested water.

* * *

Homer Myers, Jr. passed away on July 26, 2006, at his home. He is buried in the churchyard of the Zion Baptist Church in Union Grove.

A. Y. NEEL, JR.

I spoke with Mr. A. Y. Neel, Jr. at his home in the spring of 1990. We sat outdoors under a shade tree. Mr. Neel had on his trademark bib overalls and occasionally petted a dog by his feet as we talked.

* * *

The Doolie/Mayhew area of Iredell County isn't incorporated and consequently has no mayor. But if it did, though, it likely might be Avery Young Neel, Jr., or "Mr. A.Y.," as he is known to many.

He and his wife, Mary Bethel, have lived in a 100-year old house in southern Iredell for almost half a century, and he was born in an even older house on the River Road (NC Highway 150) "about three miles from the river and four miles from Mooresville."

He has many a memory about the old Catawba River from whence Lake Norman came. When he was about 6 years old, his father took the whole family down to see the river. The Catawba had risen over 40 feet during the Great Catawba River Flood of July, 1916.

"Daddy took us all out to see the water. I remember seeing a big old barn float by with a chicken on its roof—don't know if it was a hen or a rooster—but I'll never forget seeing that barn bobbin' up and down in the brown water and that chicken up there riding the roof, a-sailing down the river."

On hot summer days the Neel boys went swimming in the river. "Me and my brothers used to take a little path down to the river up above where the bridge used to be, about where the present bridge is. It was right shallow there. We went swimming' in the nude...no swimsuits back then."

He also recalls getting dressed up to go to preaching in Mooresville at the Associate Reformed Presbyterian Church, then on Main Street. "If we went to town during the week, it was in the wagon, but on Sunday we took the surrey."

Mr. A. Y attended the wooden two-room Brawley School that stood about a quarter of a mile from today's school of the same name, and then went to the old Springdale School through the seventh grade. To get a high school education, he went to Troutman High, where he graduated with the Class of 1929.

Even before he graduated, he knew what he wanted to do with his life—be a farmer. Today he is among the dwindling number of real farmers in the area.

"All I ever wanted to be was a farmer," said the man in bib overalls, sitting in a shaded swing. Then he grinned. "Oh, I did have another job once, for two weeks. I worked at a place called the Candy Kitchen in Mooresville—must have been in the late 1930s because I was already married. Anyway, I worked there for a whole week. They made candy and sold sweets and fruits and some vegetables. Worked for them a week before Christmas one week, and then did the same thing the next year. That's the only other work I've ever done besides farming—those two weeks."

Mr. A. Y. says he farms about 127 acres, which will soon be planted in soybeans and corn. He had more land, until Duke Power Company bought it and covered it with water.

"This Duke Power Company fellow came and tried to buy my land for the lake. The old fellow comes around here and makes me an offer, says he bought some property just up the road for a hundred dollars an acre. I said, 'I can't help that, but I'm not selling for that price. See here, I'm a farmer. I *use* my land. My price, see, is three hundred an acre.

"Well, he got all mad and threatened to foreclose on me and all.

"But he finally came around to my price, so I sold Duke Power the water rights at three hundred an acre, but only what was to be covered up by the lake. I sold Duke Power nine and some tenths acres, and myself, I developed 11 and some tenths.

"Mostly, though, I just like to farm," he said, looking out over the land he has known for 80 years. "I've got a few cows and some chickens. Do about all the work myself, but I can't put up hay anymore like I used to."

* * *

Avery Young Neel, Jr. passed away on November 6, 2006, at the age of 96. He was a lifelong member of the Mooresville A.R. P. Church, where he had been a deacon and an elder emeritus. Mr. A. Y. was a charter member the South Iredell Lions Club and a founding member of the Lake Norman Volunteer Department and served as a member of that organization for 40 years.

His wife, the former Mary Bethel Howard, preceded him in death, but he was survived by three sons, a daughter, a brother, a sister, nine grandchildren and ten great-grandchildren and by many friends.

The term "pillar of the community" seems to fit Mr. A. Y. about as well as his bib overalls did.

Cecil Redmond

The Centers for Disease Control and Prevention in Atlanta ought to have a whole department dedicated to helping those unfortunates stricken with Extreme Genealogy Disorder or "EGD." This affliction is usually found among those of middle age and is manifested by an unquenchable desire to find out everything possible about one's ancestors. Once contracted, the condition is usually permanent, and so far, there is no known cure.

Case in point: Mrs. Kay Johnson Trivette of Union Grove. Kay got interested in her family tree as a result of a family gathering four or five years ago. She has had various successes getting complete names of her kinfolk, important dates and so forth, each bit of family lore a new piece to the puzzle. The heartbreak of this wide-spread affliction is that eventually one runs across a question that can't be answered.

Aunt Tilley or Aunt Sally or Aunt Somebody, who knew everything about the family has passed on, church records are missing, government files are inaccessible and all hope of finding out a little more about the family's past seems to have vanished. In particular, Kay had run across a roadblock in her journey to find out about her great-uncle—her mother's mother's brother—Private First Class Cecil Roe Redmond, U.S. Army, an Iredell County resident who gave his life for his country in Europe during World War II. Specifically, she could not find when his body had been returned home and buried at New Prospect Baptist Church Cemetery.

* * *

Cecil was the son of Mr. and Mrs. David Dalton Redmond of the New Hope township. Born on May 16, 1914, he had worked on the family farm and was a member of New Hope Baptist Church. He was inducted into the U.S. Army on November 1, 1942, at the age of 28, received basic training at Camp White, Oregon, and went overseas on April 1, 1944.

Redmond first served in North Africa, but he was in Italy, as a member of the 363rd Infantry Regiment, a part of the 91st Infantry Division, when he was shot and killed on April 16, 1945.

According to an article in the June 14, 1945, *Landmark*, "A chaplain of PFC Redmond's company wrote that on the morning of April 16 there was heavy fire and Redmond was struck by a sniper. He was in action in Italy on the Po River at the time. He was buried in an American cemetery in that area."

The Landmark further stated, "The family has also heard from a lady in Mt. Airy who said her husband was right by PFC Redmond's side when he was struck and that he died instantly." Pvt. Redmond, just a month shy of his being 32 years old, was just one of the 150 or so Iredell County men known to have died during the Second World War.

Redmond's death came just days before the end of World War II in Europe. One of Hitler's generals signed a document on May 1, 1945, unconditionally surrendering all German forces in Italy to the Allies on May 2, and **all** German forces were unconditionally surrendered on May 7th.

At the time of his death Private Redmond had been in the Army for 29 months and had already been awarded the Army's Good Conduct Medal and two Purple Hearts for wounds received in action.

Back home his family held a memorial service for him on Sunday, July 15th, 1945, at New Prospect Baptist Church, but his body was still interred overseas. It would be three years and five months before Private Redmond's body was returned home, according to an article recently found in *The Landmark* of

December 13, 1948. A reburial service was held on Sunday, Dec. 12, 1948, at New Prospect Baptist. The service was conducted by the church's pastor, the Rev. R. C. Lloyd, assisted by two other ministers and full military honors were conducted at graveside by the Harmony American Legion Post. Private Redmond was survived by his parents, four sisters and four brothers and a churchful of relatives and friends.

* * *

Beginning in 1947, the Redmond family has annually held a reunion in Cecil's memory at the family homeplace. That first year there were about 200 friends and family present. Mrs. Trivette remembers attending these. In 1948 she was 6 years old and proudly signed her name to the guest register.

She recalls, "We'd have a big dinner outside under the trees and after dinner we'd march up to the crossroad and back and wave handkerchiefs. Grandma would try to have some veterans carrying the flag and as we marched we'd sing 'When the Saints Go Marchin' In.'"

"I think my great-uncle Cecil was the youngest child in his family," she said, "and was close in age to my mother, more like a brother than an uncle. He sent a letter home that was written on Dec. 29, 1944. I recently found that letter; it had been a keepsake of Mother's. In the letter great-uncle Cecil said that he was worried about my mother and that he was praying for her—Kay's father had just gone into the service—and praying for all his family and hoped by that same time next year he'd be home and the world would be again at peace. There he was in such danger and he was thinking and praying about us. His letter just touched my heart."

* * *

On Veterans Day and Memorial Day we should take the time to remember all the Cecil Redmonds—those who literally have put their lives on the line for the rest of us.

Rev. Dr. E. F. Rockwell

Iredell County has been blessed with a wide variety of interesting citizens, one of whom, the Rev. Elijah Frink Rockwell, D.D., was not born in Iredell County, but he left his mark here.

Born in Lebanon, Connecticut, in 1809, he was a Yale graduate, Class of 1834. At the time of his graduation he was 25 years old, having interrupted his own education to teach children for some time to earn money to further his education. He first came to North Carolina in 1835 to be a principal at the Donaldson Academy in Fayetteville.

After two years in the classroom he felt the calling to the ministry and decided to study theology at the seminaries of Columbia, South Carolina, and Princeton, New Jersey. He was 30 years old when he was first licensed to preach in June of 1839.

After becoming a licentiate of the Presbyterian Church, he came to Statesville in 1840 and was ordained and installed as the pastor at First Presbyterian Church—then known as "Fourth Creek Presbyterian Church"—in the spring of 1841. He remained pastor at Fourth Creek for about nine years, leaving it to become a professor of chemistry and geology at Davidson College. He later also taught Latin at Davidson before returning to Statesville in 1868 to take charge of the Concord Female College—now known as Mitchell Community College.

Concord Female College was the Presbyterian church's female equivalent of Davidson College, which was also associated with the Presbyterian Church. The young men of Davidson took the A.T. & O. Railroad to Statesville to attend teas, receptions and other social events here, and the young ladies of the Female College took the A.T. & O. to Davidson to attend dances and other social activities there.

Altogether, Rev. Rockwell was president of Concord Female College for three years, after which he and Professor H. T. Burke ran a private classical boys' school.

Rev. Rockwell resumed ministerial duties in 1872, when he became the pastor of Fifth Creek, Bethany and Tabor Presbyterian churches. He lived within walking distance of Fifth Creek Church.

After retirement from the active ministry around 1884, he became a student again, pursuing studies that interested him, particularly local history. Even though he was not a native to these parts, at the time of his passing it was said that "no man knows so much as he did of the local history of Iredell County."

In his obituary in *The Landmark* the statement was made that "It is to be regretted that he never put this knowledge into enduring form—the greater part of it died with him."

His writings and some of his sermons are still scattered, some of them in the Presbyterian Archives, some at Davidson College, and some can be found within the pages of microfilmed newspapers and journals. He was conferred the well-deserved honorary degree of Doctor of Divinity by the University of North Carolina in June of 1882.

Besides contributing local history pieces to *The Landmark,* he also wrote for scholarly journals—about Crowfield Academy, Clio's Nursery, a history of distillation in Iredell County, the Battle of Ramsour's Mill, the Battle of Cowpens, the political situation in Rowan County in 1774, a history of Fourth Creek Church, etc. According to one source, he penned more than 100 articles on important subjects and at least that number on lesser subjects, such as the shooting of the buffalo on the Sabbath, printed below.

It is some measure of the respect in which he was held that Rev. Rockwell was the person chosen to deliver the historical address in Statesville during the centennial celebration of our nation's independence on July 4, 1876.

Rev. Rockwell had been sick with a severe cold for a week in April of 1888, when he presided at a congregational meeting at Fifth Creek Church because the regular pastor, the Rev. T. J. Allison, was absent. His cold turned into bronchial pneumonia and he died at his home a week after the meeting, on April 15, 1888. He was 79 years old.

There were two funeral services held, the first at Fifth Creek Church, where there was a standing room only crowd, and then another at First Presbyterian Church in Statesville. At the time of his death, he was believed to have been the oldest member of Concord Presbytery.

He was buried first in 4th Creek Burying Ground across the street from the church. Later his wife had his body removed to the then-newly opened Oakwood Cemetery. Rev. Rockwell was married twice. He had no children by his first wife, Margarette Kirkland McNeil, but was survived by his second wife, Elizabeth Holmes Brown (died in 1902), and by their son, Joseph Huntington Rockwell (1868-1940). These last two are also buried at Oakwood.

Here is part of a short article by Rev. Rockwell which was printed in the *North Carolina Presbyterian*, year unknown:

"Not long after this year [1750] in the first settlement of the Scotch Irish in western North Carolina in what is now Iredell county, Mr. Alexander Reed...was six miles from home at church, leaving some small children, the oldest only ten years. In the absence of the parents a large buffalo came near the house, when the little boy took his father's gun, put it through between the logs of the cabin and shot the monster dead. The father, though, chastised the little fellow, the next morning, for violating the Sabbath in shooting the animal which offered himself to be shot."

In other words, the father did not mind that this son had shot a buffalo, but reprimanded the lad because the boy had shot the animal on a Sunday. How times have changed.

WILLIAM FEIMSTER SHARPE

You could walk past his headstone in the cemetery of Concord Presbyterian Church in Iredell County and take no more notice of it than of hundreds of others. It has no special markings, symbols or inscriptions. Yet this grave is almost unique, for it is the final resting place of a man who once belonged to a small, elite organization. It is the grave of a Confederate Marine veteran.

The fact that the Confederacy, in its brief four years of existence, even had a Marine Corps would be news to many people. These men were a rare breed and the fact that one of them hailed from a county as far inland as Iredell is even more remarkable. The United States Marine Corps numbered no more than four thousand officers and enlisted men during the War Between the States, and the Confederate Corps was even smaller than its Federal counterpart.

Iredell's Confederate Marine was William Feimster Sharpe of the Loray community northwest of Statesville. Mr. Sharpe was born two miles north of Loray in 1839, the last of 11 children of Silas Davidson and his wife Mary Feimster Sharpe. He was interviewed by a reporter from *The Landmark* in April of 1917, just as America was about to enter the First World War.

He had enlisted in the Confederate Army on June 29, 1862, but for reasons not clear now, was transferred to the Confederate Marine Corps. He was later promoted to the rank of sergeant and placed in charge of the 19-member Marine contingent aboard the Confederate States Ship *Palmetto State*. The *CSS Palmetto State* and three other gunboat/rams patrolled the harbor between Fort Sumter, where the Civil War began, and the peninsula on which the city of Charleston, South Carolina, is located. The ships and forts protected the "Pearl of the South" from the U.S. Navy which controlled the waters beyond the harbor.

The Union Navy was charged by President Lincoln to enforce a blockade of the Southern coast as part of what the federals called "The Anaconda Plan." Like the giant snake for which it was named, the Anaconda Plan proposed to squeeze the South to death.

The *Palmetto State* was an iron-clad ram with four-inch thick armor and carried four large cannons capable of firing 8 to 10 inch projectiles. The ship had a crew that numbered, according to Sharpe, 170 men.

Sgt. Sharpe's Marines served several purposes aboard ship: they acted as military police in enforcing order and orders, would board enemy vessels or repel boarders in hand-to-hand combat or act as sharpshooters in battle, and could also serve as a small landing force in amphibious operations. They were the only enlisted men aboard who regularly carried side arms. There was also one further duty. In case of mutiny aboard the *Palmetto State*, the Marines would be the ones to quell the insurrection.

The former Marine recalled that, in general, the discipline aboard a vessel of the Confederate Navy was more strict than the discipline that existed in the army. As an example, he mentioned that officers were then supposed to be addressed as "Mister," rather than by their rank, and he mentioned to the interviewer that he had once gotten a stinging rebuke for calling an officer, "Captain," even though that had been the man's actual rank.

The Marines, and presumably the Sailors, ate off an oil-cloth spread on the deck, and the deck had better not have any crumbs or grease spilled on it or several hours of cleaning duty would be the lot of the poor unfortunate who had been careless. It was part of the ship's daily routine that the decks were scrubbed and washed down.

As the war drew to a close, the Marines under Sergeant Sharpe alternated their duty between serving on the *Palmetto State* and manning Confederate coastal shore batteries. When the Confederates evacuated Charleston, Sergeant Sharpe and his contingent were ordered to go to Wilmington, North Carolina. Presumably, they would have helped bolster the defenses of the gigantic Fort Fisher located below the city and protecting the entrance to the Cape Fear River, but the fort and the city of Wilmington were in Union hands before Sharpe and the *Palmetto State* Marines could reach their destination.

When Charleston was evacuated by Confederate military forces, the *Palmetto State* was destroyed at the mouth of Town Creek River, above Charleston, on February 26, 1864, to prevent its capture by Union forces. The ship's chief engineer rigged the ship to explode, and when it did, the blast left "a plume of smoke in the shape of a Palmetto tree, much to the delight of the crew."

Sergeant Sharpe and his company proceeded to Whiteville, where he and the men separated. Eventually Mr. Sharpe made it back home to the red clay hills of Iredell County.

William F. Sharpe married Miss Emma Greene of Alexander County and the Sharpes had at least three children, a daughter and two sons. William Feimster Sharpe claimed to be descended from a family which had emigrated to the Snow Creek community of the Sharpesburg township of Iredell from Sharpesburg, Maryland, in the 1750s.

At the time of his death on New Year's Day, 1923, at the age of 84, Mr. Sharpe was a member of the county pension board. As mentioned before, he is buried in the cemetery of the Concord Presbyterian Church in Loray.

Pete Melitis of Mooresville, commandant of the local contingent of the Marine Corps League, a fraternal organization of Marine veterans, found the story of Sergeant Sharpe to be fascinating, and his grave remarkable, as it may likely be the oldest known grave of a Marine in Iredell County.

When asked if it mattered that it was the grave of a Confederate Marine, rather than that of a former United States Marine, Melitis, a combat veteran of the Korean War, replied, "He should be honored for his service to his country. It's all the same to us, a Marine is a Marine."

WILLIAM "LAWYER BILLY" SHARPE

One of the most important men in Iredell County's early history was a lawyer named William Sharpe. In fact, he was often referred to as "Lawyer Billy."

Sharpe was born in Rock Church, Cecil County, Maryland, in 1742. While in Maryland he was educated in classical studies and law. In 1763, at the age of 21, he moved to Mecklenburg County, N.C., and was admitted to the bar and commenced practice there. He married in 1768 and soon afterwards he and his wife moved to the area near Snow Creek in what was then western Rowan (now Iredell) County.

William Sharpe was also important in North Carolina's early affairs. By 1774 William Sharpe was secretary of the Rowan Committee of Safety. In August of 1774 the Rowan Committee of Safety adopted what is called the "Rowan Resolves," a document of 17 resolutions which, while not outright calling for a break with the British government, at least leaned in that direction.

Sharpe also represented Rowan County at the Second Provincial Congress held at New Bern in April of 1775 and at the Third Provincial Congress held at Hillsborough in August and September of the same year.

A man of actions was well as a man of words, Sharpe served as an aide-de-camp with the rank of captain to General Rutherford in his peremptory campaign against the British-allied Cherokee Indians in 1776, and in 1777 he and three others were appointed commissioners by Governor Caswell to form a treaty with them. In the Treaty of Long Island of Holston, the Overhill Cherokees gave up their lands east of the Blue Ridge and granted white settlers a corridor through western Virginia and North Carolina to the Cumberland Gap.

Sharpe served as a delegate to the North Carolina Constitutional Convention in Halifax in 1776, and was a framer the first North Carolina state constitution.

Nationally, Sharpe was elected as a delegate from the Salisbury District to the Continental Congress in Philadelphia and served three one-year terms in 1779, 1780 and October, 1781. In this position he met with and corresponded with George Washington, James Madison, Gen. Nathanael Greene, Thomas Burke and other important founders of our country.

He was a member of the North Carolina House of Commons in 1782, and in 1782 was considered for governor but was unsuccessful in this venture. He served in the lower state house again in 1784 and on November 8, 1784, Sharpe placed the first bill before the state legislature for a publicly-supported university in North Carolina. Sharpe's bill failed, but was introduced to the legislature again five years later and this time the bill had the backing of General William Richardson Davie, who had been a leader during the War for Independence. The bill subsequently passed and the University of North Carolina was created, the first state university in the United States. Gen. Davie, for whom Davie County is named, is generally recognized as being the "Father of the University of North Carolina," but William Sharpe was the one who first tried to get it established. The cornerstone for the university was laid in 1793 and "Carolina" opened its doors in 1795.

Locally, Mr. Sharpe, who also was a surveyor, was responsible for the creation of a map in 1773 of the Fourth Creek congregation. This map now hangs in the James Iredell Room of the Iredell County Public Library in Statesville. It shows many details of the early settlement of what became Iredell County in 1788, including the locations of the homes and the names of almost 200 families. The map is divided into quarters and has 11 concentric rings on a scale of a mile apart with its center point being about two miles west of the original Fourth Creek Meeting House. This map is one of the most valuable artifacts we have from our county's early days.

Surveyor Sharpe is also credited with laying out Statesville two main streets, Broad and Center and for making them wide.

Although he was a member of Fourth Creek Presbyterian Church—now First Presbyterian Church in Statesville—in 1801 what was known as "King's Methodist Episcopal Church," and later came to be known as Snow Creek Methodist Church, was organized in William Sharpe's home. In 1806 he donated five and a half acres to the trustees of this church.

Sharpe is also believed to have had a hand in the establishment of Clio's Nursery in 1774, an institution of higher education taught by Rev. James Hall.

Lawyer Billy Sharpe died at his home near Snow Creek on July 1, 1818, and is buried in the cemetery of Snow Creek United Methodist Church. He was survived by his widow, the former Catherine Ruth Reese, and 12 children. His most remarkable achievement may have been to have found the time to sire a dozen children. Many of his descendants still live in this area.

A North Carolina Highway Historical Marker honoring William Sharpe was proposed during Iredell County's bicentennial celebration and was erected in October of 1977 beside Highway 115 North at the intersection with SR 1903 (Rickert Road). The marker reads, "William Sharpe 1742-1818 Member of Continental and provincial congresses, was first legislator to advocate U.N.C., 1784. Grave is 2 miles east." It would have taken several of these markers to fully list all his accomplishments.

ERNEST AND GEORGE SLOAN

Jim Sloan, a U.S. Army veteran, was kind enough to show me some memorabilia he has from World War One: a gas mask cover, a French bugle, a magazine printed by the 81st Division, a bugler's cloth insignia, some photographs and a letter.

Two Iredell County brothers, Ernest Neal Sloan Sr. and George Norman Sloan, Jim's father and uncle, respectively, served together in the U.S. Army in the First World War. The brothers were overseas for 22 months.

Allowing brothers to serve in the same unit was contrary to War Department policy, but somehow the brothers enlisted together and stayed together. The family story is they told the officials that they might be "distantly related." George was a bugler and a communications runner and is known to have been in Company "B" of the 321st Infantry Regiment, 81st "Wildcat" Division, while his younger brother Ernest (Jim's father) was a machine gunner and was said to be in the "same unit," but it is unclear if they were in the same company, regiment or brigade.

Up through the American Civil War, brothers had often served together in the same unit. If one brother was injured or sick, his brother could do something towards helping his sibling. But this arrangement was a two-edged sword: if the brothers' unit was engaged in heavy combat, the loss to a single family could be catastrophic.

Originally composed of drafted men from North Carolina, South Carolina and Florida, the men of the Wildcat Division were trained at Fort Jackson, near Columbia, S.C., and then received further training at Camp Sevier, near Greenville, S.C.

On October 19, 1918, the division was attached to the First U.S. Army and with that organization was initiated into real combat. The 81st Division soldiers were ordered "over the top" to attack the German trenches on the very morning the armistice was to take place—November 11, 1918.

Unfortunately for the German and American troops, there was no official word that the fighting was about to cease. The Wildcats slowly advanced through the heavy fog and withering German machine gun fire and made their way between the trenches—a barren, treeless, muddy area dotted with artillery shell holes and barbed wire called "No Man's Land," and made it to the German positions. At precisely 11 a.m., firing abruptly stopped all up and down the line. The war was over.

Although in action for only about a month, the Wildcat Division sustained 1,104 casualties: 248 killed or dead from wounds and 856 wounded. Although not officially part of the 3rd Army—the Army of Occupation—it was not until June of 1919, seven months after the cessation of hostilities, that members of the division were shipped home and released from service. The 81st was officially deactivated at Hoboken, New Jersey, on June 11, 1919.

Back in civilian life George went to college and became a Methodist preacher. This calling did not last long as he had been exposed to poison gas while service in the war and developed tuberculosis and spent much time in sanatoriums. He died in 1930 at the age of 38. His obituary in *The Landmark* stated, "he was said to have been one of the most promising young ministers of his church in this state." George married, but had no children.

George's brother Ernest became a farmer and also worked as a custodian at Central School and worked for the schools' maintenance department in the summer. He was generally a quiet man and spoke little of his experiences in the Great War. Ernest survived his brother by 45 years, dying in 1975 at the age of 79. Ernest was survived by son Jim, three other sons and four daughters.

Jim said his father was "the greatest man I ever knew."

Both men are buried at Mountain View United Methodist Church Cemetery in north Iredell.

* * *

George Sloan sent the following letter, slightly edited for readability, to his home from France. The letter was written while on the march, some two weeks after the cease fire and Armistice. It has not been published previously and is published here with Jim Sloan's permission. The religious service referred to may have been a thanksgiving service, the men thanking God that they had survived and would be going home.

France, 11-24-18

Dear Father:

As this is Father's day we are all requested to write to "Dad" with the promise that it won't be censored. I have been on the front twice, first on the Vosges sector which was a quiet sector. We went into the trenches on Sept. the 19th and held this front about 21 days. Moved back for a two weeks rest and then hiked several miles and rode some in boxcars to the Historic Verdun front at which place we "went over the top" in a big drive on Oct. 10th. We had to drive over a big marsh— mud and water and lakes. On the night of the 10th I slept (?) in a water ditch partly filled with water. Under a heavy shell fire early in the morning I was told to get on my pack. We was going to move up; I got up and plunged into the chilly water the shells were falling all around and I was expecting every one that came whistling over to have my name on it. I can't imagine how I ever got through alive.

So we went forward until 11:00 a.m. when orders came to cease firing. We found that we had advanced about 2 kilo[meter]s, lost five men and about 8 wounded in Co. B. The Germans told us that they laid down the heaviest barrage on us that morning they ever put on this front and never knew of anyone advancing our Infantry under such heavy shelling.

We were fighting the 5th Prussian Guard, Germany's very best troops. I don't want to seem to brag but the 81st Division did something that the famous 26th [Division] failed to do. The French told our general before we started to drive that it was impossible to drive over such a marshy district, but when the firing stopped we was across and had them on the run toward German soil. Sounds good, Eh?

We have hiked many, many miles since coming here. We are on a 200 kilo hike now. It is likely we will sail for the U.S. soon. My feet is sore but I am too ambitious to "fall out." It is very cold and don't often get by any fire, sometimes have to sleep on the frozen ground. I am so cold now I can't half write.

Well, I have preached to my comrades some. While we were in the trenches I held services for them. I am trying to live out my good training wherever I go. I feel like I want to tell you this.

The first time I held services the commanding officer and officers gathered around me in a barn yard. I was feeling the best I ever felt in my life.

We open[ed] by having prayer and it wasn't long before you could hear weeping all around. The Spirit seemed hovering over us. After the prayer I talked and it seemed I got lost in myself. I forgot all about my captain being a big college professor and the officers being college graduates. As soon as I finished the captain made the remark that without exception that was the best service he ever attended. I never heard such high tribute paid me as he did. I give God all the glory. This is the best news I could think of to write you for Xmas, so I close by hoping you all will have a real fine Yuletide.

Your devoted son

Geo. N. Sloan

Co. B, 321st Inf.

* * *

During and right after the First World War the conflict was known as "The World War," or "The Great War." Many also believed that it would be "The War to End All Wars."

As we now know, it was not.

RALPH SLOAN

We in Iredell County have been fortunate in having had a good number of men and women to record our common history.

The Rev. Dr. E. F. Rockwell, who taught at Mitchell College and was pastor at First Presbyterian Church, Statesville, might be considered our first bona fide historian. Others who have written local history include dentist Dr. Phillip F. Laugenhour, Minnie Hampton Eliason and Homer Keever, who wrote columns in *The Daily Record* and later in the *Record & Landmark* for nearly 30 years.

More recently Mac Lackey Jr. penned history columns for the "Iredell Neighbors" section of *The Charlotte Observer*. Other recent historians include William C. "Bill" Moose, Mildred Miller and the late "Red" Watt.

I would like to tell a little about another Iredell historian: Ralph Clifton Sloan. Most people who knew Ralph Sloan probably remember him best as a men's clothier or for his dry cleaning business on East Water Street. He was also once the editor of *The Mascot*, Statesville's first daily newspaper.

Born in 1889 in Stony Point, Sloan became a Statesville resident in 1892, when his family moved here. His formal education was limited to the eighth grade under Professor D. Matt Thompson at the old Mulberry School. Sloan was a keen observer of human nature and had a prodigious memory. Rather than writing what might be called "formal" history, Sloan, in his later years, wrote sketches of the city and the county of his youth.

He began writing his reminiscences in the *Record & Landmark* in the fall of 1966 and continued contributing them for several years, and then only wrote occasionally through November of 1976. He passed away in May, 1981, at the age of 92.

One of the problems in making a study of local history is that old newspapers often left out addresses. The papers felt no need to mention the location of, say, a new building, as that was the only building being erected at the time and everyone in town knew where the structure was going up.

But here we are, 90 or more years later, and we are lucky if an author put in something that gives a clue as to a building's location, such as, "across the street from the Methodist church," or "at the corner of Front and Center streets." The latter location would, of course, leave one wondering *which* corner.

Ralph Sloan did Statesville a great service when in the late 1960s he started at various landmarks in town, such as the depot, and in his imagination walked up the east side of Center Street to the Square, giving a description of who lived in each house along the way or what business was located there, what they made or sold, who owned it and who worked there.

A week or so later, Sloan took up where he had left off and described the other side of the street. He frequently inserted such asides as, "where the Metropolitan Life Insurance Co. is now located."

And where was that? All you have to do is look in a city directory—available at the county library—for the year Sloan's article was published. He also wrote many thumbnail sketches of prominent as well as less prominent Iredell County citizens of 90 or more years ago.

A good example of Sloan's contribution to local history is his column, "How It Was in the Old-Time Grocery Store," from the *Record & Landmark* of January 4, 1968. A number of grayer heads may recall some of the businesses mentioned below. Here is a portion of Sloan's column:

"Some of the nostalgic memories which linger with me are the days when I clerked in two of the early-day grocery stores in Statesville. In those days before transportation was so easy, most of the food stores were located in the heart of the uptown business section.

"There were several small neighborhood stores located in various sections of the town. Most of the sales were delivered in a horse-drawn vehicle or in an old time two-wheel push cart. Each morning the larger stores sent out the deliveryman to the better customers' homes to solicit orders.

"Cash and carry came years later. Of course, if the credit of the customer did not warrant a charge account, the sale was cash on delivery. On many occasions the goodness of a merchant's heart governed whether a customer could get credit.

"Among the old grocery stores I recall Turner's located on the corner where Holmes Drug now is [1968]. Down the street where Ralph Sloan, Inc., is located was Alexander Brothers, operated by Moffat and Rufe Alexander. Across the street Eagle and Milholland were located just to the rear of the Statesville Drug Store. Around the corner where Belk's Gift Shop operates was the location of J. B. Gill, one of the better and larger stores in town.

"Down in the old Iredell Hotel building, which stood on the site of today's Woolworth's, J. P. Phifer & Son also operated a nice grocery business.

"Kimball and Dayvault [where Sloan first worked] were also in the Iredell Hotel building.

"In the old St. Charles Hotel building there was a small place operated by J. W. Marshall. In the same building Hunter Moore operated a grocery store and meat market. On West Broad, Fry and Phifer conducted a grocery store in the building now occupied by Lester's. Across the street,

in the building occupied by Jo-Ann's, Thad Summers conducted a good-sized store.

"In the building occupied by First Union National Bank, Frank Sherrill, the one-armed man, operated one of the better grocery stores. It was a curiosity to see his dexterity in handling groceries, to see him, with one arm, weigh up merchandise, wrap it up with paper and securely tie it with twine. He operated the store until his death. W. P. McLain later became owner. Eventually June and Francis McAuley took it over and were very popular in the business.

"In the building where Louis Marrett is located, D. J. Kimball for years operated a grocery store. In later years he moved into the location now occupied by Parks Realty Co. In the building now occupied by Plyler's Men's Shop, Jesse and A. R. Sherrill opened a nice grocery and successfully operated it for years.

"This makes a total of 12 grocery stores that were at one time located in the heart of the uptown business section. Today [1968] the nearest is the A&P on South Center and the Winn-Dixie on East Broad. The first chain grocery to open in Statesville was then called the Great Atlantic and Pacific Tea Co., now the A&P. It was located in one of the store rooms where the Penny Building stands. It was a small average grocery store when they opened."

* * *

The part of the above that is in quotation marks is about a fourth of the column Ralph Sloan wrote on the old-time Statesville groceries. Copies of Sloan's columns are in a binder and can be read in the James Iredell Room of the main Iredell County Public Library in Statesville. They are a valuable, interesting part of our history.

GRAY SLOOP

After referring to itself as "Port City of Lake Norman," for some time now Mooresville ha. taken to calling itself "Race City, USA." Nearly a century ago there was a Mooresville man whose life and achievements might serve to bolster Mooresville's new sobriquet. His name was Gray Sloop.

Gray Sloop was born in Mooresville in August of 1889, the only son of Augustus J. and Dovie Ann Sloop. Gray's father passed away in July of 1904, leaving the 15-year-old as the man of the family.

It is unclear just when young Sloop began making a name for himself in racing circles, but he was well-established as a motor sportsman by 1913. In late June of that year he left for Elgin, Illinois, just outside of Chicago, to participate in the Elgin Motorcycle Race to be held on the Fourth of July. This race was described as a 250-mile contest over an eight-mile course, and was billed as the first nationally-sanctioned motorcycle race and also the first 250-mile motorcycle race in the United States.

At the time of the Elgin race Sloop was riding a Reading-Standard cycle, specially built for him by the company in Reading, Pa. Mooresville's weekly newspaper, *The Enterprise*, noted, "Mr.

Sloop is the only man from the South entering the [Elgin] races, so far, and we predict for him one or more of the capital prizes." First prize in the Elgin Race was $500 in gold and a two-foot tall trophy, the "V Ray Cup."

The Statesville *Landmark* carried more information about the coming race. "*The Motorcycle,* a magazine published in Springfield, Mass., in its latest issue, speaking of the unusually strong line-up for the national motorcycle race at Elgin, Ill., on July the Fourth, said, after giving a list of the most important entrants, 'One of the latest entries to be received is from Mooresville, N.C., and is signed "Gray Sloop." This entry puzzled the contest committee for some time and Chairman Hill was inclined to believe that some one had worked in a yacht by mistake until he looked into the matter. Then he learned that Gray Sloop is a youngster who sprang from nowhere this year and romped off with the motorcycle championship of North Carolina. Sloop will ride a Reading Standard machine in the Elgin race and he is being talked of as a dark horse who is likely to spring surprises.'"

Sloop didn't win at Elgin, but that didn't stop him.

The race was won by a Texan, Charles "Fearless" Balke, who, with a blistering average speed of 55 mph over public roads, led an Indian Motorcycles sweep of the first five finishing positions. Out of 45 cyclists who had registered for the Elgin race, 43 began it and just ten completed it.

Sloop was not among those completing the course. According to a Chicago newspaper, Sloop had to make the eighth-mile qualifying run three times before he qualified, this due to brake malfunctions. His troubles continued during the actual race.

"Sloop dropped out of the race," reported the paper, "in the twentieth lap, after breaking over ten chains on his machine.

The chains were the cause of many falls of the different riders, none of whom were injured."

On June 8, 1914, just short of his 23rd birthday, "Fearless" Balke was killed in an accident at the Hawthorne dirt track near Chicago. Motorcycle racing was a dangerous business.

In early July of the next year Gray Sloop did very well in what was billed as the "Southern Championship Race" from Birmingham to Atlanta and back, an endurance race. By this time Sloop was not only riding Harley-Davidson motorcycles, he was selling them in Mooresville.

Reported *The Enterprise*, "Mr. Gray Sloop returned Tuesday night from Birmingham, Ala., where he participated in the Fourth of July motorcycle races. He won not only first place, but the world's championship, making the total distance of 462 miles from Birmingham to Atlanta and return in 12 hours and 20 minutes. While en route he had twelve changes of tires and changed one wheel. His part of the prize money was considerable."

Later that same month Sloop and his modified Harley took on Charlotte's Archie Templeton, piloting an Indian motorbike, in a two-contestant, 226-mile race from Charlotte to Columbia, S.C., and back, for a $200 prize.

Templeton completed the second half of the race, about 113 miles, in 2 hours and 56 minutes, whereas Sloop had trouble with his French racing motor just four miles short of the finish line in downtown Charlotte.

It is interesting to note that both Templeton and Sloop were "on their own" when it came to avoiding speeding tickets, other traffic and other "unforeseen difficulties."

At the Charlotte finish line, where about a thousand spectators had gathered, Templeton graciously remarked to Sloop, "Hard luck, old man. You raced a good race."

Sloop replied in kind, "Same back at you. A little hard luck on my part, but you deserve full glory for the race."

Next we hear of Sloop as the big winner of the professional 50-mile race held on Labor Day, 1914, on the Isle of Palms, near Charleston, S.C.

"Riding against time on a Harley-Davidson," reported *The Enterprise* of September 10, 1914, "he rode one mile at the speed of 92 miles an hour. His winning time was 55 minutes and 45 seconds, with 20 hairpin turns, which gives him the championship of North and South Carolina."

It is a wonder that Sloop did so well, as about a week prior to the Isle of Palms race, Sloop was in an accident with his motorbike and two-horse surrey wagon in Mooresville.

"Mr. Sloop," *The Enterprise* informed its readers, "was knocked senseless to the ground by the impact from the tongue of the surrey. His left arm struck the pole and the muscles were cut pretty severely. While down, a horse stepped on his hip."

After regaining consciousness, Sloop somehow managed to get back on his cycle, which was relatively undamaged, and get medical help.

The young man certainly had grit.

Sloop's last race was run on Thanksgiving Day, 1914. It was the Savannah 300 Road Race in Savannah, Georgia. This was only the second time the race had been held, and Sloop had ridden in the previous year's race. The course wound through the city and consisted of 27 laps of 11 miles. Holding third place, Sloop had just completed the third lap when he lost control of his Harley, the same machine on which he had won the Isle of Palms Race, and ran over a small embankment was hurled through the air. He broke his back, neck, hip and leg and was dead when assistance reached him.

The Enterprise quoted a Savannah newspaper:

"An examination made after the race showed a broken handle bar had been the cause of the accident which cost the life of Sloop. It was found Sloop had fallen on Norwood Avenue and cracked the right side of his handle bar. On Dale Avenue the bar had cracked completely off and Sloop entered the dangerous curve at Waters Road and Estill Avenue with only the left handle bar to his machine.

"When he ran into the rough ground, this caused him to loose control. He was thrown from his machine and went into the air.

"When descending the back of his neck struck a guy wire with such force as to cause a fracture of the neck. He then dropped between the machine and the tree. During the investigation after the race the piece of broken handle bar which had fallen from Sloop's machine was found on Dale Avenue by members of the Harley-Davidson racing stable."

Thus ended the life of the 25-year-old motorcycle racing enthusiast from Iredell County.

His death fell like a pall over his hometown. Twenty-five young men of the town met the train carrying his body from Savannah to Charlotte and from the Queen City escorted his remains home to Mooresville. His grave in Willow Valley Cemetery was covered with flowers.

"For many years he had been the dependence of his widowed mother and his [two] sisters, and the burden of grief falls heavy upon them," reported *The Enterprise*, which also referred to his handsome appearance, his affable and congenial spirit, and his simple life of purity and nobility.

His racing skills and potential in the new sport were known and admired to such an extent that an article reporting his demise was carried in the *New York Times.*

Although his name is unknown there today, Gray Sloop was the first to make Mooresville, "Race City, USA."

Drs. Eustace and Mary Martin Sloop

A local couple began to make a huge impact on the lives of the people of Avery County about a century ago. You may have heard of the school at Crossnore in Avery. It was founded in 1913 by Dr. Eustace Sloop, originally of Mooresville, and his wife, Dr. Mary Martin Sloop, originally of Davidson.

Rather than devoting their lives as medical missionaries to helping people in a foreign country, the Sloops dedicated themselves to helping the poor and disadvantaged of the Appalachian Mountains in North Carolina.

They came to Avery County in 1908, on mule back. Mountain travel, at that time and place, was by either by foot, human or animal. When the Sloops arrived, Crossnore was little more than a wide, level clearing at an altitude of more than 3,500 feet, the site of a country store operated by a fellow named George Crossnore.

The two set about addressing five interrelated problems: the marriage of girls as early as 13; the production of moonshine as the area's largest industry; illiteracy; the absence of medical and dental services; and the lack of roads which would allow the people to get their products to market.

The Sloops began with a boarding school. Then came a small hospital; then came their encouragement of a revival of mountain crafts, particularly weaving, to be sold to the outside market. Then came the first electrical generator; then came the development of the Irish potato as a cash crop...I'm getting ahead of my story.

Born in Davidson in 1873, Mary Martin was the daughter of a Davidson chemistry and geology professor and at 18 years of age—in 1891—was a graduate of Statesville Female College, better known today as Mitchell Community College.

After graduation she returned to Davidson and took some pre-med courses there, the school's only co-ed, with the intention of becoming a medical missionary to Asia.

After a year as the first woman admitted to the Medical College at Davidson, Mary continued her studies at the Woman's College of Pennsylvania, graduating from that institution in 1906.

The Presbyterian Church turned Mary down in her bid to become a foreign medical missionary because of her advanced age—she was 33 at the time—and the belief that she would not be able to manage the physical rigors of the calling. Little did they know of the grit in the diminutive Mary Martin.

Eustace Henry Sloop was born near Mooresville in January of 1878 and graduated from Davidson College in 1897. Sloop returned to Davidson when the North Carolina Medical College operated there and again ran into Mary Martin.

The couple married in July, 1908, in Blowing Rock, and soon began a medical practice in the mountain village of Plumtree. After three years at that location the duo moved a short distance to Crossnore, which became their home on December 11, 1911.

Dr. Eustace directed his efforts to help the mountain people through his medical practice, while Mary—although also a physician—became more involved in educational and social issues, although their efforts at times combined or overlapped.

Dr. Mary was an untiring letter-writer and made frequent trips to Raleigh to button-hole legislators about roads and to pester members of the Department of Public Instruction for more money for buildings and teachers in Avery County. A member of the Daughters of the American Revolution, she persuaded many chapters of that national organization to "adopt" Crossnore as a pet project.

The Crossnore School was begun in 1913. Dr. Mary got the school changed from a 4 1/2 month school to a full 9-month school and had it chartered as a nondenominational school. The addition of a high school department soon followed. The school featured manual arts training classes as well as the standard academic curriculum.

By around 1930 Crossnore School occupied more than 70 acres and was valued at $90,000. One of the ways the school made money was through the sale of "gently used" clothing.

With the help of others, Crossnore Presbyterian Church was organized in 1918 and built on land donated by the Sloops. A weaving program was instituted in 1920. Garrett Hospital, originally a 20-bed facility, was begun in 1928.

In describing her relationship with her husband, whom she always called "Doctor," Mary Sloop stated, "We just seemed to drift into the sea of matrimony, and, once in it, we've never had any desire to venture out of those waters."

For half a century these two devoted their lives to uplifting their less fortunate brothers and sisters. Dr. Eustace Sloop passed on to his reward on February 6, 1961, and Dr. Mary Martin Sloop joined him less than a year later, on January 13, 1962.

In October of 2006, a five-mile stretch of US Highway 221 was officially named the "Dr. Mary Martin Sloop Memorial Highway."

There is a further link between Crossnore, the Sloops and Iredell County. Renowned artist Benjamin F. Long IV, who grew up in Statesville and did the fresco in the Statesville Civic Center, also did the fresco, "Suffer the Little Children," which graces a wall in the E. H. Sloop Chapel on the campus of the Crossnore School. The children in the painting are said to be modeled on actual students of the Crossnore School.

In her 1953 book with Legette Blythe, *Miracle in the Hills,* Mary Sloop revealed a bit of her philosophy: "In the mountains you never see all around you...But I don't have the feeling of being fenced in. Instead, I feel on top of the world, even though I may be in a sheltered little valley. To me the mountains are inspiring, uplifting, challenging. They seem to beckon to higher things."

All of us should be thankful that the Sloops didn't ignore this summons from the mountains.

NORMAN SMALL

Moor Field on the southern end of Mooresville's Main Street holds the spirits of the fans and the boys of many summers. Great plays were made here, as well as great blunders. Once thousands of fans crowded under the sun or under the lights to watch their hometown heroes, the Moors, struggle in a game that some say is very much like life itself; all of us are capable of great deeds and great errors.

This plot of grass and sand was once the home turf of the mill-sponsored team, the Mooresville Moors, who played professional minor league baseball from 1937 through 1953. The Moors tested their mettle against teams from other textile towns in the Carolina piedmont like Concord, Cooleemee, Hickory, Landis, Lexington, Salisbury, Statesville and Thomasville.

One of the most outstanding Moors to ever catch a ball, run the bases or swing a bat at Moor Field was Norman "Butch" Small.

Chris Holaday in his authoritative 1998 book, *Professional Baseball in North Carolina*, has said this about the local lads: "The Mooresville Moors were the most successful team in the history of the N.C. State League, if not the most successful team ever in the state. In their fourteen years in that league, they won three pennants, three post season championships and went to the playoffs every year but three."

If the Moors were the most successful minor league team in the state during those halcyon years, what would that say about the man many consider to be the finest player the Moors ever fielded?

Norman Woodnutt Small was born in Glen Cove, Long Island, New York, on November 16, 1913, the son of Harry and Mary Elizabeth Woodnutt Small. After setting records with his high school ball team, he began his professional career in 1934 as a pitcher in the St. Louis Cardinal's Class D farm team in Martinsville, Virginia, "the Manufacturers." He lost his first game, but won the next nine in a row that summer. After tearing a ligament in his throwing arm, he left the mound for the outfield. Even with this injury, he led the Bi-State League, of which Martinsville was a part, in hitting that season.

In 1935 he came to North Carolina and played center field for the Class B Asheville Tourists. At mid-season he was sent back to Martinsville to replace an outfielder who had been injured. He began the 1936 season playing for the White Roses of York, Pennsylvania, but eventually his contract was bought by the Moors and he came to Mooresville where he soon met Sarah Sherrill, a local girl, and niece of the Moors' manager, Byron Hager. Although the Moors came in at seventh place with a 35 and 64 record that year in the so-called "outlaw" Carolina League, Small impressed all who saw him play with his intensity, his athleticism and his grit.

In June of the 1937, the middle of the season, Small's contract was sold to the Durham Bulls for $2,500. At the time he had a batting average of .350. In spite of losing one of the best all-round players, the Moors went on to grab the league championship, their first, in September. Small must have been cheering his friends back on the Moors team and thinking of them. He was also thinking a lot about Miss Sarah Sherrill.

The September 2, 1937, issue of the old *Mooresville Enterprise* tells more about Butch and Sarah: "A wedding which has caused much interest throughout sports circles in the state took place last Sunday afternoon at the Durham ball park, Durham, when Miss Sarah Small of this city became the bride of Mr. Norman Small of Long Island, N.Y. The ceremony was witnessed by thousands of ball fans and friends of the bride and groom from all sections of the state, and during the ceremony, which took place just prior to the game, the immense throng sat in perfect silence while the vows were spoken. A chaplain of the United States Army heard the vows and amplifiers were used so that all might hear. An orchestra played ' O Promise Me.'

"At third base she was joined by the groom, walking with him to home plate where an altar had been improvised.... The game that afternoon was between the Bulls and the Asheville team, and the players came from their dug-outs, crossing each other, to form a line for the couple to pass through after the ceremony. They stood with their bats crossed, forming an archway."

This sounds much like a scene in the 1988 Kevin Costner movie, "Bull Durham."

Len Sullivan of the *Mooresville Tribune* interviewed Norman Small in 1961. Recalled Small about the day of his wedding, "I had a pretty good day all around. I married Sarah and got three for four—a single, a double and a triple."

In 1938 Small was again traded, this time to Cincinnati, and after a brief stint with the minor league Red Hawks in Waterloo, Iowa, was sent as a center fielder to Cincinnati's Class B farm team, the Reds, in Columbia, S.C. Next he played with the Meridian, Mississippi, Scrappers of the Southeastern League in 1939, but returned to Mooresville in 1940. Small, who finished the season with an impressive .346 batting average, 25 home runs and 115 RBIs, and a Salisbury player were the unanimous choices for the *Salisbury Post's* North Carolina State League's All-Star Team, selected by the eight managers of the circuit.

As a team, the Moors did not fare as well as Small, and finished the season in fourth place with a 60 and 51 record and by being in the top four, qualified for the playoffs but lost to the Lexington Indians four games to one.

In July of 1941 *Mooresville Tribune* Editor Tom McKnight summarized Small's contribution to the Moors, "...It has been

Norman Small...who has been largely responsible for making baseball in Mooresville what it is today from the standpoint of the fans. Always colorful, always a potential fence-buster, Norman has been the greatest drawing card in the local park, and among the best around the loop."

Once again Norman Small led the Moors with a .332 batting average and 18 homers in 1941 play. The Moors moved up a notch and concluded the regular season in third place (57-43), but in post-season play, the Moors were defeated by the Salisbury Giants, four games to three.

The 1942 season saw the Moors improve their standings again, moving into second place by the season's conclusion, with 61 wins versus 39 losses. Once more, however, they botched the playoffs, this time to the Landis Millers. Small, however, led the league in 1942 in home runs (32), RBIs (107) and hits (144). His batting average was .376.

Following the 1942 season Small left the Moors and went into spring training with the New York Giants in early 1943. This might have been the well-deserved break into the major leagues that he had hoped for. Wanting to see him in action, he played as a center fielder in 52 games with the Giants' AAA farm team of the International League, the Jersey City Giants, just one rung on the ladder, just one step, below the majors.

Small was hitting .309 in May before being drafted into military service. He served in the 97th Infantry "Trident" Division, part of General George Patton's Third Army in Europe, and then served in the Pacific in the occupation of Japan. He had attained the rank of sergeant before being discharged in 1946.

Back in the States, he played one month again in Jersey City, was released early, and returned to Mooresville in May of 1946. Small was at the top of his form and back in Mooresville, where he wanted to be.

The 1946 baseball season was to be a time of rebuilding for the Moors. During 1945 they had been part of the short-lived "Victory League," and as a farm team for the Boston Braves were known that year as the "Mooresville Braves," the only time in the team's history when they were not the "Moors." As such they had finished the season in sixth place of eight teams.

Now, in 1946, they were the Moors again and went on to win five more than they lost, finishing fourth place in the regular season and qualifying for the playoffs. They went on to take the league championship from the Concord Weavers in the finals. This was a big upset, as the Weavers had concluded the regular season 19 games ahead of the Moors. Norman Small, who managed the team that year and in 1947 and 1948, led the league with 100 runs, 31 doubles and 18 homers to his credit. He also took on the duties of team manager midway in the season.

"Manager Bob Crow slugged umpire Bob Weaver in June, so the management gave me the club. We were in sixth place. By the end of the season we had moved up far enough for a place in the playoffs and we won by beating Landis in seven games and Concord in six," Small later recalled.

The golden year for hometown ball was probably 1947. The Moors really had the talent that year. Players and male fans were back from the war and had settled in as civilians and ball players and television had not yet invaded local living rooms. WBT in Charlotte would not sign on until June of 1949. People wanted to get out of their houses in the summer—no one had air-conditioning—and the local ball park was the place to go.

The 1947 season opened on May 1 at Moor Park. In a full-page ad, *The Tribune* featured player/manager Norman Small, summarizing his statistics for the fans. They were impressive. Reported the *Tribune*, "...Small has hit 158 home runs, 66 triples, 268 doubles. He has an all-time batting average of .332 for his

13 years in baseball. He has never been ejected from a game... has been known...for his keen competitive spirit and his fine sportsmanship."

In 1947 the Moors won the pennant and the championship of the N.C. State League, their third time, with a final tally of 68 and 43. The Moors brimmed with talent. Besides Small, there was Hoyt Wilhelm from nearby Cornelius with his mesmerizing knuckleball, Ross Morrow's batting skills and the equally impressive pitching talents of Tom McCall and Stony Point's Dave Jolly.

The Moors played as semi-pros for the 1954 season in the Granite Belt League and Norman Small was listed as a player in some pre-season publicity. It is doubtful, however, if he played in more than a handful of games, if any. After a few pre-season articles, there was no further coverage of that year's team in *The Tribune.*

During a textile slump the Mooresville Mills management undertook some cost-cutting measures. In January of 1954 the mill management stunned the town by announcing that they would no longer be sponsoring a baseball team. The mill had supported a ball team since at least 1919.

That announcement was the death knell of an era in Mooresville. No longer would E. T. "Pig" Christenbury sell tickets at the gate. No longer would O. C. Stonestreet Sr. paint ball scores on the plate glass windows of his cafe and give free steak dinners to homerun-hitting Moors.

* * *

Although born on Long Island, New York, Small always considered Mooresville his home. To quote from his 1961 *Tribune* interview again, he said, "I knew when I came here in 1936 that

I had found a home. Mooresville is the friendliest town I have ever seen."

Butch Small was called out by the Ultimate Umpire on Christmas Eve, 1995, and is buried in Glenwood Cemetery, Mooresville, beside his Sarah, who preceded him in death by a little more than a year. They had no children. Norman was 82 years old and had outlived most of his contemporaries.

The Mooresville Tribune carried his obituary in its Dec. 27, 1995, issue. It was brief, just 22 column-lines, and it contained only one sentence about his baseball career: "Mr. Small was a former manager and ball player for the Moors Baseball Team."

In his many seasons he had consistently given his best to at least a dozen different teams in 1,703 minor league games and had worn the blue and white of the Mooresville Moors for about half his career. He had a lifetime batting average of .323 and had 486 home runs to his credit. Some said he could have gone into the majors but preferred to have a home and be with his wife. He had been a man with whom the locals identified and respected. "Hero" may not be too strong a word.

Mooresville resident Tex Millard, who scouted players for the Washington Senators, Cincinnati Reds and St. Louis Browns, penned a couple of books about baseball. In his 1982 book, *They Came to Play,* he stated that Butch Small was "the most popular player who ever played for Mooresville...and the best player I ever saw in minor league baseball."

An umpire once summed up Norman "Butch" Small as "a gentleman off the field, a sportsman on it," which is not a bad epitaph for anyone.

HERM STARRETTE

There is an old story, a myth maybe, that in the olden days hardcore baseball fans would gather in country stores, barber shops, hardware stores and similar places in the depths of winter to discuss their baseball team's prospects for the coming season. The men involved in these informal get-togethers were collectively referred to as the "Hot Stove League."

So, pretend you are in a country store of yesteryear. Prop your feet up near the pot-bellied stove, grab a MoonPie and an RC Cola and think about a local lad who has done pretty well for himself, Herman Paul "Herm" Starrette.

Starrette began his involvement with our national pastime in the old ball field behind Cool Spring Elementary School in the early 1950s, coached by teacher Paul Brendle. He pitched in every game from 1953 to 1956 for Cool Spring's Red Devils. The team won the county championship in 1955. "I had a good slider," he explains.

When his class made its annual senior trip to New York, it took in a game at Yankee Stadium. Starrette says he sat there in the bleachers, daydreaming about being a player out on that green, green field. He told his fellow classmates that someday he would be out there and they said, "Yeah, you'll be out there, as a water boy!"

Starrette graduated from Cool Spring High in spring of 1956. Nine years later, in 1963, Herm Starrette was in the bullpen at Yankee Stadium, wearing an American League Baltimore Orioles uniform, warming up to pitch against the New York Yankees, including Roger Maris and Hall-of-Famer Mickey Mantle, in front of 56,000 fans on a Saturday afternoon.

* * *

Born in Statesville in November of 1936, Herm listened to Orioles and Cardinals games on the radio with his father, Rob, who also took him and his siblings to see the old Statesville Owls games.

"I came from a sports-oriented family; ever since I can remember, I wanted to play baseball," he says.

After high school he played for Lenoir-Rhyne College Bears on a baseball scholarship but left L-R when he was offered a position with the Baltimore Orioles. He signed with them on June 13, 1958.

For nine years, 1958 to 1966, he was a right-handed pitcher with the Orioles organization. From 1963 to 1965, he appeared in 27 Major League Baseball games and pitched in 46 innings.

But it is as a pitching coach that Herm Starrette will likely be best remembered. He was a pitching coach with the Rochester Red Wings, the Orioles' AAA farm team, then was pitching coach for the Atlanta Braves in 1974 and served in a variety of positions with seven major league teams, ending up with the Boston Red Sox.

His greatest claim to fame may be that he was pitching coach for the world champion Philadelphia Phillies in 1980 and consequently has a World Series ring with a diamond in it commemorating that series.

He also has a 1970 World Series ring for his contributions to the Orioles as their minor league pitching coordinator.

In 1980 the Phillies defeated the Kansas City Royals in a six-game series, October 14 to October 21, capturing their first World Series title. The series was notable historically in that it was the first World Series played entirely on artificial turf.

Starrette has been out of Major League Baseball for some time now, retiring as a farm system official and coach in the Red Sox organization.

Herm married Betty Sigmon, an Iredell County lady, in 1960. They have a daughter and son-in-law, Lisa and Scott Bass, and a granddaughter, Laura Bass.

Sitting around the kitchen table at his home in the Cool Springs community, Herm and I talked about baseball and life. There is an old baseball on the table. Herm holds it, turns it, rubs it, as he talks.

Looking out a large kitchen window, he remarked that as a boy he used to pick cotton in the field that is now his yard. I asked him what the best thing about baseball was.

"The best thing about the game of baseball, for me," he said as he picked at the stitching of the ball in his hand with a fingernail, "is that it helped me to grow up, taught me to be a better person; I learned to communicate with people. One thing that you find out quickly is that you're not the best in the world. Baseball, maybe all sports, toughens you mentally and you have to be tough mentally to play sports."

How about Football versus Baseball as a game?" I asked.

"Professional baseball teams play 162 games a season, not counting pre-season exhibitions and play-offs. A professional football team plays 16 games in a regular season.

"There's no clock in baseball. Yeah, sometimes the game gets slow, but as Yogi Berra said, 'It ain't over till it's over.' I've seen teams come back from being five or six runs behind to win the game in the last inning. Life can be like that, too."

He continued: "There were three people who helped me the most in my game. The first was my high school coach, Paul Brendle. We are still good friends. Earl Weaver was my manager for three years in the Orioles and George Bamberger, who was an instructor for the Orioles' minor league teams. They helped me understand the finer points of the game. I also owe a lot to Jerry Fox, my catcher at Cool Spring, who encouraged me to go on to college and play ball there."

I asked if he had a favorite baseball movie.

He mentioned several and then said, "Honestly, I like any baseball movie that has someone playing Babe Ruth in it."

Herm doesn't go to many games today, but he is working with a couple of promising high school boys, pro bono, and now and then he speaks to youngsters at schools, telling them how important an education is.

"I'm proud of what I accomplished," he said, tossing the ball in the air.

RICHARD N. SUMMERS

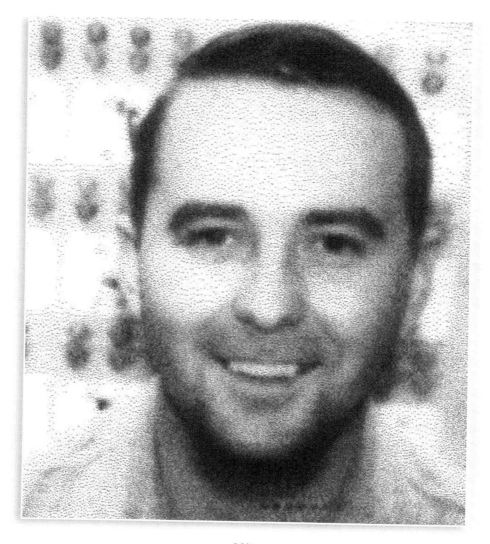

Richard Norman Summers was a casualty of what the history books now call "The Cold War," the political conflict between the forces of democracy and the forces of the Communism. Summers died in 1968, but not in Vietnam, although that war was consuming American lives at a horrific rate that year. Summers' name is not to be found on Iredell County's Vietnam Memorial. Not all those who gave their lives for this country died in the heat of battle.

Richard Summers was a Yeoman 3rd Class aboard the nuclear attack submarine *USS Scorpion* (SSN-589) when it and its 99-man crew became overdue in port in late May, 1968.

Besides the hot, shooting war in Southeast Asia, there was an intense Cold War going on between the United States and its allies and the Soviet Union and its allies. A very critical part of that undeclared but very real conflict was the ceaseless gathering of intelligence about the other side's military hardware. An integral part of this potentially lethal cat-and-mouse-game was played out between American and Soviet submarines. Their toys were the most deadly and stealthy their respective technologies could devise.

A FREE SPIRIT

The youngest of the seven children of Charles and Hila Summers, Richard liked to make people, particularly his family, laugh at his antics. Like many boys of the time he built plastic models of cars and airplanes, even models of submarines. His sister Carolyn also remembered that her brother had liked submarines from the time he was a young boy. His older brother Bill, who had served in the Navy, encouraged him to go in that direction and told him that if he were going to be a Sailor, the best duty was aboard submarines, which have the reputation of having the best food in the Armed Forces.

Larry King, Richard's best friend and the driver of Summers' school bus, recalled his friend's enthusiasm for life. "He was a fun guy, he liked to have fun. He loved life, he really did." King went on to describe his friend as "an above average boy, quick and witty."

King said, "He could do all right in school just by listening well in class, but there was a bit of the daredevil in him. He liked fast cars and was a good mechanic. Everybody liked Richard."

Summers' sister, Carolyn, said much the same thing, characterizing her brother as a "free spirit." She said her brother didn't have time for a lot of extracurricular activities, as he had to help on the family dairy farm and later at the little gas station/ grocery her father operated near the intersection of Highway 115 and Scotts Road. Still, Summers did fairly well at Scotts High School.

His football coach and geography teacher, Kenneth Wilson, remembered Summers well, even recalling where Summers sat in his classroom. Wilson recalled, "I remember him as being a unique person, an independent, quick thinker, with a mind of his own. That was a neat time to be in education and there were some really good, sharp kids at Scotts."

His senior year Summers was recognized as having the "Most School Spirit," was president of the school's Future Farmers of America chapter and was a member of the student council. His favorite teacher was probably Tom Setzer, the strict but respected agriculture teacher, who had taken Richard under his wing.

SUBMARINER

After graduating from Scotts in the spring of 1964, Summers took some classes at Mitchell College and worked at the Forest Heights Service Station. He joined the local unit of the Naval Reserve in November of 1965 and went on active duty in March of the following year. He graduated from the Navy's Yeoman School in Maryland in May, 1967, and finished Submarine School in Connecticut that August.

A Navy yeoman is like a company clerk in the Army. Yeomen do secretarial and clerical work, maintain files and service records and perform other office duties.

Summers joined the *USS Scorpion*'s crew in August of 1967. The ship had then been in service for seven years, having been commissioned on July 29, 1960. In 1962 it set an underwater endurance record of 70 days.

LAST CRUISE

Scorpion left its home port of Norfolk, Virginia, on February 15, 1968, to take part in training exercises in the Mediterranean. Sixth Fleet exercises concluded, the ship headed homeward. Its last radio transmission on May 21 gave its position as some 250 miles south of the Azores. *Scorpion* had been expected to arrive in Norfolk between May 24 and May 27. It was officially listed as overdue at 1300 hours (1 p.m.) on May 27. After being overdue for 24 hours, the Navy began a search.

THE SEARCH

Some 60 ships and an uncounted number of aircraft combed the sea for signs of the lost submarine. Newspapers reported this hunt as "the largest search in naval history."

The Navy initially concentrated its efforts in the area around Norfolk, where the relatively shallow seabed might have allowed a damaged submarine to survive. Hopes ran high on May 31 when it was reported that a metallic object the size and shape of a submarine had been detected at a depth of 180 feet, about 70 miles east of the Virginia capes, but this turned out to be the wreck of a World War II German U-boat.

The next cause for hope came when a radio transmission using the name "Brandywine," the code name for *Scorpion*, was intercepted. Further investigation, however, revealed that there were at least eight vessels operating in the Atlantic using that name at that time.

When *Scorpion* was not located near our coast, the search was extended along the vessel's presumed course across the North Atlantic. The Navy brought out its most sophisticated hardware, including vessels capable of reaching vast depths. By then hopes for the recovery of the vessel and its 99-man crew were gone.

Carolyn remembered how the news of her brother's death affected her mother, who found out about the fate of *The Scorpion* on the 6 p.m. TV news: "My mother quit living on the day she heard the news. It was her child, her baby. Out of seven children, he was her baby. Momma died about two years later.

"I put (his death) in the back of my mind for a long time. I just couldn't even think about it—my sweet baby brother."

QUESTIONS REMAIN

An official inquiry held during the first week of June revealed that *Scorpion* had reported a problem: she was taking on seven gallons of water a minute through a leak in the propeller shaft. Sources said this was not considered a "significant" problem, though the ship had been scheduled to be dry docked for repairs when it reached Norfolk. There was also some conflicting testimony that the leak had been corrected or at least brought under control by the crew.

There were other theories as well. One was that a problem in the sub's electrical system had led to the failure of the propulsion system.

There was also speculation that a Mark 37 torpedo might have malfunctioned and inadvertently have self-activated in one of the torpedo tubes during a routine inspection. This particular model torpedo was found to have a serious defect in its batteries and the official naval inquiry listed this as the most likely cause of the loss of the $40 million ship and its crew.

NO CLOSURE

The mystery of the loss of the *Scorpion* has not diminished over the years, but rather increased. Several books have been written about *The Scorpion* in recent years: *Blind Man's Bluff: The Untold Story of American Submarine Espionage* (1998); *Silent Steel: The Mysterious Death of the Nuclear Attack Sub USS Scorpion* (2006); *Scorpion Down: Sunk by the Soviets, Buried by the Pentagon—The Untold Story of the USS Scorpion (2007);* and *All Hands Down: The True Story of the Soviet Attack on the USS Scorpion* (2008).

Most recently *Stalking the Red Bear: The True Story of a U.S. Cold War Submarine's Covert Operations Against the Soviet Union* was published in 2009. While not about *The Scorpion,* but rather a fictitious nuclear sub, the book explains some of the challenges faced by today's submariners.

Another book, *Red Star Rogue: The Untold Story of a Soviet Submarine's Nuclear Strike Attempt on the U.S.,* published in 2005, also suggests that *Scorpion* may have been deliberately sunk by the Soviets in retaliation for the sinking, caused by us, of one of their submarines in March, 1968.

Red November: Inside the Secret U.S.-Soviet Submarine War, by W. Craig Reed (2010), lay the blame on leaking hydrogen from defective TLX-53-A main storage batteries, and estimates a explosive yield of "not more than 20 pounds of TNT each," which in a confined space would have been ample to sink the *Scorpion.*

A variation of this last hypothesis is that *Scorpion* and a Soviet sub accidentally collided in the depths.

The whole truth about the last hours of *The Scorpion* will probably never be known. The Navy has officially stated that the ship was lost on May 22, 1968, probably due to an explosion.

Whatever the cause, on June 6, 1968, the Navy officially ordered flags to be flown at half mast at all U.S. Navy installations and on all Navy vessels. A memorial service for the 12 officers and 87 enlisted men of *The Scorpion* was held in Norfolk that same day. Eight members of Richard Summers' family attended the service.

Locally, services for the young sailor were held at Concord Presbyterian Church in Loray on October 27th. An honor guard composed of members of the local Naval Reserve unit, of which Petty Officer Summers had once been a member, was present at the service.

About the same time that the local service was being held, parts of the hull of *The Scorpion* were located by the research ship *USNS Mizar* at a depth of 10,000 feet, some 400 miles west of the Azores, and the deep-submersible *Trieste* was able to take photographs of the debris field on the ocean floor. Even though the photographs were of poor quality, they were clear enough to identify the ship, which had been missing for five months by then.

The Woods Hole Oceanographic Institute made an investigation of the wreckage 30 years after her sinking and the results of that study have not lessened the mystery surrounding the ship. There is no closure in sight.

Petty Officer Third Class Richard Norman Summers, USN, was survived by his parents, by sisters Dorothy, Mary Julia and Carolyn, and by brothers William, James and Donald. There is a grave marker to his memory in the Summers' plot in Iredell Memorial Gardens.

A tradition of long standing in the Navy's "Silent Service" is that those submarines and their crews, such as in the case of *Scorpion*, are not referred to as deceased, but are said to be "On Eternal Patrol."

TED TAYLOR

A very interesting man passed away at his home in California on October 26, 2006. His name was Theodore "Ted" Taylor. "Never heard of him," you say?

To be perfectly honest, when I read of his passing in an email to the *Record & Landmark*, I was unfamiliar with his name, too. His daughter Wendy, though, helped fill me in: He was probably the most prolific author to ever call Iredell County his homeplace.

Born in Statesville on June 23, 1921, he was the last of six children of Edward and Eleanora Langhans Taylor. He never intended to become a writer and never graduated from high school, but became involved with newspapers at an early age. The newsrooms of five different papers were his GED and college diploma. He said, "I loved the excitement of writing under pressure, the smell of fresh ink, and the rumble of the presses."

He became a sports writer and then served as a lieutenant in the Merchant Marine and the Navy in World War II. During a part of that time he served aboard a tanker transporting gasoline across the North Atlantic. Think for a moment of what a German U-boat torpedo would do to a slow-moving tanker filled with 73,000 barrels of high-octane aviation gasoline.

Taylor fell in love with the sea and the islands and they were featured prominently in many of his short stories and novels. Taylor eventually penned more than 50 books, many of them for young readers. His first book, *The Magnificent Mitscher*, was a biography of American World War II Admiral Marc "Pete" Mitscher, and came out in 1954.

After the war, Taylor, still in the Navy, was present at the testing of atomic weapons at Bikini Atoll. That experience led to another book, the historical novel, *The Bomb* (1995).

His autobiography appeared in 2005, *Making Love to Typewriters* (Ivy House Publishing Group, Raleigh) and in that work Taylor presents us with some excellent verbal photographs, given in the quotes below, of growing up in Statesville in the 1920s—the family moved to Virginia in 1931. There is a copy of *Making Love to Typewriters* in the Iredell County Public Library.

Regarding autobiographies, Taylor once wrote, "Writing one's own history is eventually frightening—an entire compressed life on the chopping block."

Things were different in the 1920s. For instance, how many of today's mothers would have allowed the following:

"Mother said that she thought it was fine when I told her I'd gotten a paper route. I was up at 4 in the morning to walk to the Vance Hotel and wait for the Greyhound driver to toss off the *Greensboro Daily News.* Moving through the still darkness at age nine, not once did I think of harm. Then off to school I trudged in knickers and cap."

At about this same age, he and several chums constructed a raft and started on a cruise down the old Catawba River like Huckleberry Finn. Wrote Taylor, "Never once did my mother ask, 'Where are you going?' Off to explore, of course. A very religious lady, she trusted God that I'd come safely home. Several times I came close to joining Him."

Because his father was frequently gone from home seeking work during the Great Depression, young Taylor found a friend in a next door neighbor, "Next we lived in a house on Walnut Street owned by a Dr. Anderson who lived next door in a truly grand house. His children were adults, gone from the hearth, and Dr. Anderson, an elderly man, became my companion on many occasions. He took me to Ringling Brothers, Barnum and Bailey, or whatever circuses came to town; he took me to carnivals and to other events exciting to children."

Ted Taylor's first job with a newspaper came when at age 13 he did a high school sports column for his hometown paper in Portsmouth, Virginia. His pay was fifty cents a week.

In between books, Taylor worked as an editor, as a publicist, a film director and producer. He seemed to prefer writing for himself; he did well in the motion picture industry and work there allowed him to travel around the world.

He also worked with some of Hollywood's legends, such as Clark Gable, Frank Sinatra, Steve McQueen, William Holden, Charlton Heston, Tippi Hedren and Jerry Lewis, to name but a few.

His best known book was his award-winning novel, *The Cay*, written in 1968, which was made into a Universal Picture of the same title in 1974, starring James Earl Jones. Taylor claimed to have written the book in just three weeks; the boy in the story was based on a pal he knew in Statesville. It eventually sold over five million copies, won eleven literary awards and was required reading in schools in many states.

Ted Taylor put down his pen for the last time on Thursday, October 26, 2006, at his home in Laguna Beach, California. He was 85.

Besides his daughter, Wendy, he was survived by his wife, Flora, two sons, a stepdaughter, two stepsons, five grandchildren and two great-grandchildren.

He acknowledged that his early experiences in Iredell County fired his imagination and supplied him with a palette of personalities for his fictional adventures.

He wrote, "I roamed fields and muddy creeks and other interesting places around and about town; the abandoned headquarters of the volunteer cavalry...the old brickyard, the strong-smelling building where chewing tobacco had once been manufactured; numerous drainpipes and other places of mystery."

Not all, but some parts of "the good old days" were very good for little explorers in knickers and cap.

DAVID LAWRENCE THOMAS

Technically, Second Lieutenant David Lawrence Thomas's name should not appear on the memorial to Iredell County's Korean War and Vietnam War dead which stands on the lawn of the Hall of Justice, as he died about three months after the Department of Defense's cut-off date for the Korean War. He died in the service of his country during that thin slice of time between the Korean War and the beginning of our country's involvement in Vietnam. Also, Lt. Thomas had not been part of the air war over that peninsula in far-off Asia.

Officially, for government purposes, the Korean War, or "Police Action" as it was euphemistically called, lasted from June 27, 1950, to July 27, 1954. But the young lieutenant's death October 21, 1954, was just as real, just as tragic to his family and friends as if he had been shot down over "MiG Alley."

As his brother told it, the F-94C Lockheed "Starfire" jet fighter simply dropped out of formation and headed into the ground. Witnesses reported that there was no apparent attempt to bail-out of the aircraft by either officer, nor was there any radio transmission indicating there was trouble.

The two Air Force officers in the jet, the pilot and the radar-systems officer, died on impact.

The pilot was Lt. Charles D. Vrmeer of Oakland, California. The man in the rear seat, the radar operator, was Second Lieutenant David Lawrence Thomas, of Mooresville. The date was October 21, 1954, and the place was the foot of the Bear Paw Mountains near Cleveland, Montana.

Thomas, 23, was one of six children of Theodore and Lovell Phifer Thomas of West Moore Avenue, Mooresville. He was born in Mooresville in 1931 and was a 1949 graduate of Dunbar High School. For two years he had attended North Carolina College in Durham, now known as North Carolina

Central University, and had been in the Air Force for three years, having enlisted in 1951.

The flight was a routine training flight, said Thomas' brother, retired Air Force Major Felton A. Thomas, a resident of Fayetteville, North Carolina. "I suspect that the jet went down due to a failure in the oxygen system, which would explain why they didn't attempt to eject, call for help, or try to alter the path of the aircraft," said his brother.

Lt. Thomas had been a member of the 29th Fighter Interceptor Squadron, a part of the Air Force's Air Defense Command, stationed at Great Falls Air Force Base in Montana. He had been married only seventeen days at the time of his death.

Final rites for Lt. Thomas were held at Mooresville's Reid Memorial Presbyterian Church on October 28, a week after his death. As a young man Thomas had joined Reid's Memorial by Profession of Faith.

Thomas was buried, with full military honors, at the National Military Cemetery in Salisbury.

The program for Thomas' funeral at Reid's Memorial Church contains a sentence summing up his life and career: "His short life was a life of service to Church, School, Community, State and Nation."

After the Vietnam War, Iredell citizens wanted a permanent marker put up to record the names of those who had made the ultimate sacrifice in the two post-World War II conflicts. There were errors and omissions made in several of the names submitted for the memorial.

Lt. Thomas, 23, died in the line of duty for his country and his name is now, literally, set in stone. Would it really matter had he died three months earlier?

D. MATT THOMPSON

You could walk right past the grave of D. Matt Thompson in Statesville's Oakwood Cemetery and never notice it. The headstone—there is no foot stone—is plain and rectangular and is almost flush with the ground. It reads simply, "D. Matt Thompson June 5, 1845-June 30, 1925." You would have thought a man as important as "Professor" Thompson would have a more grandiose marker for his final resting place.

David Matthew Thompson was born on June 5, 1844, near Long's Mills in Randolph County, the son of Samuel and Elizabeth Moser Thompson.

In 1862 at the age of 18 he volunteered for Confederate military service, joining Company "H" of the 3rd North Carolina Infantry Regiment. He was severely wounded at the Battle of Gettysburg and was afterwards transferred to Company "F" of the Second North Carolina Cavalry. While in the Second Cavalry Regiment at Deep Bottom, Virginia, on August 15, 1864, he received his second severe wound, which permanently crippled his left arm. At war's end he was a sergeant in the Provost Guard at Richmond, Va.

Returning home, he worked on the family farm for several years and then entered Sylvan Academy in Alamance County. He next attended Cook County Normal School in Chicago. Iredell historian Homer Keever states that Thompson also earned a master's degree from Rutherford College.

Coming back to North Carolina, Thompson began a distinguished career in education. He taught in a private school, then at Sylvan Academy. Next, he founded the Aurora Academy in Chatham County and conducted that school until he was made principal of the Rock Spring Seminary in Lincoln County in 1873.

Thompson married Miss Lizzie Rice of Randolph County in August of 1872, and from this union there were three sons:

Holland, who became a history professor; Walter, who became the superintendent of the Methodist Orphanage in Winston-Salem; and Dorman, who became a Statesville attorney.

Thompson stayed at Rock Spring for almost ten years, then served as the county superintendent and chairman of the board of education of Lincoln County. By 1884 he was principal of the Piedmont Seminary in Lincolnton.

From here Thompson went to be the superintendent of the public schools in Gainesville, Florida, and it was from Florida that he came to Statesville.

In 1891 he was interviewed and elected as the first superintendent of the newly-formed Statesville Graded Schools, a position he would hold for almost thirty years. His salary was $1,000 per year.

It is interesting to note that the staunchest opponent of the Statesville City Schools was none other than *The Landmark*'s publisher and editor, J. P. Caldwell. In the February 2, 1883, issue Caldwell wrote, "We are very well acquainted with all the arguments in favor of a popular [tax-supported] education, and we concur in every one of them; but for all that, we make bold to say that as the case now stands, the taxpayers are paying as much money in this interest as they can well afford to pay. We set our face as a flint against any scheme to amend the constitution so that more tax can be levied for school purposes."

Basically, Editor Caldwell felt that learning beyond the "Three R's" was a luxury and tax money shouldn't be used for that purpose. Caldwell changed his mind after hearing a speech by State School Superintendent Charles D. McGiver and became a great supporter of the city school system.

The Statesville Graded Schools opened for students on September 23, 1891. The first day's attendance figures were 170 white students and 32 black students, but the system grew rapidly. By March of 1893 there were 393 white students and 212 black students enrolled.

There was no one building large enough for all the students, so school for white children was held in separate locations: a building across the street from where the Mulberry School would be built, the old Male Academy Building, and in what was described as a "new" school building near the cemetery in the eastern part of town.

Black children were educated in two locations: an old Negro school building and in the black Baptist church.

Therefore, Professor Thompson's first order of business was to begin the construction of new school buildings. By January of 1893, the school building on Mulberry Street was completed. It featured separate rooms for the different grades, first through seventh, hence the term, "graded school."

A new school for black students was also completed, "a very good frame building, both for the cost of about $12,000."

An eight grade was added to the Mulberry School and then in 1907 a ninth grade was added, giving Statesville its first high school.

Thompson's office was in the Mulberry School building, rather than in an office downtown, and "Professor Thompson," as he was called, actually taught classes.

In November of 1920, Thompson was struck by an automobile while crossing Center Street in front of the Federal Building—now Statesville City Hall. He never recovered from the injuries and died while a patient at the State Hospital in Morganton a little more than four years later. He was succeeded as superintendent by Robert MacDonald "Mac" Gray.

At the time of his passing the Statesville schools served about 2,300 students. A new high school building was ready to open on West Front Street, now Mitchell Community College's Continuing Education facility.

In 1927 the city school board unanimously decided to name the new school building "D. Matt Thompson High School" in the professor's honor and memory.

The Front Street building had already opened in January of 1922, at which time the building on Mulberry Street became an elementary school. A new school for black students had also recently opened on Garfield and Green Streets.

D. Matt Thompson High School served Statesville from 1922 through 1946, and then was used as a junior high school until 1986. The property was acquired by Mitchell Community College that year and the college began holding classes there in March of the next year, following renovations and up-grades.

In his July 2, 1925, obituary, *The Landmark* remarked that by a conservative estimate, Prof. Thompson had taught some 10,000 students.

Perhaps the Professor's most lasting monument was not a cold, horizontal slab of stone in Oakwood Cemetery, but an educated, upstanding citizenry in Iredell and surrounding counties.

JAMES R. WALKER SR.

Here's another of what used to be known as a "Horatio Alger story," a story of a person born to humble circumstances who rose to success through dogged determination and just plain hard work, sometimes called "pulling yourself up by your own bootstraps." This story is appropriate for February, which is Black History Month, but it also stands as a lesson for all of us any time of the year.

James Robert Walker Sr. was born on January 10, 1885, in a log cabin in Henderson, Kentucky. His parents died while he was an infant and he was raised by grandparents.

In a 1955 *Record & Landmark* interview, he said that he had no recollection of his father at all and the only recollection of his mother was "so vague I often think it's a dream. I realize, though, that my parents, who were living in Henderson at the time of my birth, were very poor."

As a young man he attended St. Clement's Mission, an Episcopal school in Henderson, and studied there through the seventh grade.

In 1904, when he was 19, he entered Hampton Institute in Hampton, Virginia. He worked on the institute's 600-acre farm as a milker his first year, working during the day and attending classes at night. His grandparents died during his freshman year, which added to his financial difficulties.

One of his instructors inspired him to persevere. The Rev. J. M. Munday took Walker and some other students to a classroom window, pointed to a drunkard staggering down the street, and told the group that they could be like the drunkard or they could "be another Booker T. Washington."

While at Hampton, Walker saw the obituary and a photograph of Paul Laurence Dunbar, the black poet, on the door of the institute's library. Walker's daughter, Muriel, related what happened next: "At that moment he felt a sharp blow on the shoulder and a voice in his ear told him, 'You're next, write!'"

When his academic education was interrupted by the lack of funds, he found employment at the shipyards of Newport News, Virginia, making a dime an hour for a ten-hour day.

In 1913 he was accepted as a student at North Carolina Agricultural and Technical College in Greensboro. After two years there, his education was interrupted again and he left NCA&T, returning to the shipyards in Newport News during World War I.

After the war he returned to NCA&T. To pay for his classes he took the worst job at the college: tending pigs on the college's farm. According to the *Record & Landmark* interview, Walker said that he "would haul slop in a horse-drawn wagon and stayed in the animal barns instead of on campus his first year. Working thusly, he attended night school throughout his first year and then, in his second, entered day school."

He did this until he graduated valedictorian of the Class of 1921 with a degree in Agriculture. His commencement speech was aptly entitled, "In Spite of It."

For two years following graduation, Walker taught at the Hereford County Training School in Ashokie, N.C. Busy as he was, he jotted down verse in his spare time.

The year 1923 was a pivotal one in Walker's life. He moved to a place near the Iredell/Rowan county line and taught at the R. A. Clement School in Cleveland, N.C. He continued to teach there and in area schools for the next twenty-five years. That same year, 1923, he married Ethel Lee Dockery, daughter of the Rev. Zander A. Dockery, of Statesville, a leader in Iredell County black education and religion. The couple eventually had three sons and five daughters.

In 1923 Walker self-published 1,000 copies of his first book of poetry, *Poetical Diets*. Walker continued to teach in segregated black public schools until his retirement in 1948.

From 1948 to 1953, he served as a special instructor with the Veterans' Administration Farm Program in North Wilkesboro.

In 1953 he began to give "poetry reading tours" at black high schools and colleges within the state, an activity he pursued for at least a dozen years. With the black community he was respectfully known as "Professor Walker."

In 1955 Comet Press of New York published his second book of poems, *Be Firm My Hope*.

Walker was quoted as saying, "I'm not a racial poet, but one who writes for the sake of humanity." Of his *Be Firm My Hope*, he said, "The entire volume is dedicated to humanity with divine intuition as its motive. Even when I'm at my work I will look toward the sky and say, 'Reveal it to me, Master,' and then I write as the Lord would have me do."

New York's Carlton Press published his third volume of poetry, *Musings of Childhood*, in 1960 and published his *Menus of Love* in 1963 and then his *Speak Nature* in 1965.

His wife passed away in 1981 and two years later Walker, then 98, died at the home of a daughter in New Jersey. *Rural Life*, to be his sixth book of verse, was unpublished. The poet and his wife are buried in Statesville's Belmont Cemetery.

At the time of Professor Walker's death, he and his wife were survived by their eight children, twenty-five grandchildren and twenty-four great-grandchildren.

Besides being a poet, Walker was an elder and a Sunday school teacher at Broad Street Presbyterian Church in Statesville, a church his father-in-law pastored. It was Walker who suggested the name, "Calvary Presbyterian Church," when Broad Street Presbyterian and three other local churches merged in 1967. Broad Street Presbyterian Church stood about where the offices of the *Record & Landmark* stand today on East Broad Street. The old church building, which was for some time abandoned, was demolished in the fall of 1955 and some of the bricks were reused in the foundations of the R&L building.

Two of Professor Walker's shorter poems are given below:

BLOW, WINTRY WINDS

Blow, O wintry winds, from north and west,
Give humanity the zero test;
Challenge man to answer duty's calls—
Skate on frozen lakes or throw snowballs;
Go to church on square or on the hill,
Or benumb man's heart to do God's will;
Blow, O wintry winds, your aftermath
Makes snowbound road and frozen path
To prevent success of mankind weak;
To make firm the highway strong men seek
As they upward climb to reach the crest

Of life's mountain called—success, there rest
In the confines of the home above—
Made sublime by God's eternal love.

—*from Speak Nature*

PRESS ON

Press on, press on, O mighty man,
Think not to stop, the goal's beyond;
Though great your deeds, though wise you plan,
There's more to come with morning's dawn.

Your deeds, though great, you can't perfect,
Though they for you great laurels win;
Where ends your work, your intellect,
The man tomorrow will begin.

As so today we set the gauge,
Tomorrow's work is thus begun;
But other hands it will engage,
And greater work will then be done.

The rest assured, my fellowman,
Where we here end our work and will,
Some other ones will from our plan
Do work as great and greater still.

—*from Be Firm My Hope*

S. Clay and LuTelle Sherrill Williams

Anyone thinking about who might have been the most successful person to have ever called Iredell County home must consider Samuel Clay Williams as a leading contender.

S. Clay Williams, as he preferred to be called, the son of Thomas Jefferson Williams and wife, Ada McCulloch Williams, was born on his father's farm just south of Mooresville in 1884.

Williams' father was an important early businessman in Mooresville and represented Iredell County for two terms in the state legislature.

Clay Williams went to Davidson College and graduated from that institution, a Phi Beta Kappa, with a bachelor's degree in 1905. After serving as principal of the small Davidson High School, Williams enrolled in the Law School of the University of Virginia, graduating with an LL.B. degree in 1908. While in law school he played the guard position on the university's football team in 1906 and 1907.

Williams married LuTelle Sherrill, daughter of Mooresville Cotton Mills owner James Elbert Sherrill and Emma Harris Sherrill, in 1910. Their wedding was the social event of the season, if not the decade.

The couple had two children, Margaret (Mrs. Thornton Brooks) and S. Clay, Jr., who became a physician.

After being in a partnership with another lawyer for five years, Williams was invited to join the R. J. Reynolds Tobacco Company by Mr. Reynolds himself, as an assistant general counsel in 1917.

Williams' subsequent rise in the corporation was remarkable. He rose to the vice presidency of the company in 1925 and to its presidency in 1931, succeeding Bowman Gray. He rose to become vice chairman of the board in 1934 and became chairman of the board in 1935, a position he would hold until his death in February, 1949.

369

Besides his duties within R. J. Reynolds, Williams took on the duties of Chairman of the National Labor Board for 1933-34, served on the Business Advisory Council of the U.S. Department of Commerce and was chairman of that group.

President Franklin D. Roosevelt successfully persuaded Williams to serve as the head of the National Recovery Administration (NRA), one of Roosevelt's agencies that were created to help end the Great Depression. Williams headed the NRA from September of 1934, to March of 1935.

Time magazine carried an extensive article on Williams in February, 1935. In May, 1935, in the midst of the Great Depression, S. Clay Williams was reckoned to be the highest-paid North Carolinian in the nation, having been paid a salary of $60,000 the previous year at R. J. Reynolds Tobacco. This salary was just $15,000 less than the salary of the President of the United States.

The local paper, the *Mooresville Enterprise*, regularly ran articles about S. Clay Williams, keeping its readership informed of the local man's doings in the corporate business world.

In 1941 President Roosevelt considered the creation of the office of Minister of the U.S. Embassy in London, and offered the position to Williams. Williams respectfully declined, but the two remained friends.

It was Williams' wife, however, who may be remembered more in Mooresville than her husband.

Mooresville attorney Zeb Vance Turlington persuaded Mrs. Williams, an old friend, to donate her parents' homeplace on South Main Street as a permanent site for the Mooresville Public Library. Previously, the library had been located in at least a dozen sites around town.

The story about the library's first permanent home appeared in *The Enterprise* on February 2, 1939. The $15,000 building—very expensive for 1939—was formally opened on December 12, 1939.

At Mrs. Williams' request, some of the original architectural details from the Sherrill home were incorporated into the new library building. Mrs. Williams also made handsome donations to the library in both money and in hand-selected volumes from time to time.

Other charitable work by Mrs. Williams includes the S. Clay Williams Music Scholarship at her alma mater, Converse College, in Spartanburg, S.C., established in 1966 in honor and memory of her husband.

Clay preceded his wife in death by 37 years, passing away in February, 1949, at his country home located midway between Winston-Salem and Mocksville. The country estate was built in eastern Davie County in the late 1920s by Williams who named the place, "Win-Mock," as it was midway between WINston-Salem and MOCKsville.

Mr. Williams, in addition to his position at R. J. Reynolds, was also a director of the American Telephone and Telegraph Company at the time of his passing. He and Mrs. Sherrill had donated $100,000 to Davidson College, his alma mater, earlier in the week of his death.

LuTelle Sherrill Williams passed away on May 3, 1986, at the age of 100. She was reckoned to have been the last surviving charter member of Mooresville's Mary Slocumb Chapter of the Daughters of the American Revolution. One of her last acts was a $104,000 bequest to the Mooresville Public Library.

The Williamses are buried in Greensboro's Green Hill Cemetery.

CHAD WOOTEN

In these newspaper columns I have written about some of the people who have called Iredell County home. I have written about poets, local historians, entertainers, athletes, educators, scientists and physicians—all in all, a pretty varied group.

This column is about a person I, and many others, admired greatly.

* * *

A 1983 graduate of North Iredell High School, he lived with his parents, Bill and Betty Sue, and worked at Piedmont Farm Systems of Statesville as a salesman. He never wrote a book and he never won any trophies or major awards or other recognitions that I know of.

His chief achievement was getting out of bed each morning, with substantial help, getting dressed and getting into a wheelchair—both again with much help—and so on with all the things we do every day, and then being as much of a person as his crippled body would allow him to be. His name was Chad Wooten.

Chad was a quadriplegic. He died November 9, 2011, at the age of 46, from indirect complications from an accident that happened 25 years before. He had been working underneath a pickup truck which rolled back over him, leaving him paralyzed below the upper chest. He was able to move one arm a little.

My wife and I did not know Chad until we started attending Fifth Creek Presbyterian Church in the Cool Springs community. Chad was a lifelong member of Fifth Creek. Almost every Sunday he would come to church in the special van driven by his father and wheel his way up the ramp to the doors of the church.

He stayed in the back of the sanctuary during the service. Usually he could be spotted wearing a smile and a misshapen cowboy hat. After preaching was done Chad usually came back to the kitchen of the church's fellowship hall for coffee and snacks and fellowship. Someone had to hold the coffee cup for him to reach or feed him the cake or pie a bite at the time. No one minded doing this.

Now here's the funny thing: After you spoke with Chad a few times and got to know him, you forgot that he was paralyzed and confined to a wheelchair. And you soon found out that although his body was deteriorating, there was nothing in the least wrong with his mind. His strength of mind overcame his disabilities.

Chad was elected as an elder in the church. This position of responsibility was not given to him out of a sense of guilt or pity, but because those who knew him valued his wisdom and judgment. Chad had developed his mind so that it took in the long view. Most of the congregation considers having known Chad as a blessing to themselves. He was an inspiration.

He participated in almost all activities of the church, including taking part in what Fifth Creek Church optimistically calls its annual talent show. Chad took part by singing and telling jokes. He had a good, clear, but not strong, voice.

Just take a moment and consider how easy it would have been for a person with Chad's disabilities to have sunk into a deep pool of self-pity—to withdraw upon oneself like a sea creature going into its shell. But Chad never did this.

How much courage did it take for him to get up every morning and face reality? I don't know and can scarcely think about what it would be like without shuddering. The saying "There but for the Grace of God go I" comes to mind.

And so when I have an ache or pain or didn't sleep well or something doesn't go the way I wanted it to, I think about Chad Wooten and feel ashamed of myself.

Chad loved the history of the American West, cowboys and horses. Horses can run with the wind and cowboys are the iconic symbol of American self-reliance.

At the conclusion of Chad's funeral service, his aunt, Karen Campbell, who is the minister of music at Fifth Creek, played the closing theme song to the old Roy Rogers TV show, "Happy Trails to You," on the piano. We all sang along, some through tears, and thought of Chad Wooten in his floppy old cowboy hat, no longer confined to a wheelchair, but free to run with the wind, laughing, somewhere beyond the sunset.

Happy trails to you, partner!

MONROE NATHAN WORK

There are those who rise to prominence and bloom, so to speak, on home soil, while other people flower and attain recognition far from their home ground. Monroe Nathan Work (1866-1945) was representative of the latter.

Born in Iredell County on August 15, 1866, he was the youngest of eleven children of Alexander and Eliza Hobbs Work, both of whom had been slaves. Work's grandfather, Henry Work, a brick mason, had become a free man and moved to Michigan. There he bought a farm and set about purchasing his wife and ten children and bringing them North.

As the story goes, each freed family member worked to buy the other family members still in bondage. Alexander, Monroe's father, was one of three still in bondage when slavery was abolished.

When Work was one year old, in 1867, his family left Iredell and moved to Cairo, Illinois. Nine years later the family moved again, this time to Ashton, Sumner County, Kansas, where Monroe completed his elementary education.

He worked as a farmer until his mother's death in 1889, when he was 23. It was only then that he was able to attend high school. As might be expected from someone nearly a decade older than his classmates, he became discouraged and almost abandoned his goal of completing his education.

Superintendent David Ross Boyd, later the first president of the University of Oklahoma, encouraged Work to tough it out. Subsequently Work graduated at the head of his racially integrated class at the high school in Arkansas City in 1892.

Interested in both teaching and preaching, he entered the Chicago Theological Seminary in 1895 and graduated from that institution in 1898. Deciding on a life in academia rather than that of a man of the cloth, Work next entered the University of Chicago, working his way through school waiting tables, collecting and returning clothing for a laundry service and doing janitorial work.

His persistence paid off. He was awarded the Bachelor of Philosophy degree in 1902 and the Master of Arts degree in 1903, the first African American to receive a Master's from that university. In 1901, while still an undergraduate he wrote a paper, "The Negro and Crime in Chicago," which was published in the prestigious *American Journal of Sociology*. It was the first paper authored by an African American in that scholarly publication.

In 1903 Work accepted a position as a teacher of English and education at Georgia State Industrial College in Savannah at a salary of $800 a year. It was in Savannah that he became interested in researching the history of his race. He once said that no group had suffered more because of lack of knowledge of themselves.

He taught in Savannah for five years and found a wife there, Florence Evelyn Henderson. She was to be his helpmate for the rest of his life. The couple had no children.

Work began to write in his chosen field of study, eventually attracting the notice of Booker T. Washington, who invited him to join the faculty of Tuskegee Institute (now Tuskegee University) in Alabama. There in 1908, Monroe Work established and became Director of Tuskegee's Office of Records and Research. He held this position for the next 30 years—collecting, recording and organizing information on the Negro in America and then on the Negro in Africa.

Even though Work never did any classroom teaching at Tuskegee, he is regarded as a true pioneer in Afro-American studies and could, with much justification, be called, "The Father of Black Studies."

In 1912 he edited and published the first volume of *The Negro Year Book*, a collection of economic, sociological and historical information about the Negro, which included a bibliography of 408 classified references.

Work continued collecting bibliographic entries and subsequent editions of the *Year Book* reflected his ever-expanding bibliography.

In 1928 came the publication of his magnum opus, *Bibliography of the Negro in Africa and America,* which contained over 17,000 entries. One reviewer called the work, "The whole history of the Negro race in outline."

This was the first work of its kind: one volume named the works and publications on Negroes from all parts of the world, from ancient times to 1928, and categorized the works by 74 carefully chosen subtopics. Twenty years of meticulous research had gone into its production.

Among other honors, Monroe Nathan Work was awarded the Harmon Award in Education in 1928, the University of Chicago Alumni Citation in 1942 and was awarded an honorary Doctor of Letters degree from Howard University in 1943.

Dr. Work retired in 1938 but continued to contribute to Tuskegee until his death on May 2, 1945. He was buried on the Tuskegee campus.

A workaholic before the term was invented, Dr. Work published many articles on Negro life and history. His *Year Book* went through eleven editions and he compiled the annual Tuskegee reports on lynchings, regardless of the race of the victim, in the United States. These annual reports of Mr.Work probably did more to stop lynchings in the United States than any other single factor.

As historian Earle E. Thorpe has noted, his contributions to knowledge "give him rank among the top Negro historians produced in this country...and contributed greatly to establishing Negro history as a recognized and respectable field of study."

Biographer Jessie P. Guzman, writing four years after Work's death, commented on his steadfastness and drive. "He was a man of diligence and industry," stated Guzman. "In his own quiet way, he appeared tireless. He worked day in and day out, so that he and his name became synonymous."

All of us who call Iredell County home should know the name and the contributions of Monroe Nathan Work.

BIBLIOGRAPHY AND SUGGESTED READING

GEORGE AMOX

Interview with George Amox on July 3, 2006, at Statesville Record & Landmark office, Statesville, N.C.

Stonestreet, O. C., "A Patriotic Stand" Statesville Record & Landmark, July 4, 2006.

GERRI BENFIELD

"Woman Earning Place on Local EMS Staff" Statesville Record & Landmark, January 2, 1978.

Interview with Geraldine Benfield in September, 2005, in Statesville, N.C.

Stonestreet, O. C., "Unwitting EMS Pioneer Never Gave Up" Statesville Record & Landmark, September 4, 2005.

J. D. BESHEARS

Interview with J. D. Beshears on October 15, 2009, at Barium Springs, N.C.

Stonestreet, O. C., "A Survivor's Story" Statesville Record & Landmark, November 11, 2009.

DORIS BETTS

"Superlatives Are Announced" Statesville Daily Record, October 1, 1949.

Waugh, Doris, "Hitting the High Spots" Statesville Daily Record, October 22, 1949.

Keever, Homer, "Early Betts Writing Turns Up in Column" Statesville Record & Landmark, June 4, 1958.

Betts, Doris, "The Novelist's Task: To Keep People from Ending" Greensboro Daily News, February 18, 1962.

Betts, Doris, The Astronomer and Other Stories. Baton Rouge: Louisiana States University Press, 1965.

Simon, Pamela, "Work Is Nominated for Award" Statesville Record & Landmark, April 8, 1974.

Simon, Pamela, "Doris Betts: Still Learning, Changing, Growing" Statesville Record & Landmark, December 9, 1978.

"Author Comments on Associate Reformed Presbyterian Members, History" Statesville Record & Landmark, April 8, 1990.

"Betts Writes to Local Students" Statesville Record & Landmark, April 4, 1995.

Redding, Sandra, "The Storylines of Doris Betts" Our State, May, 2000.

Sidener, Carrie J., "The Life and Legend of a Southern Writer" Statesville Record & Landmark, May 29, 2005.

"NC Author Doris Betts Dies at 79" Statesville Record & Landmark, April 24, 2012.

Stonestreet, O. C., "Betts Never Forgot Her Hometown" Statesville Record & Landmark, May 2, 2012.

REVEREND AND MRS. A. S.BILLINGSLEY

"Trouble Between Pastor and People" The Landmark, May 16, 1884.

"The Late Rev. Dr. Billingsley" The Landmark, October 12, 1897.

"Mrs. Billingsley at Home—Mr. Billingsley's Will" The Landmark, October 26, 1897.

"Lot Bought for the Hospital" The Landmark, February 24, 1899.

"The A. S. Billingsley Hospital—Cornerstone Laid" The Landmark, October 10, 1899.

"The Late Dr. Billingsley and Wife" The Landmark, May 29, 1900.

"The Billingsley Hospital" The Landmark, July 17, 1900.

"The Billingsley Hospital Opened" The Landmark, September 4, 1900.

"The Billingsley Hospital" The Landmark, September 7, 1900.

"The Billingsley Hospital Company" The Landmark, September 21, 1900.

"The Billingsley Memorial Academy and Industrial School" The Landmark, August 9, 1901.

"Billingsley Memorial Academy" The Landmark, June 26, 1903.

"Billlingsley Academy" in Presbyterian Magazine, Vol. 13, No. 1, January, 1907.

"Billingsley Hospital May Be Taken and Conducted by the Civic League" The Sentinel, January 15, 1914.

Dockery, Rev. Z. A., "Billingsley Academy, the Colored High School" The Landmark, September 3, 1915.

Caldwell, Arthur B., History of the American Negro and His Institutions. Volume 4 (North Carolina). Atlanta: A. B. Caldwell Publishing Company, 1917.

"Take Over Billingsley [hospital]" The Landmark, February 10, 1920.

"Will Sell the Billingsley [hospital]" The Landmark, May 27, 1926.

"Negro Hospital Group Now Planning Clinic" Statesville Record & Landmark, June 6, 1956.

Keever, Homer, "Negroes of Statesville Taught by Billingsleys" Statesville Record & Landmark, July 29, 1959.

Keever, Homer, "Billingsley Hospital Had Checkered Career" Statesville Record & Landmark, August 13, 1959.

"Blacks Organized Many Churches in Iredell" Statesville Record & Landmark, April 8, 1974.

Morrison, Jettie, "Black Heritage Recalled in Iredell" Statesville Record & Landmark, July 1, 1976.

Lackey, Mac, "Builders of Black Churches" Iredell Neighbors [Charlotte Observer], February 25, 1990.

Moose, Bill, "Reverend Billingsley's Life Made a Difference for Freedmen" Statesville Record & Landmark, November 17, 1991.

Watt, W. N., Statesville: My Home Town, 1789 - 1920. Statesville, N. C.: The Author, 1996.

Stonestreet, O. C., "Northern Missionary's Work 'Anything but Pleasant'" Statesville Record & Landmark, December 9, 2012.

Stonestreet, O. C., "The Rev. and Mrs. Billingsley Come to Statesville" Statesville Record & Landmark, December 16, 2012.

Stonestreet, O. C., "Billingsley Hospital: An Institution Ahead of Its Time" Statesville Record & Landmark, December 23, 2012.

Stonestreet, O. C., "The Founding of Billingsley Memorial Academy" Statesville Record & Landmark, December 30, 2012.

DAVID HENRY BRANTLEY

United Daughters of the Confederacy, Battle of Bentonville Chapter, Collected Testimonies: "I, D. H. Brantley, Will Give a Short Sketch" Mooresville, NC: n.p., 1913.

"David Henry Brantley" in North Carolina Troops, 1861-1865, A Roster. Volume X. Raleigh, N.C.: Division of Archives and History, 1985.

"David H. Brantley, Aged Citizen Dead" Mooresville Enterprise, October 8, 1925.

Stonestreet, O. C., "Local Man Makes Long Journey Home" Mooresville Tribune, November 20, 1996.

PAUL BRENDLE

"Paul Brendle Enters Baseball's Hall of Fame" The Landmark, April 12, 1948.

"Brendle Tosses One-Hit Game" Statesville Daily Record, April 17, 1948.

Owens, Mike, "From the Pressbox" Statesville Record & Landmark, June 14, 1983.

Interview with Paul Brendle in March, 2011, at his home in Cool Springs, N.C.

Stonestreet, O. C., "Checking in with Paul Brendle, 'Mr. Baseball'" Statesville Record & Landmark, April 3, 2011.

Stonestreet, O. C., "Life, Baseball at Times Synonymous for Brendle" Statesville Record & Landmark, April 10, 2011.

L. B. BRISTOL

"Mr. L. B. Bristol Dies Today from Heart Disease" The Landmark, April 4, 1935.

Lackey, Mac, "Mayor Led City's Progress: 'Forward March Statesville' Was Bristol's Motto" Iredell Neighbors [Charlotte Observer], July 28, 1985.

Lackey, Mac, "Igniting Progress: Bristol Brought Business, Fire Inspections to Statesville" Iredell Neighbors [Charlotte Observer], August 4, 1985.

Stonestreet, O. C., "Ticket to Statesville's Past" Statesville Record & Landmark, February 18, 2007.

STAN BROOKSHIRE

"Stan Brookshire" Statesville Record & Landmark, October 11, 1990.

http://www.charmeck.org/Departments/Mayor/Past+Mayoes/Stanford+R.+ Brookshire.htm December 31, 2007.

Stonestreet, O. C., "Iredell Natives Leave Mark on Queen City" Statesville Record & Landmark, January 13, 2008.

J. P. CALDWELL

"An [sic] Hebrew Congregation Organized" The Landmark, August 31, 1883.

"Popular Education" The Landmark, February 2, 1883.

"Jos. P. Caldwell Dead" The Landmark, Nov. 23, 1911.

Bryant, H. E. C., "Joseph Pearson Caldwell" The Landmark, January 6, 1933.

"J. P. Caldwell Marker Will Be Located Here" The Landmark, July 22, 1948.

Keever, Homer, "Editor Caldwell Right about News" Statesville Record & Landmark, January 22, 1965.

Watt, W. N., Statesville, My Home Town, 1789 - 1920. Statesville, N.C.: The Author, 1996.

Keever, Homer M., "Joseph Pearson Caldwell Jr.," in Dictionary of North Carolina Biography. Volume I. Edited by William S. Powell. Chapel Hill: University of North Carolina Press, 1979.

Reese, Joel, "The Strange Case of Cabinsville" Statesville Record & Landmark, June 17, 2011.

Stonestreet, O. C., "J. P. Caldwell's Influence Grew Beyond Statesville" Statesville Record & Landmark, September 23, 2012.

MARTIN CAMPBELL

"Martin Campbell, Negro Noted for His Strong Religion, Weird Songs" Mooresville Enterprise, November 4, 1937.

"Martin Campbell's Church To Be Opened Next Sunday" Mooresville Enterprise, October 6, 1938.

"'Uncle Martin' Raises Money to Complete Church" Mooresville Enterprise, October 13, 1938.

"Uncle Martin Campbell Our Only Centurian [sic]" Mooresville Enterprise, December 18, 1941.

"Martin Campbell, Wants Wife" Mooresville Enterprise, May 14, 1942.

"Special Musical at 'Uncle' Martin's" Mooresville Enterprise, August 20, 1942.

"Oldest Citizen of Mooresville Dies at Age 106" Statesville Daily Record, September 21, 1944.

"Uncle Martin Campbell Dies at Age of 106" Mooresville Enterprise, September 21, 1944.

Campbell, James L., From Slavery to the 21st Century As Seen Through the Eyes of a Grandson. Mooresville, N.C.: Performance Business Services, 2000.

McGuire, Erinn, "Overcome, Indeed" Statesville Record & Landmark, November 6, 2003.

Menster, Jennifer, "Slave's Grandson, 92, Writes Book" Statesville Record & Landmark, undated.

Jacobus, Casey, "Troutman Mainstay Wrapping Up" Iredell Neighbors [Charlotte Observer], April 7, 2004.

Stonestreet, O. C., "'Uncle Martin' Campbell: A Well-Known Mooresville Character" Record & Landmark, February 10, 2013.

MILTON CAMPBELL

Keever, Homer, "Early 1800's Saw Rapid Progress of Education in Iredell County" Statesville Daily Record, September 11, 1950.

Keever, Homer, "Public Schools Got Start Early in 1840s" Statesville Record & Landmark, March 21, 1957.

Keever, Homer, "Early Vote in Iredell County on Public School Act Led to Education System" Statesville Record & Landmark, June 20, 1974.

Stonestreet, O. C., "Milton Campbell: Forgotten Man" Iredell Neighbors [Charlotte Observer], August 22, 2004.

BUCK CLAYWELL

http://www.historycentral.com/NAVY/DE/Cecildoyle.html. November 23, 2007.

http://www.ussindianapolis.org/woody.htm   November 23, 2007.

http://www.discovery.com/exp/indianapolis/haynes_trans.html November 23, 2007.

http://www.ussindianapolis.org/story.htm   November 23, 2007.

Interview with Buck Clayton in December, 2007, in his home in Statesville, N.C.

Stonestreet, O. C., "Iredell Veteran Witnessed 1945 Disaster" Statesville Record & Landmark, December 9, 2007.

"William 'Buck' Claywell Jr." Statesville Record & Landmark, December 27, 2012.

HARRY P. DEATON

"Final Announcement" Mooresville Enterprise, August 31, 1906.

"Comments of the Press" Mooresville Enterprise, September 7, 1906.

"Home Again" Mooresville Enterprise, May 12, 1910.

"Our Fortieth Anniversary Edition" Mooresville Enterprise, September 7, 1939.

"Mrs. Harry P. Deaton Died Sunday Morning" Mooresville Enterprise, June 6, 1940.

"Harry P. Deaton Passed Away Last Thursday Afternoon" Mooresville Enterprise, November 1, 1945.

"Editor Frank Freeze Died Early Saturday" Mooresville Enterprise, November 21, 1946.

"The Enterprise Publishes Their Final Issue Today" Mooresville Enterprise, February 27, 1947.

"Final Issue" Mooresville Enterprise, February 27, 1947.

Jones, Everette, "Harry P. Deaton, Enterprise Publisher" Mooresville Tribune, May 1, 1991.

Stonestreet, O. C., "Harry P. Deaton: The Mooresville Enterprise Editor" Mooresville Tribune, April 2, 1997.

SIDNEY DIXON

"Notice" Statesville American, February 3, 1877.

"Vindicated" Statesville American, October 30, 1880.

Gamma, "Notes from Mooresville" The Landmark, January 22, 1886.

"The Mayor and Austin's Cow" The Landmark, June 2, 1887.

"The Farmer and Planter" The Landmark, October 20, 1887.

"The Poet Laurate Warned" The Landmark, October 30, 1890.

"The Airship" The Landmark, February 21, 1891.

"State News" The Landmark, March 28, 1902.

"It Was the Bard of Coddle Creek" The Landmark, April 1, 1902.

"People Air-Minded Many Years Ago" Mooresville Enterprise, March 24, 1932.

"History As It Was" The Landmark, April 22, 1932.

"Once More Unto the Breach" The Landmark, July 26, 1932.

"Iredell County Once Boasted a Famous Poet" The Landmark, October 18, 1932.

"'The Haunted Barn' Tale of Wheat Threshing Told in Verse by S. L. Dixon" The Landmark, July 27, 1939.

"Down in Iredell—Annual Visit" The Landmark, January 17, 1947.

"Reminiscing—The Bard of Coddle Creek" Statesville Daily Record, September 8, 1952.

McKnight, Tom, "Community Chaff: Smiley Jetson Brown," Mooresville Tribune, February 23, 1956.

"S. L. Dixon" in North Carolina State Troops, 1861-1865: A Roster. Volume VIII. Raleigh, N. C.: Division of Archives and History, 1981.

Stonestreet, O. C., "To Uncle Sidney's Memory" Mooresville Tribune, June 7, 2000.

Stonestreet, O. C., "Iredell Poet's Verses Rife with Controversy" Statesville Record & Landmark, December 30, 2007.

MARTHA H. DOBSON

Interview with Martha Dobson in January, 2008, at Statesville Record & Landmark offices, Statesville, N.C.

Stonestreet, O. C., "Teacher Almost Joined Doomed Crew" Statesville Record & Landmark, January 27, 2008.

BEN DOUGLAS

"Douglas, 86, Dies" Statesville Record & Landmark, July 28, 1981.

http://www.charmeck.org/Departments/Mayor/Past+Mayors/Ben+E.+Douglas.htm December 31, 2007.

Stonestreet, O. C., "Iredell Natives Leave Mark on Queen City" Statesville Record & Landmark, January 13, 2008.

J. H. FESPERMAN

Fesperman, J. H., The Life of a Sufferer: An Autobiography. Utica, N.Y.: The Young Lutheran Company, 1892.

Jordan, Weymouth T. Jr., Comp. "Joseph H. Fesperman" in North Carolina Troops, 1861-1865: A Roster. Volume IV. Raleigh, N.C. Office of Archives and History, 1973.

"The Record of Deaths—Mr. Fesperman and Others" The Landmark, May 1, 1917.

Stonestreet, O. C., "J. H. Fesperman, Warrior for Christ, Reluctant Soldier" Mooresville Tribune, November 10, 1999.

CORA FREEZE

"Rufus Wilburn Freeze Dead" Mooresville Enterprise, January 15, 1920.

"Basketball Games During Past Week" Mooresville Enterprise, December 2, 1920.

"Commencement Over" Mooresville Enterprise, May 5, 1921.

"Teaching Staff for Schools Announced" Mooresville Enterprise, July 22, 1926.

"Mrs. Rufus W. Freeze Passes at Her Home Here" Mooresville Enterprise, February 6, 1936.

"The Little Chicken Pluckers Who Started a School Library" Mooresville Tribune, December 16, 1976.

Jones, Everette, "Teacher 'Miss Cora:' 'I Thank My Maker for the Privilege'" Mooresville Tribune, October 1, 1986.

"Monday Memorial Service for Cora Freeze, Teacher" Mooresville Tribune, November 11, 1987.

Sullivan, Len, "We Thank Our Maker for Miss Cora" Mooresville Tribune, November 11, 1987.

Stonestreet, O. C., "Remembering 'Miss Cora' Freeze" Record & Landmark, October 14, 2012.

SHELLEY FRONTIS

"Frontis-Williams Wedding" Raleigh News & Observer, December 21, 1902.

Frontis, Shelley, "Mooresville and Her Progress" Mooresville Enterprise, April 27, 1911.

"Frontis Mooresville Mayor" The Landmark, April 29, 1913.

"Mayor Frontis at Charlotte" Mooresville Enterprise, September 7, 1916.

Frontis, S., "For Billy Norman, Jr." Mooresville Enterprise, August 23, 1923.

Frontis, S., "Six Kids at Enochville" Mooresville Enterprise, Augugust 30, 1923.

Frontis, S., "Escapades of Borel Frontis" Mooresville Enterprise, September 7, 1923.

Frontis, S., "Mush and Ham" Mooresville Enterprise, October 16, 1924.

"Dr. Frontis Addressed Statesville Kiwanians" ["Men from Cabin Doors" poem] Mooresville Enterprise, March 26, 1925.

Frontis, S., "Dinner in the Grove" Mooresville Enterprise, September 23, 1926.

Frontis, S., "My Eczema" Mooresville Enterprise, December 9, 1926.

Frontis, S., "A Childhood Reminiscence" Mooresville Enterprise, September 10, 1931.

McNeely, Rankin, "Digging Up the Past—an Interview with Dr. Shelley Frontis" The Rounder, October 21, 1937.

"Dr. Shelley Frontis, 70, Died Friday, January 31" Mooresville Enterprise, February 6, 1941.

Stonestreet, O. C., "Dentist Wrote of 1900s" Iredell Neighbors [Charlotte Observer], July 23, 1989.

Stonestreet, O. C., "Dr. Shelley Frontis: Mooresville's Poet Laureate" Mooresville Tribune, October 16, 1996.

Stonestreet, O. C., "'Mush and Ham' Refreshes Memories" Statesville Record & Landmark, August 5, 2007.

STEPHEN FRONTIS

Clark, Edith M., "Stephen Frontis," in Dictionary of North Carolina Biography. Volume II. Edited by William S. Powell. Chapel Hill: University of North Carolina Press, 1986.

Stonestreet, O. C., "19th Century Minister Founded Area Schools" Iredell Neighbors [Charlotte Observer], July 9, 1989.

STEPHEN FRONTIS JR.

"Death of Prof. S. Frontis" The Landmark, August 11, 1892.

"Mrs. Stephen Frontis Passes" Mooresville Enterprise, February 19, 1925.

Stonestreet, O. C., "2nd Generation Frontis Ran Mooresville School" Iredell Neighbors [Charlotte Observer], July 16, 1989.

Stonestreet, O. C., "Town's First School Puts Mooresville on the Map" Mooresville Tribune, September 29, 2004.

JAMES GAY

Keever, Homer, "State's Published Poetry Began in Iredell" Statesville Record & Landmark, April 7, 1962.

Walser, Richard, "Introduction" to James Gay's A Collection of Various Pieces of Poetry Chiefly Patriotic. Charlotte, McNally & Loftin, 1964.

Walser, Richard, "James Gay," in Dictionary of North Carolina Biography. Volume II. Edited by William S. Powell. Chapel Hill: University of North Carolina Press, 1986.

"Earliest Book" Statesville Record & Landmark, March 17, 1993.

Stonestreet, O. C., "James Gay, Iredell County's First Poet" Record & Landmark, October 28, 2012.

MAC GRAY

"R. M. Gray Resigns as Superintendent of Schools" The Landmark, April 10, 1941.

"Mr. Robert Mac Gray" The Landmark, July 14, 1941.

"Robert Mac Gray Taken Suddenly Friday Afternoon" The Landmark, July 14, 1941.

"Robert Mac Gray Taken Suddenly" Mooresville Tribune, July 17, 1941.

"High Auditorium Named Mac Gray" The Landmark, July 12, 1948.

Stonestreet, O. C., "Just Who Was Mac Gray, Anyway?" Statesville Record & Landmark, May 6, 2007.

JAMES HALL

Foote, William Henry, Sketches of North Carolina, Historical and Biographical... (1846)

Sprague, William B., "James Hall, D.D.," Annals of the American Pulpit; or Commemorative Notices of Distinguished American Clergymen of Various Denominations... Volume III. New York: Robert Carter & Brothers, 1860.

"Rev. James Hall's Memory Honored" The Landmark, June 17, 1929.

Hall, Nell K., "The Reverend James Hall" The State, February 19, 1944.

Dudley, Harold J., "Dr. Hall Pioneer Pastor in Iredell" Statesville Record & Landmark, April 13, 1963.

Wiest, Timothy J., "James Hall," in Dictionary of North Carolina Biography. Volume III. Edited by William S. Powell. Chapel Hill: University of North Carolina Press, 1988.

Lackey, Mac, "Bethany Church Grew Up with the Nation: Soldier-Scholar Was Founder" Iredell Neighbors [Charlotte Observer], October 15, 1989.

Raynal, Henry Middleton, Old Fourth Creek Congregation: The Story of First Presbyterian Church, Statesville, 1764-1989. Statesville, N.C.: First Presbyterian Church, 1995.

Stonestreet, O. C., "First Presbyterian Was Led by a Fighting Parson" Iredell Neighbors [Charlotte Observer], September 17, 2003.

Stonestreet, O. C., "The Many Contributions of the Rev. Hall" Statesville Record & Landmark, March 7, 2010.

LEONARD HAM

Interview with Leonard Ham in August, 2005, at Pat's Coffee Shop, Mooresville, N.C.

Stonestreet, O. C., "His Service, His Memories" Statesville Record & Landmark, August 14, 2005.

"Leonard Ham" Mooresville Tribune, April 9, 2010.

EDWARD HARRIS

Crawford, Jon G., "Edward Harris," in Dictionary of North Carolina Biography. Volume III. Edited by William S. Powell. Chapel Hill: University of North Carolina Press, 1988.

Stonestreet, O. C., "Grave of Iredell Judge Found in Lumberton" Statesville Record & Landmark, November 15, 2009.

KEN HARRIS

http://www.charmeck.org/Departments/Mayor/Past+Mayors/Kenneth+R.+Harris.htm

Stonestreet, O. C., "Add Another Iredell Man to the List" Statesville Record & Landmark, March 16, 2008.

Morrill, Jim, "Former Charlotte Mayor Harris Dies" Charlotte Observer, January 18, 2009.

SARAH HEINZERLING

"Mrs. Heinzerling Is One of Contributors to N. C. Poetry Review" The Landmark, July 28, 1933.

"Poetry Society Meets with Mrs. Heinzerling" Statesville Record, May 4, 1934.

Heinzerling, Sarah A., The Pines of Rockingham and Other Poems. Boomer, N.C.: Pearson Printing Company, 1934.

"Songs of Iredell Title of New Book" The Landmark, October 11, 1934.

Heinzerling, Sarah A., Songs of Iredell. Statesville, N.C.: Brady Printing Company, 1934.

Heinzerling, Sarah A., The Call. Statesville, N.C.: Brady Printing Company, 1936.

"'Songs of Iredell' Tell Lyrical Story of Green Hills" Statesville Daily Record, April 6, 1950.

"Mrs. Heinzerling Today Observing Her 90th Birthday" Statesville Daily Record, September 11, 1952.

"Poetess Dies at Home Here" The Landmark, March 12, 1954.

Stonestreet, O. C., "Iredell Poetess Rediscovered" Statesville Record & Landmark, July 22, 2007.

MARY C. HOLLIDAY

"For the Negro Schools" The Landmark, October 26, 1915.

"Dr. Mary Bethune Heard by Large Crowd of People" The Landmark, April 1, 1946.

"Mary C. Holliday, Dean of Congress" The Landmark, June 19, 1950.

Eisele, Douglas. "Mrs. Mary C. Holliday Praised as Educator" Statesville Record & Landmark, May 31, 1956.

"Tribute Paid Memory of Former Educator" Statesville Record & Landmark, April 11, 1968.

"Hollidays Helped Iredell Blacks from 20's Through 40's" Iredell County News, February 16, 1984.

Reese, Joel, "Woman Remade Black Education in Iredell County" Statesville Record & Landmark, March 22, 2006.

Stonestreet, O. C., "Mary C. Holliday, an Iredell Education Pioneer" Statesville Record & Landmark, February 26, 2012.

MORDECAI HYAMS

"The Late Prof. M. E. Hyams" The Landmark, May 21, 1891.

Powell, William S., "Mordecai E. Hyams," in Dictionary of North Carolina Biography. Volume III. Edited by William S. Powell. Chapel Hill: University of North Carolina Press, 1988.

Troyer, James R., "The Hyams Family, Father and Sons, Contributors to North Carolina Botany" in The Journal of the Elisha Mitchell Scientific Society, 117 (4), 2001.

Freeze, Gary R., "Roots, Barks, Berries and Jews: the Herb Trade in Gilded-Age North Carolina" Essays in Economic Business History, 13:107-127, 2005.

"Wild Flower of Mystery" The Blooming News, April, 2011.

Stonestreet, O. C., "Statesville's Mordecai Hyams Found 'the Botanical Holy Grail'" Statesville Record & Landmark, May 6, 2012.

DOTTY AND WILLIE JOLLY

"US District Attorney Talks to Lions Club" Statesville Daily Record, October 23, 1945.

"Jolly Sisters Have a Christmas Party" The Landmark, January 1, 1948.

"They Love It" Statesville Daily Record, February 14, 1949.

"Radio Roundup" Statesville Daily Record, June 7, 1949.

"Cowgirls Return" Statesville Daily Record, November 3, 1949.

"Friends Go All Out in Helping Alexander Get Its New Hospital" Statesville Daily Record, December 8, 1949.

"Jolly Sisters Gone Again" Statesville Daily Record, February 25, 1950.

"Annual Picnic Set by Olin Company" Statesville Daily Record, June 28, 1950.

"Sing in Greenville" Statesville Daily Record, July 20, 1950.

"Charlotte Appearance" Statesville Daily Record, August 5, 1950.

"Play to Feature Square Dance" Statesville Daily Record, September 19, 1950.

Yount, Marion Ruth, "Hitting the High Spots" Statesville Daily Record, September 26, 1950.

"Fourth of July Picnic at Sloan's Mill" The Landmark, July 2, 1951.

"Personal Appearance" Statesville Daily Record, January 8, 1952.

"On Television" Statesville Daily Record, May 3, 1952.

"Added Attraction at Ball Game Monday Night" Mooresville Tribune, May 8, 1952.

"Personal Appearances" Statesville Daily Record, May 16, 1952.

"Rally Program Details Given" Statesville Daily Record, October 10, 1952.

"Jolly Sisters on Television" Statesville Daily Record, December 10, 1952.

"Off to Augusta" Statesville Daily Record, February 23, 1953.

"Marathon Show" Statesville Daily Record, September 18, 1953.

"Jolly Good" The Landmark, October 8, 1953.

"Civitans Hear Jolly Sisters" Statesville Daily Record, February 19, 1954.

"Jolly Sisters at Food Fair" The Landmark, April 30, 1954.

"Jolly Sisters on TV" Statesville Daily Record, June 23, 1954.

"Olive Hits Republicans at North Iredell Rally" Statesville Daily Record, October 20, 1954.

"Dinner Dance at Country Club" Statesville Daily Record, November 18, 1954.

"Family Night Dinner" Statesville Daily Record, December 21, 1954.

"Jolly Sisters Back" Statesville Record & Landmark, April 22, 1955.

"Entertainers Return" Statesville Record & Landmark, September 6, 1955.

"Iredell Girls Record for National Release" Statesville Record & Landmark, October 15, 1955.

"Iredell Singer Plans Air Force Base Tour" Statesville Record & Landmark, January 6, 1960.

Owens, David L., "Dottie Keeps Her Dixie Drawl" Greensboro Daily News, January 22, 1961.

"Iredell Singer Begins New Southwest Tour" Statesville Record & Landmark, September 16, 1961.

"Southern-Type Singer Appears at Legion Club" The Huntsville [Ala.] Times, May 10, 1962.

"South Is More Jolly, Contends Singer Dottie" The Valley Voice, Florence, Ala., May 25, 1962.

"Jolly Sister Singing Again" Statesville Record & Landmark, May 31, 1969.

"Rev. Jolly Is Stricken" Statesville Record & Landmark, April 21, 1971.

"Grace Jolly Celebrates 100th Birthday" Statesville Record & Landmark, November 29, 1994.

"Grace M. Jolly" Statesville Record & Landmark, December 19, 1996.

Telephone conversation with Robert G. Carney Jr., Shelby, NC, March 1, 2011.

Telephone conversation with Dorothy Jolly Parker, Deerfield, Ill., March 7, 2011.

Telephone conversation with Robert G. Carney Jr., Shelby, NC, March 8, 2011.

Interview with Mrs. Ethel Campbell, Statesville, NC, March 10, 2011.

Stonestreet, O. C., "Fondly Remembering the Jolly Sisters, Willie and Dottie" Statesville Record & Landmark, March 20, 2011.

Stonestreet, O. C., "The Jolly Sisters Hit the Highway" Statesville Record & Landmark, March 27, 2011.

HOMER KEEVER

"Keever Added to Sports Staff" Statesville Daily Record, December 4, 1950.

"Optimists Hear Homer Keever" Statesville Daily Record, May 13, 1953.

"Keever Discusses Early History of Iredell County" The Landmark, May 14, 1953.

"Keever Elected to NCEA Board" Statesville Record & Landmark, March 4, 1961.

"Methodist Conference Names Keever to Historian Post" Statesville Record & Landmark, June 4, 1963.

"Keever Urges Microfilming" Statesville Record & Landmark, July 10, 1965.

"Keever to Leave Classroom" Statesville Record & Landmark, May 30, 1968.

"Keever Wins Second Place" Statesville Record & Landmark, December 9, 1968.

"Keever Wins Citizenship Award" Statesville Record & Landmark, May 19, 1972.

"Keever Stricken" Statesville Record & Landmark, September 12, 1979.

"Alta A. Keever" Statesville Record & Landmark, June 20, 1989.

Stonestreet, O. C., "Keever Put County's History, People into Print" Statesville Record & Landmark, April 12, 2002.

PHILLIP F. LAUGENOUR

"Dr. P. F. Laugenhour Dead" The Landmark, February 8, 1916.

"Dr. Laugenour Dead" The Sentinal, February 10, 1916.

"Dr. P. F. Laugenour Called by Death" The Sentinal, February 10, 1916.

MacLean, Constance, "Dr. Lagenour [sic] Known for Unusual Methods of Research" Statesville Record & Landmark, July 2, 1976.

McLean, Constance, "Dentist, Now Deceased, Was Fascinated by Family's and County's History" Statesville Record & Landmark, Bicentennial Edition.

Lackey, Mac, "Dentist's Records Something To Sink Your Teeth Into" Iredell Neighbors[Charlotte Observer], February 10, 1988.

Bristol, Mabel Laugenour, "Philip Fletcher Laugenour" in Heritage of Iredell County. Volume I. Statesville, N.C.: Genealogical Society of Iredell County, 1980.

Stonestreet, O. C., "An Early Iredell Historian: Dr. P. F. Laugenour" Record & Landmark, December 2, 2012.

AUGUSTUS LEAZAR

"Death of Mrs. A. Leazar" The Landmark, August 23, 1895.

"Death of Hon. A. Leazar" The Landmark, February 21, 1905.

"Hon. A. Leazar Dead" Mooresville Enterprise, February 24, 1905.

"Leazar Portrait Presented" The Landmark, June 6, 1911.

"Why Not a New County" Mooresville Enterprise, April 5, 1923.

"Mr. Leazar and the State Prison" Mooresville Enterprise, August 13, 1925.

Keever, Homer, "Efforts to Divide Iredell into New Counties Failed." Statesville Daily Record, June 1, 1950.

Keever, Homer, "Birth of Lillington Is Blocked" Statesville Record & Landmark, May 28, 1964.

Fountain, A. M., Place Names on the North Carolina State University Campus. Raleigh, Volume I, 1978.

Walser, Richard, The Watauga Club. Raleigh: Wolf's Head Press, 1980.

Jordan, Weymouth T. Jr., Comp. "Augustus Leazar" in North Carolina Troops, 1861-1865, A Roster. Volume X. Raleigh, N.C.: Division of Archives and History, 1985.

Stonestreet, O. C., "Augustus Leazar: Iredell County Son, Soldier, Scholar, Statesman" Iredell Neighbors [Charlotte Observer], November 20, 1988.

Steelman, Lala Carr, "Augustus Leazar," in Dictionary of North Carolina Biography. Volume IV. Edited by William S. Powell. Chapel Hill: The University of North Carolina Press, 1991.

Stonestreet, O. C., "Lillington, the County That Never Was" in Tales from Old Iredell County, Statesville, N.C.: 2012.

GUS LEAZAR

"Mr. Augustus Leazar Receives Cadetship Appointment" Mooresville Enterprise, February 11, 1909.

"Mooresville Citizens Going Abroad" The Landmark, June 7, 1910.

"Aviator Gus Leazar Doing Stunts" Mooresville Enterprise, June 12, 1919.

"New School Buildings" The Landmark, July 15, 1919.

"Gus Leazar Gets Airplane License" Mooresville Enterprise, July 24, 1919.

Goodman, Vernie, "News of Mooresville" The Landmark, September 23, 1919.

"Leazar-Dunn" Mooresville Enterprise, June 7, 1923.

"Gus Leazar Gets Higher Air Post" Mooresville Enterprise, February 6, 1930.

"Gus Leazar Sent to Atlanta Airport" Mooresville Enterprise, November 27, 1930.

"Augustus Leazar, Mooresville Native, Passes in Raleigh" Mooresville Tribune, February 11, 1960.

Parramore, James C., First to Fly: North Carolina and The Beginnings of Aviation. Chapel Hill: The University of North Carolina Press, 2002.

Stonestreet, O. C., "Gus Leazar: A Forgotten Pioneer" Statesville Record & Landmark, January 11, 2009.

SAMUEL MASCOTTS

Miller's Statesville, N.C. City Directory, Volume XV, (pp. 235), Asheville, N.C., 1944-1945.

"Little Sammy Is Found at Harm'ny" The Landmark, May 3, 1945.

"Sammy the Dog Killed By Car" Statesville Daily Record, August 24, 1946.

Moore, W. M., "Tearing Down Station Brings Back Memories" Statesville Daily Record, September 1, 1953.

Jackins, Carmen, "Once Upon a Time, Sammy Was a Familiar Sight" Iredell Citizen, April 15, 1998.

"It Was Just a Spark, but It Ignited Blaze To Start SFD" Statesville Record & Landmark, April 24, 2002.

Stonestreet, O. C., "Goodbye, (Fire)man's Best Friend" Statesville Record & Landmark, April 22, 2007.

Swicegood, Donna, "Preserving the Memory of Sammy" Statesville Record & Landmark, November 4, 2008.

Swicegood, Donna, "Mascot Gets New Home" Statesville Record & Landmark, October 18, 2011.

MARY MAYO

"Mary Mayo Riker Wins Statewide Broadcast" Statesville Record, February 3, 1939.

Sample, Sue Horner, "Future Looks Good to Mary Mayo" Statesville Record & Landmark, December 1, 1955.

"Profiles of American Singers: Mary Mayo" The New Yorker, February 27, 1978.

"Long Musical Career Recalled" Statesville Record & Landmark, December 16, 1985.

Reese, Joel, "Professional Singer One of the County's Talents" Statesville Record & Landmark, August 10, 2005.

Stonestreet, O. C., "Remembering Mary's Angelic Voice" Statesville Record & Landmark, February 4, 2007.

JOHN MCCONNELL

Laugenour, Philip F., "Baker Cemetery Centre Congregation" The Sentinel, May 25, 1916.

"Duke Will Move Ancient Graveyard" Mooresville Tribune, March 30, 1961.

McConnell, Joel P., The McConnell Families of Davidson's Creek Settlement, Iredell County, North Carolina, 1748-1982. Mooresville, N.C.: The Author, 1983.

Stonestreet, O. C., "The Wandering Spirit of John McConnell" Statesville Record & Landmark, September 30, 2007.

THOMAS JEFFERSON MCKINLEY

Johns, Henry T., Life with the Forty-ninth Massachusetts Volunteers. Washington, D.C.: Ramsey & Bisbee, Printers, 1890.

"Five Score and Twelve" The Berkshire [Mass.] Courier, December 24, 1896.

"Said He Was Born in Statesville" The Landmark, January 1, 1897.

"The Late Jefferson McKenley" Berkshire [Mass.] Courier, January 7, 1897.

Martin, Frederic Rowland, "Old Jeff" in The Companionship of Books and Other Papers. New York: G. P. Putnam's Sons, 1905.

"49th Massachusetts Infantry in the Civil War" in The Union Army, Volume I, Federal Publishing Company, 1908.

La Fontana, Rox, "The Long Search" The Berkshire [Mass.] Courier, July 15, 1971.

Drew, Bernard, Great Barrington-Great Town-Great History. Great Barrington, Massachusetts: Great Barrington Historical Society, 1999.

Hart, Charlotte Kay, "Samuel Hart and His Descendants" in The Heritage of Iredell County, Volume II, Statesville, N.C.: Genealogical Society of Iredell County, 2000.

Stonestreet, O. C., "The Interesting Life of Thomas Jefferson McKinley" Statesville Record & Landmark, March 17, 2013.

Stonestreet, O. C., "Thomas J. McKinley Remembered as Honorable Man" Statesville Record & Landmark, March 24, 2013.

PHIL MCLAUGHLIN

"Motion Picture To Be Filmed" Mooresville Enterprise, May 9, 1935.

"Filming Started on Local Picture" Mooresville Enterprise, May 16, 1935.

"Mooresville's Movie Will Be Screened Three Days at the Carolina" Mooresville Enterprise, May 23, 1935.

"World Premiere of 'Mooresville's Hero'" Mooresville Enterprise, May 30, 1935.

Interview with Philip McLaughlin in August, 1992, at his home in Mooresville, N.C.

Stonestreet, O. C., "Mooresville's Silver-Screen Hero" Mooresville Tribune, August 19, 1992.

"Carl McLaughlin" Mooresville Tribune, August 21, 2011.

ALEXANDER MEANS

"He Was a Native of Statesville" The Landmark, November 10, 1903.

"Dr. Foard Knew Dr. Means—Other Reminiscences" The Landmark, November 13, 1903.

Powell, William S., "Alexander Means," in Dictionary of North Carolina Biography. Volume IV. Edited by William S. Powell. Chapel Hill: University of North Carolina Press, 1991.

Stonestreet, O. C., "An Extraordinary Man: Iredell's Alexander Means" Statesville Record & Landmark, May 13, 2012.

J. P. MILLS

"John Pinkney Mills, 88, Dies After Useful Career" Mooresville Enterprise, March 7, 1940.

Stonestreet, O. C., "He Helped Mooresville Blossom" Iredell Neighbors [Charlotte Observer], March 9, 2005.

QUINCY SHARPE MILLS

"Mr. Q. S. Mills Promoted" The Landmark, March 23, 1915.

"New York Officer Missing in Action" The New York Times, Aug. 28, 1918.

"Lieut. Q. S. Mills Killed" The Landmark, September 6, 1918.

"Other Editors Thought" The Landmark, September 10, 1918.

Luby, James, One Who Gave His Life: War Letters of Quincy Sharpe Mills. New York: G.P. Putnam's Sons, 1923.

Mills, Quincy Sharpe, Editorials, Sketches and Stories. New York: G. P. Putman's Sons, 1930.

Knox, Katherine Noe, "Quincy Sharpe Mills," in Dictionary of North Carolina Biography. Volume IV. Edited by William S. Powell. Chapel Hill: University of North Carolina Press, 1991.

Stonestreet, O. C., "Quincy Sharpe Mills Died for His Country" Record & Landmark, November 11, 2012.

HOMER MYERS JR.

"Homer Myers Jr." Statesville Record & Landmark, July 28, 2006.

Interview with Homer Myers Jr. in August, 2006, in his home in Union Grove, N.C.

Stonestreet, O. C. "Pilot Saved Comrades from Shark-Filled Water" Statesville Record & Landmark, August 7, 2006.

A. Y. NEEL JR.

Interview with A. Y. Neel Jr. in his home near Mooresville, N.C., 1990.

Stonestreet, O. C., "80-Year-Old Iredell County Farmer Cultivates a Love for the Land" Lake Norman Magazine Guide, 1990.

"A. Y. Neel" Mooresville Tribune, November 8, 2006.

CECIL REDMOND

"Cecil Redmond Killed in Action in Italy April 16" The Landmark, May 10, 1945.

"Cecil Redmond," The Landmark, June 14, 1945.

"Memorial Sunday for PFC Redmond" Statesville Daily Record, July 14, 1945.

"Redmond Reunion Held Sunday" Statesville Daily Record April 29, 1947.

"Redmond Homecoming in New Hope on May 30" The Landmark, May 20, 1948.

"Reburial Rites Sunday for Pfc. Cecil Redmond" The Landmark, Dec. 13, 1948.

Telephone conversation with Mrs. Kay J. Trivette, February 11, 2013.

Conversation with Mrs. Kay J. Trivette at the Cook Shack, Union Grove, February 13, 2013.

Stonestreet, O. C., "Pfc. Cecil Redmond Died for His Country" Record & Landmark, February 17, 2013.

E. F. ROCKWELL

"Rev. E. F. Rockwell, D.D." The Landmark, April 19, 1888.

"Rev. E. F. Rockwell, D.D." North Carolina Presbyterian, May 27, 1897.

"J. H. Rockwell" The Landmark, June 17, 1940.

"Rockwell Notes Descendants of Martyrs Among Early Settlers of This Community" Statesville Daily Record, September 11, 1953.

McGeachy, Neill R., "Elijah Frink Rockwell," in Dictionary of North Carolina Biography. Volume V. Edited by William S. Powell. Chapel Hill: University of North Carolina Press, 1994.

Raynal, Henry Middleton, Old Fourth Creek Congregation: The Story of First Presbyterian Church, Statesville, 1764-1989. Statesville, N.C.: First Presbyterian Church, 1995.

Stonestreet, O. C., "The Rev. Dr. E. F. Rockwell: A Man for All Seasons" Statesville Record & Landmark, October 7, 2012.

WILLIAM F. SHARPE

"Was a Marine Sergeant" The Landmark, April 10, 1917.

"Funeral of Mr. W. F. Sharpe at Loray" The Landmark, January 4, 1923.

Stonestreet, O. C., "Loray's Sharpe Served Aboard Confederate Ship" Iredell Neighbors [Charlotte Observer], January 12, 2003.

WILLIAM "LAWYER BILLY" SHARPE

Wheeler, John H., Historical Sketches of North Carolina, 1584-1851. New York: Frederick H. Hathcock, 1925, reprint. Philadelphia: Lippincott, Grambo and Co.,1851.

Rumple, Jethro, A History of Rowan County, North Carolina. Baltimore: Regional Publishing Co., 1974. First published in 1881 by J. J. Bruner, Salisbury.

Keever, Homer M., Iredell, Piedmont County. Statesville, NC: Iredell County Bicentennial Committee, 1976.

"Marker Is Dedicated To Pioneer in Iredell" Record & Landmark, October 31, 1977.

Raynal, Henry Middleton, Old Fourth Creek Congregation: The Story of the First Presbyterian Church, Statesville, 1764-1989. First Presbyterian Church: Statesville, N.C., 1995.

Cashion, Jerry C. "William Sharpe" Dictionary of North Carolina Biography. Volume V. Edited by William S. Powell. Chapel Hill: University of North Carolina Press, 1994.

Stonestreet, O. C. "A Look at the Life of William 'Lawyer Billy' Sharpe" Statesville Record & Landmark, August 25, 2013.

ERNEST AND GEORGE SLOAN

"Rev. George Sloan Dies in Wilkes" The Landmark, March 10, 1930.

"Sloan, 79, Succumbs" Statesville Record & Landmark, August 9, 1975.

Interview with Jim Sloan [son of Ernest N. Sloan] in May, 2011, at his home in Statesville, N.C.

Stonestreet, O. C., "Brothers Weathered Great War Together" Statesville Record & Landmark, May 30, 2011.

RALPH SLOAN

"Rites Set for Sloan" Record & Landmark, May 5, 1981.

Stonestreet, O. C., "Ralph Sloan's Contributions to Local History" Statesville Record & Landmark, August 2, 2009.

GRAY SLOOP

"Will Enter the Big Race" Mooresville Enterprise, June 5, 1913.

"Will Enter Big Race" Mooresville Enterprise, June 26, 1913.

"To Be in Motor Cycle Race" The Landmark, June 27, 1913.

"An Election Next Monday" The Landmark, July 1, 1913.

Day, Donald S., "Balke, on Indian, Wins Elgin Race" The Inter-Ocean Newspaper (Chicago, Ill.), July 5, 1913.

"Local Briefs" Mooresville Enterprise, July 10, 1913.

"Won First Prize and World's Championship" The Landmark, July 10, 1914.

"Gray Sloop Accepts Challenge" Mooresville Enterprise, July 23, 1914.

"Archie Templeton Won Motorcycle Race from Gray Sloop" Mooresville Enterprise, July 30, 1914.

"Motorcycle Collided with Surrey" The Landmark, September 1, 1914.

"Motorcycle and Surrey Collided" Mooresville Enterprise, September 3, 1914.

"Gray Sloop Wins Races at Charleston" Mooresville Enterprise, September 10, 1914.

"Killed in Cycle Race" The New York Times, November 27, 1914.

"Met Death in Savannah" The Landmark, November 27, 1914.

"Lee Taylor Wins Motorcycle Race" Atlanta Constitution, November 28, 1914.

"Instantly Killed at Savannah" Mooresville Enterprise, December 3, 1914.

Stonestreet, O. C., "Gray Sloop: A Man Ahead of His Time" Mooresville Tribune, July 13, 2005.

EUSTACE AND MARY SLOOP

Sloop, Mary Martin with Legette Blythe, Miracle in the Hills. New York: McGraw-Hill Book Company, 1953.

"Dr. Mary Sloop Succumbs at 88" Statesville Record & Landmark, January 15, 1962.

Inscoe, John C., "Mary T. Martin Sloop," in Dictionary of North Carolina Biography. Volume V. Edited by William S. Powell. Chapel Hill: University of North Carolina Press, 1994.

Arthur, Billy, "The Angels of Avery County" The State, March, 1996.

Smith, Scott, "They Help Us Learn To Be Happy" Our State, October, 1996.

http://www.crossnoreschool.org/aboutus.html January 4, 2010.

Stonestreet, O. C., "Crossnore: A Century of Miracles" Statesville Record & Landmark, January 31, 2010.

NORMAN SMALL

"Small-Sherrill Wedding in Durham Ball Park" Mooresville Enterprise, September 2, 1937.

"Small, Moor Outfielder Is Sold to Durham" Mooresville Enterprise, June 17, 1937

"Mooresville's Babe Ruth" Mooresville Tribune, July 10, 1941.

"Norman Small Sold to New York Giants" Mooresville Enterprise, September 24, 1942.

"Tribune's Diamond Dust" Mooresville Tribune, May 16, 1946.

"Slugging Norman Small with 365 home Runs to His Credit Shoots for Minor Loop Mark" Mooresville Enterprise, April 9, 1953.

Sullivan, Len, "'The Sand Is Out of My Shoe,' Says Retired Baseball Hero Butch Small" Mooresville Tribune, April 13, 1961.

"Sarah Sherrill Small" Mooresville Tribune, September 21, 1994.

"Norman Small" Mooresville Tribune, December 27, 1995.

Holaday, J. Chris, "Norman Small" in Professional Baseball in North Carolina: An Illustrated City-by-City History, 1901-1996. Jefferson, N.C: McFarland & Company, Inc., 1996.

Utley, R. G. " Hank," "Norman Woodnut Small—A Baseball Odyssey" Ragtyme Sports, May, 1996.

Stonestreet, O. C., "A Local Baseball Giant Named Small" Statesville Record & Landmark, May 20, 2007.

Stonestreet, O. C., "The Forgotten Baseball Legend, Continued" Statesville Record & Landmark, May 21, 2007.

HERM STARRETTE

Interview with Herm Starrette at his home in January, 2010, in Cool Springs, N.C.

Stonestreet, O. C., "Herm Starrette: Playing the Games of Baseball and Life" Statesville Record & Landmark, January 17, 2010.

RICHARD N. SUMMERS

"Big Armada Hunting 'Overdue' Sub" Statesville Record & Landmark, May 29, 1968.

"Local Sailor on Scorpion" Statesville Record & Landmark, May 29, 1968.

"Radio Voice Heard" Statesville Record & Landmark, May 30, 1968.

"Ships Looking for Scorpion Find Mystery" Statesville Record & Landmark, May 31, 1968.

"Underwater Research Units Hunt for Sub" Statesville Record & Landmark, June 1, 1968.

"Leak in Sub Is Revealed" Statesville Record & Landmark, June 6, 1968.

"Missing Sub Off Its Course" Statesville Record & Landmark, June 7, 1968.

"Missing Submarine's Crew Praised In Memorial Services" Statesville Record & Landmark, June 10, 1968.

"Service Set for Summers" Statesville Record & Landmark, Oct. 26, 1968.

"Hull of Sub Is Located" Statesville Record & Landmark, Oct. 31, 1968.

Craven, John Pina, The Silent Sea: the Cold War Battle Beneath the Sea. New York: Simon & Schuster: 2001.

Stonestreet, O. C., "Recounting the Death of a Cold Warrior" Statesville Record & Landmark, November 12, 2006.

TED TAYLOR

Taylor, Ted, Making Love to Typewriters. Raleigh, N.C.: Ivy House Publishing Group, 2005.

Miller, Stephen, "Theodore Taylor, 85, Children's Novelist" New York Sun, October 30, 2006.

Bernstein, Adam, "Theodore Taylor, 85; Author of 'The Cay'" Washington Post, October 30, 2006.

Stonestreet, O. C., "Iredell-born Author Passes in California" Statesville Record & Landmark, November 19, 2006.

DAVID L. THOMAS

"Local Negro To Receive AF Commission" Mooresville Tribune, May 21, 1953.

"Air Force Officer from Mooresville Killed in Crash" Mooresville Tribune, October 28, 1954.

Telephone conversation with Felton A. Thomas (brother) December 27, 2002.

Letter from Felton A. Thomas, January 7, 2003.

Letter from Felton A. Thomas, January 21, 2003.

Stonestreet, O. C., "He Died for His Country" Statesville Record & Landmark, February 27, 2003.

D. MATT. THOMPSON

"The Statesville Graded School" The Landmark, June 1, 1893.

"Funeral for Prof. Thompson" The Landmark, July 2, 1925.

"Prof. Thompson Ranked High as an Educator" The Landmark, July 2, 1925.

"Prof. Thompson [editorial]" The Landmark, July 2, 1925.

"D. Matt Thompson's Memory Is Lauded" The Landmark, May 9, 1927.

"Professor Thompson Is a Part of Statesville" The Landmark, July 23, 1931.

Keever, Homer, "City's First Graded School in 1891" Statesville Record & Landmark, November 4, 1955.

"David M. Thompson" in North Carolina Troops, 1861-1865: A Roster. Volume II Cavalry. Raleigh, N. C.: State Department of Archives and History, 1968.

"David M. Thompson" North Carolina Troops: 1861-1865: A Roster. Volume III. Raleigh, N. C. State Department of Archives and History, 1971.

Lackey, Mac, "1st Superintendent Left His Mark on Statesville's Public School System" Iredell Neighbors [Charlotte Observer], August 20, 1986.

Keever, Homer M., "David Matthew Thompson," in Dictionary of North Carolina Biography. Volume VI. Edited by William S. Powell. Chapel Hill: University of North Carolina Press, 1996.

Stonestreet, O. C., "Remembering 'Professor Thompson'" Statesville Record & Landmark, August 26, 2007.

JAMES R. WALKER SR.

Walker, James R. Sr., Be Firm My Hope. New York: Comet Press, 1955.

Eisele, Douglas, "Local Poet Struggled for Education" Statesville Record & Landmark, June 9, 1955.

Walker, James R. Sr., Musings of Childhood, New York: Carlton Press, 1960.

"City Library Honors Statesville Writers" Statesville Record & Landmark, April 23, 1963.

"Walker Publishes New Poetry" Statesville Record & Landmark, November 15, 1963.

Walker, James R. Sr., Menus of Love. New York: Carlton Press, 1963.

"James R. Walker Publishes New Book of Poetry" Statesville Record & Landmark, November 15, 1963.

"Postoffice Poet Writes of God" Charlotte Observer, August 15, 1965.

Walker, James R. Sr., Speak Nature. New York: Carlton Press, 1965.

Fuller, Bill, "Statesville's Poet Started in 1905" Charlotte Observer, August 15, 1965.

Jackson, Dot, "Poets Sometimes Don't Eat Well So He Wrote Between Teaching" Charlotte Observer, March 21, 1971.

"Funeral Services Slated for Former Teacher, Poet" Statesville Record & Landmark, December 8, 1983.

Stonestreet, O. C., "'Professor Walker' Also an Iredell Poet" Statesville Record & Landmark, February 17, 2008.

S. CLAY AND LUTELLE WILLIAMS

"S. Clay Williams Is Made President R. J. Reynolds Co." Mooresville Enterprise, May 14, 1931.

"Elevated to Presidency" Mooresville Enterprise, June 18, 1931.

"Recovery: Midway Man" Time, February 25, 1935.

"Clay Williams Quits Recovery Board Post" The Landmark, March 7, 1935.

"S. Clay Williams Declares NRA Has Been Good Thing" The Landmark, March 18, 1935.

"S. Clay Williams Highest Paid North Carolinian" Statesville Daily Record, May 21, 1935.

"Mr. Williams Looks Ahead" Mooresville Enterprise, May 23, 1935.

"S. Clay Williams May Be Appointed Minister to London" Mooresville Enterprise, January 30, 1941.

"Clay Williams Says He Has to Walk Miles for a Camel" Mooresville Tribune December 21, 1944.

"Clay Williams Puts Pack of Camels on Senate Desk and Starts a Riot" Mooresville Tribune, March 22, 1945.

"Clay Williams of Twin City Assails U.S. Price Control; Ruin Free Economy" Mooresville Enterprise, May 16, 1946.

"S. Clay Williams Passes Suddenly of Heart Attack" Statesville Daily Record, February 26, 1949.

"Rites Held Sunday for S. Clay Williams" Mooresville Tribune, March 3, 1949.

"Mrs. Williams Gives Library to Town for Fee Simple" Mooresville Tribune, November 9, 1967.

"Mrs. Williams, Donor of Local Public Library, Taken in Death" Mooresville Tribune, May 14, 1986.

Bair, Anna Withers, "Samuel Clay Williams," in Dictionary of North Carolina Biography. Volume VI. Edited by William S. Powell. Chapel Hill: University of North Carolina Press, 1996.

Stonestreet, O. C., "Mr. and Mrs. S. Clay Williams: Influential Iredell Folks" Statesville Record & Landmark, March 14, 2010.

CHAD WOOTEN

"Chad Wooten" Statesville Record & Landmark, November 11, 2011.

Interview with Mrs. Betty C. Wooten [Chad's mother] in her home in May, 2012, in Cool Springs, N.C.

Stonestreet, O. C., "Remembering Chad Wooten: A Life of Inspiration" Statesville Record & Landmark, May 20, 2012.

MONROE NATHAN WORK

Thorpe, Earl E., Black Historians: A Critique. New York: William Morrow & Co., 1971.

Johnson, E. D., "Monroe Nathan Work," in Dictionary of North Carolina Biography. Volume VI. Edited by William S. Powell. Chapel Hill: University of North Carolina Press, 1996.

Reese, Joel, "Statistics Were His Weapon Against Racism" Statesville Record & Landmark, February 22, 2006.

Stonestreet, O. C., "A Favorite Son: Monroe Nathan Work" Mooresville Tribune, March 31, 2006.

28030656R00249

Made in the USA
Charleston, SC
29 March 2014